*On Improving
the Status
of Women*

Theodor Gottlieb von Hippel, 1741–1796

Theodor Gottlieb von Hippel

On Improving
the Status
of Women

Translated and edited with an introduction by
TIMOTHY F. SELLNER

Wayne State University Press
Detroit, 1979

Original title: *Über die bürgerliche Verbesserung der Weiber*
English translation copyright © 1979 by Wayne State University Press, Detroit, Michigan
48202. All rights are reserved. No part of this book may be reproduced without formal
permission.

Library of Congress Cataloging in Publicaton Data

Hippel, Theodor Gottlieb von, 1741–1796.
On improving the status of women.

   Translation of Über die bürgerliche Verbesserung der Weiber.
   Includes bibliographical references and index.
   1. Women—Social conditions. 2. Women's rights—History. 3. Equality.
I. Sellner, Timothy F., 1938–   II. Title.
HQ1121.H62513   301.41′2   78–23302
ISBN 0–8143–1622–0

For Vicki and Susannah

Contents

On Improving the Status of Women

I   *Form and Substance of the Present Treatise*   53

Difficulty of writing on the proposed subject. Reasons for the author's choice of the present form. An appeal to an enlightened readership. Discourse with an imaginary noblewoman concerning the substance of the present treatise. Woman's right to grace and mercy. Improvement of the status of women recommended as the best means for ending enslavement of that sex. Purpose of the present treatise. Improving the condition of women compared with improving that of the Jews. Society presupposes equality between the sexes.

present day. How women face death. Observations
concerning friendship. Women seen as a beneficent
influence on politics. Reproach of a lack of discretion
among women answered. Potential of women for
mathematics. Potential of women for animal husbandry
and agriculture. Improvement of the condition of women
advocated as a further step in the perfection of the human
race. Necessity for legislation to achieve this end. Women
as judges, legislators, and lawyers. Talent of women for the
healing arts. Necessity for women doctors. Moral reasons
given for the necessity of women as hairdressers (for
women) as well as designers and tailors of women's
clothing. Return to a more natural use of cosmetics
recommended. Concluding dialogue between the author
and an imaginary male opponent in which the frequently
heard objections to women and their emancipation are
discussed at some length.

Appeal to men to apply the ideas proposed in this treatise
and to bring about the improvement in the status of the
female sex. Results to be expected from such improvement.
Some final observations on what the author hopes to
achieve by his treatise.

Preface

During the last few years I have often had the opportunity to give a lecture contrasting the present work with the *Vindication of the Rights of Woman* by Mary Wollstonecraft. On several such occasions I was asked how I had chanced upon this work by Hippel after it had lain for almost a century and a half in obscurity.

While the rediscovery offered only a small part of the romance associated with such monumental finds, for example, as Tischendorf's rediscovery of forty-three leaves of the Codex Sinaiticus in a wastebasket in St. Catherine's Monastery at Sinai in 1844, nevertheless to relate the incident here in some detail is perhaps justifiable in the interest of satisfying a legitimate claim by potential readers to information about a work which proposes to lay its own claim to their time and attention—Hippel's diatribes in Chapter VI of the work against readers who were so desperately seeking to ferret out information about its author notwithstanding.

The tale begins some years ago in a now-defunct Ann Arbor bookshop. I happened to discover on a back shelf, amid a row of dusty volumes, a worn and coverless copy of a work with the promising title *Über die bürgerliche Verbesserung der Weiber*. In a neat twentieth-century hand—probably that of a modern book dealer—a penciled name identified the author of this anonymous work, whom I recognized as a minor eighteenth-century novelist who wrote in the manner of Lawrence Sterne. Another name in an earlier hand identified a previous owner as a certain "Countess Henckel." It soon became apparent that more information was available on the book's early owner than on the book itself: Countess Henckel (Gräfin Eleonore Ottilie Henckel-Donnersmarck, 1756–1843) had been the wife of one of the generals of Frederick the Great who had later become governor of Königsberg, at which time she had probably known the author Hippel personally. In 1804, after the death of her husband, she became Oberhofmeisterin (a position equivalent to Lord High Steward) at the court in Weimar and later the grandmother of the girl whom Goethe in 1816 picked to become the wife of his only son, August.

The book itself, however, proved more difficult to characterize. To be sure, some work had been done on Hippel's literary endeavors before the First World War, but precious little after that. Moreover, almost nothing seemed to exist regarding his role in the history of the idea of the emancipation of women. With time, I was able to draw together several short articles on this subject in some rather obscure German journals, a biography of the first forty years of the author's life, and a single English book which devotes itself chiefly to Mary Wollstonecraft but contains a brief chapter on Hippel—all of which appeared before 1920.

In the meanwhile, however, a single reading of the work was enough to convince me of its value for the history of ideas, and it soon became apparent that I was dealing with a major, but completely unknown, treatise on a subject of considerable interest and importance, whose translation and republication, it seemed, would serve to shed much light on the historical development of the idea of equal rights for women. In addition, the work, with its chiefly masculine orientation, gave promise of providing a useful complement to the work of present-day women feminists striving to achieve full equality in society.

This book is thus not a scholarly treatise, nor is it merely a historical curiosity, the fossil relic of an earlier period of oppression whose injustices have all been corrected and whose prejudices are no longer permitted to determine the actions of individuals or governments. There is, in fact, nothing in this work which is not directly applicable, even today, to the problem in microcosm, the denial of equal rights to the female sex, and in macrocosm, the imperfections in man and in the institutions of human society.

If the most basic relationship in the life of any human being is that between him and his God, then certainly next in importance can only be the relationships between him and the members of the opposite sex, both within and outside the marriage bond. Hippel would have us rethink for ourselves the latter relationships in all their manifold aspects. The present work, to use his own words in another context, is to be a "powerful sermon of repentance and belief," designed to persuade us to exchange some of our most deeply cherished notions for those more in consonance with the laws of God and nature. But even with the attainment of that end, Hippel's work would not yet have come to full fruition, for he would not have brought us to the final enlightened stage in which repentance and belief, united with our determination to "go, and sin no more," are finally translated into action.

Acknowledgments

I wish to express my sincere gratitude for valuable help received from the following:

Professor James C. O'Flaherty, Professor Wilmer D. Sanders, and Mrs. Hannelore T. McDowell of the Department of German, Wake Forest University, for their insightful interpretation of the most obscure passages in the present work; Professor Robert W. Ulery of the Department of Classical Languages for his tireless help in tracking down Hippel's classical references; Dr. Joseph Kohnen of Luxemburg City, Luxemburg, for a stimulating correspondence concerning Hippel, as well as for hitherto unpublished information concerning the present status of the latter's papers; Professor O. M. Olivo of the Institute of Bologna for information unavailable elsewhere on the work of Ercole Lelli at that institution; Professor William B. Willcox of Yale University and The Franklin Papers for his efforts directed at identifying the Franklin quote; the Columbia University Library, the Yale University Library, the British Library, the Bibliothèque Nationale, the Oesterreichische Nationalbibliothek, and the Stadt- und Universitätsbibliothek in Frankfurt am Main for the use of their materials and facilities; the Wake Forest University Library, and in particular Mrs. Patricia B. Giles, Reference Librarian, for continual assistance in the location of some of the most elusive information for the many notes contained in this volume; the Graduate Council of Wake Forest University for a grant to assist in the publication of this work; and most importantly, Mrs. Mary C. Reid for her dedicated typing and preparation of the final manuscript during the long summer months when it was being prepared for publication.

15

Translator's Note

The present translation is based on the first edition of *Über die bürgerliche Verbesserung der Weiber*, published in Berlin in 1792. Of the 429 pages constituting the text of this small octavo edition, a total of approximately seventy-two have been deleted at various points, for the reason that they contained material not directly pertinent to the woman question. This has proven advisable in view of Hippel's discursive style of writing, and in order to preserve continuity of expression several sentences of the text have had to be transposed as well. I have not indicated these omissions by ellipsis marks in the text, since they occur too frequently and would have disturbed the continuity of Hippel's argument. I have provided an annotated table of contents to assist the reader.

I have endeavored to explain in my Introduction Hippel's reasons for having chosen the form he did, and believe that if he is truly to be allowed to have his say, then he ought to be permitted to say it in the way in which he chose to express himself. This choice of form, of course, presents exceedingly difficult problems for the translator. In my opinion there is only one other author in the German language whose prose is more difficult to translate, and that, not surprisingly, is Hippel's close friend and sometime mentor, Johann Georg Hamann.

Thus I have tried my best to walk a fine line between consciously antiquated speech and very modern idiom, all the while striving for clarity of expression. There are times, however, when Hippel appears to seek ambiguity intentionally (particularly in the first two chapters). In such cases, I could do no better than to render the ambiguity into English as felicitously as possible. Perhaps the reader will fault me for this, translation being a subjective art, but I believe this has the compensating advantage of eliminating any distortions in the text, which are a far greater fault in themselves.

Introduction

At the end of the seventeenth century, Mary Astell, an early defender of the female sex, lamented that "the Men by Interest or Inclination are so generally engaged against us, that it is not to be expected, that any one Man of Wit should arise so generous as to engage in our quarrel, and be the Champion of our sex against the Injuries and Oppressions of his own."[1] Nearly two hundred years later, the philosopher Friedrich Nietzsche, one of the most thorough-going misogynists of the nineteenth century, was grumbling that by his time there were already "enough idiotic friends and corrupters of woman among the scholarly asses of the male sex" preaching the emancipation of woman and thus advising her to "defeminize herself . . . and ape all the stupidities from which 'man' in Europe, 'European manliness,' is suffering."[2] Between the two statements lies perhaps the most significant phase in the history of the women's movement: it went from the plaintive expression of a few isolated voices to the decision of the New Zealand legislature to grant full legal rights to women in 1893—the first nation in the world to do so.

The role played by men in this movement, both as theoreticians and active participants, is now for the most part known to us.[3] Never as numerous as their feminine counterparts, the male advocates of an alteration in the condition of women nonetheless included such people as Diderot, Helvétius, D'Holbach, Condorcet, Paine, Godwin, and John Stuart Mill. Moreover, it is possible that the well-meaning opinions of Voltaire and Rousseau, as well as the prurience of John Wilkes and

19

perhaps even John Cleland, played some part in calling attention to the plight of women during this period.

The works of the defenders of women from the beginning to about the middle of the eighteenth century can best be classified as apologetics for their supposed physical frailty, excessive vanity, frivolousness, and innate need for dependence. For the most part these works are general in nature, and not addressed to either sex specifically. In some cases, an author, such as D'Holbach, felt compelled to appeal directly to women, calling upon them to desist from all that was frivolous and superficial and thereby to earn the respect of men.[4] Choderlos de Laclos even went so far as to advise women that there could be no improvement in their situation unless they finally began to confront their male oppressors.[5] The majority of writers, however, recognized the difficulty of such courses of action, in the face of a society which assumed that females possessed less human reason than males and therefore were entitled to only a modicum of education and limited, if any, civil rights.

Since medieval times, the interpretation placed on Aristotle's assessment of human moral qualities in the *Politics* was that the virtues and characteristics of the human race were distributed between the sexes in differing measures of quantity and quality—thus the courage of a man would consist in commanding, and of a woman in obeying.[6] Opponents of this line of reasoning had long countered with the ideas of Plato, who has Socrates conclude that reason is universal in human nature and that therefore education ought to be able to develop the potential of each of the sexes in a like manner.[7] In general, the Aristotelian viewpoint was adopted by those wishing to assign a subordinate position to the female sex, the Platonic by those wishing to improve its status, although it must be stated that modifications of the Aristotelian position were also adopted by a significant number of males writing in support of feminism.

Toward the end of the century the debate over the question intensified, in a barrage of pamphlets, brochures, and articles in literary magazines. In many of these works one can hear themes which will later be developed more fully: equal rights for women, equal opportunities for education, and citizenship and suffrage for all. The failure of the French Revolution and the Constitution of 1791 to accord a change in the rights or status of women, however, stimulated the appearance of the two most important feminist documents of the period in France: Condorcet's essay *Sur l'admission des femmes aux droits de cité* of 1789 and the pamphlet *La déclaration des droits de la femme et de la citoyenne*, published by Olympe de Gouges in September 1791. In the following year the first comprehensive treatises on the subject of woman's status, education, and natural rights were published: Mary Wollstonecraft's *A Vindication of the Rights of Woman*, which appeared in London in 1792, and an anonymous work, published in Berlin in the same year, whose author was posthumously identified as the German essayist and writer of humorous novels Theodor Gottlieb von Hippel.

Wollstonecraft's work has been so aptly described by Humphreys as a "passionate force springing from a generous, impulsive nature, disdaining refinements of style, concerned with 'things, not words,' and burning its way through the dry faggots of rationalism."[8] It was an immediate sensation. She directed her appeal mainly to middle-class women, and it is clear that her choice was dictated by her own sex and class. Yet while it lay within the power of women to accept her admonishments and attempt to divest themselves of all that was frivolous in order to gain the respect of men and deserve equal treatment,[9] it was certainly *not* within their power to effect any true change in their status by themselves. "Just as in America there is no Negro problem but rather a white problem," Simone de Beauvoir once observed, "just as antisemitism is not a Jewish problem, it is our problem; so the woman problem has always been a man's problem."[10] It remained necessary to address the actual source of the oppression of the female sex in a manner calculated first to gain an audience and then to win converts. Condorcet's plea for equal rights for women, for example, in essence an outline of the arguments traditionally offered by the male sex as a justification for the subjugation of women, also contained its author's supposed "refutation" of each of these arguments. Yet when he argued that "the rights of men result simply from the fact that they are rational, sentient beings, susceptible of acquiring ideas of morality, and of reasoning concerning those ideas," and then drew the conclusion that "women, having these same qualities, have necessarily the same rights,"[11] he was merely begging the question. The idea that most women possess the faculty of human reason required for the proper exercise of the rights implied by citizenship was a difficult one for the male of the eighteenth century to accept. It would have required a delineation of proof which adhered to all the rules of rational inquiry in order to merit even tacit acceptance. Hippel's work provided, as far as was possible, that delineation of proof.

Nevertheless, the work is far from being a mere supplement to the *Vindication* written by a male and intended for a male audience. Hippel's treatment of the legal rights of women, his attempt to describe the history of the subjection of the female sex, his observations concerning the natural superiority of women for certain endeavors, his suggestions for the improvement of women's education and for their admission to citizenship, his exhaustive refutation of the arguments in favor of maintaining the status quo, and his lengthy index of women of the period whose talents had been recognized—all testify to the broad scope of the treatise and its unique position in feminist literature.

It has recently been argued that Mary Wollstonecraft's *Vindication of the Rights of Woman* can be regarded as the manifesto of the feminist movement.[12] In view of the special status which the work has acquired in the last few decades, it would be difficult to deny this work its rightful place in the history of the idea of equal rights for women. And yet it seems no less difficult to deny that the present work also represents a singular document in the history of this idea. These two works, which complement each other in a remarkable way, ought perhaps to be considered *together* as comprising the first truly complete manifesto of feminism.

Theodor Gottlieb von Hippel was born on January 31, 1741, in the small East Prussian town of Gerdauen. His father was a school superintendent with noble antecedents, although his forebears had allowed the patent of nobility to expire and no longer included the prefix "von" in their surname. His mother came from a family of artisans in the surrounding area. In his somewhat idealized autobiography written in 1790–1791, Hippel maintains that his father, paternal grandfather, and father-in-law were ministers, a statement which must be viewed as a manifestation of his lifelong respect and admiration for this profession. Although this utterance is not literally true, it seems clear that the Pietistic orientation of his upbringing and the deep spiritual convictions of his parents were the reason for the desire of the young Theodor Gottlieb and his only brother, Gotthard Friedrich, to enter the ministry. Theodor entered the University of Königsberg in the autumn of 1756, shortly before his sixteenth birthday, to study theology. By 1760 he had taken all his preparatory courses for that degree, but he never completed these studies. That year he received an invitation from an acquaintance, a Russian lieutenant named Von Keyser, to accompany him on a political mission in Russia. Keyser's father was a vice-admiral who lived in some splendor in the town of Kronstadt, and it was Hippel's stay in this household, more than anything else in an exceedingly illuminating journey, which brought about a radical change in his life. Here he first became acquainted with the world of polite society and met men not of mere learning, but of influence and reputation. He returned home the next February in a state of crisis. Unable or unwilling to return to the study of theology, he accepted a position as tutor for a wealthy family in Königsberg. Contact for a second time with the manners and way of life of the titled and rich—this time on an intimate basis—further exacerbated the crisis in Hippel's being during this difficult period. There he fell in love with the daughter of his employer. Since a love affair of this sort could never come to fruition because of the difference in their stations in life, Hippel was obliged to give up both his position as tutor and his love. In the words of Friedrich Schlichtegroll, who completed Hippel's autobiography after the latter's death, he then "seized upon the idea of someday becoming her equal in both wealth and social position."[13] Proof for this statement is lacking, but Hippel from this moment on pursued his career with a relentlessness and singleness of purpose not previously discernible in his character. Worldly success, wealth, and reputation seemed now to be his only goals, and in 1762 he returned to the university, to take up the study of law, a more useful vehicle for the attainment of these ends.

For a year and a half Hippel tolerated the most severe deprivations and poverty in order to finish his degree. To improve his already pleasant speaking voice and increase his effectiveness as a courtroom orator, he took private lessons in declamation from the director of a local theatrical troupe. In 1765 he was finally able to obtain a position as a lawyer in the Königsberg court of justice. From this point on, there was little to hold him back in his career as a bureaucrat. He was practiced in manners, a hard worker, a born orator who often overpowered his opponents with his keenness of understanding and the brilliance of his logic, and a man who seemed born to lead others. He rose quickly in the government of Königsberg from the position of Counselor in Criminal Affairs, to City Counselor, to Director of the Criminal Court, and then to Director of Police. In 1780 he was appointed a member of the commission to oversee the introduction of Prussian state law, and later received a gold medal for his contribution to this project. That same year, at the age of thirty-nine, he was appointed Governing Mayor of the city, the largest and most important in East Prussia.

The death of Frederick the Great in 1786 and ascension of his nephew, Frederick William II, brought no change in the favorable light in which Hippel was viewed at the Prussian court in Berlin. During his short stay in Königsberg in 1786, Frederick William II decorated him personally for his services to the state, and later that year he was also given a promotion to the titular office of City President, which he held until his death. In 1790, by means of secret negotiations with the court of the

Holy Roman Emperor, Joseph II, he secured the right to renew the hereditary patent of nobility for himself and his family, a piece of snobbery for which he was roundly criticized by his middle-class friends. Three years later he was called to Danzig by his friend Baron von Schroetter, then the highest civil official of the province of Old Prussia, to supervise the incorporation of Danzig into the political organization of Prussia, the result of the second partition of Poland in 1793. Although Hippel accomplished this task with distinction, the change in his strictly regulated way of life and the pressures of the assignment were disastrous to his health. His constitution became permanently weakened, and before he left Danzig in March of 1794 he had developed an infection which caused him to lose an eye. He died in Königsberg on April 23, 1796, of, according to the official reports, "dropsy of the chest."

The events of Hippel's life, however, reveal little of the complicated and contradictory nature of his inner being, for his writings and letters present a sharp contrast to the man known to even the most intimate of his friends. Much in the manner of Franz Kafka a century and a half later, Hippel carried on a full literary career in addition to his official duties, and it is his nightly "scribbling" which most clearly reveals this contrast. For example, he once wrote that a liar was "the most detestable person" he could imagine, and "a lie one of the grossest crimes," [14] yet his attempts at preserving his anonymity as a writer were carried on with such intensity that he himself and several close friends—to their occasional acute embarrassment—were often forced into outright denials when confronted by the inquisitive. His most famous work was a treatise on marriage, and he recommended this institution with enthusiasm to all who would listen, yet he remained a bachelor. He gleefully pilloried secret societies in his writings, yet was an active Mason throughout his adult life. Although confident, even dictatorial, in his demeanor, he often complained to his closest friend, Johann Georg Scheffner, of hypochondria, melancholy, and fits of weeping. He upbraided others for their greed, yet when he felt called upon to defend himself in his autobiography against even his friends' charges of stinginess and greed, he nonchalantly replied: "How I acquired my fortune is often even a puzzle to me. In truth I can say that it fell to me from heaven above." [15]

In spite of his reputation as a capable public official, Hippel's background and character frequently caused those around him—sometimes with justification, but occasionally out of envy or pique—to suggest that he had an overweening lust for power and the perquisites of high office. Yet he wrote to Scheffner shortly after he was elected Mayor of Königsberg:

> With a heart heavier than lead I report to you that I am [now] Counselor and Governing Mayor.— . . . God! if you knew what I have suffered since Wednesday [the day of his election] until yesterday evening, you would pity me. . . . The worst of it is that on top of everything else people actually envy me! . . . I do not possess the soul of a mayor. But what am I to do? Send it [the patent] back? Prostitute myself even further? I have kept silent and not thanked God, and thus I go to meet my fate.[16]

Nowhere are the contradictions in Hippel's being more clearly manifested, however, than in his acceptance of the philosophical principles of the Enlightenment, which sought to subject all aspects of human life to critical analysis by human reason, and also of a Christian faith requiring belief in concepts which cannot be subjected to such investigation. It seems apparent that Hippel's ability and willingness to tolerate such a contradiction lay in the nature of his religious beliefs. The Pietistic movement within the Lutheran church to which his father belonged sought to counteract the coldness and formality of orthodox liturgy by emphasizing the spontaneous, effusive outpouring of Christian spirit in an informal liturgical setting. By placing great stress on emotional preaching, the Pietists had gradually developed a specific "sentimental" vocabulary and manner of expression of which Hippel himself made use during his student years in his own sermons, and which finds its way into all his literary works. He is still known today as one of the most successful German representatives of the sentimental novel in the mode of Samuel Richardson and Lawrence Sterne—a kind of novel which required of its readers that they both laugh and weep, as well as experience the full range of human emotions in between. That he was quite conscious of this stylistic influence can be seen from a letter to Scheffner of January 20, 1778:

> One comes to the realization that this world is a vale of tears, and that every intelligent person must ask of joy: "You are mad, and what do you do to make yourself laugh?" I believe firmly that one can find both laughing and weeping people in the world who are equally intelligent. I don't know who has the

> advantage, but at least I feel that the laugher is a thousand thousand times less satisfied with himself and the world than the weeper; at least I believe that the Christian religion, if it is to make us truly happy, requires that our eyes be filled with holy tears. . . .Christ the Lord wept, and his moral aim, according to the interpretation of His followers [i.e., those New Testament writers who included no references to the laughing Christ], is the propagation of tears. . . . Everything considered, such is also the state of happiness in the world, where nothing can exist without hope, and [yet] who can hope without tears, who can without [tears] . . . feel a longing for heaven?[17]

Thus in spite of the fact that Hippel, as a child of the Enlightenment and the eighteenth century, believed in the power of human reason to better all aspects of human life, including the status of women, it is precisely this "longing for heaven" and the actions and beliefs attendant to this longing—belief in God and the efficacy of prayer, an awareness of one's own mortality, and even a belief in the world of ghosts and spirits—which required him to abandon the principles of reason and even renounce his faith in its power when he was confronted with a question whose answer lay outside the scope of human understanding.[18] This is particularly true in the case of human mortality, the most constantly recurring single theme in Hippel's thought and writings.[19] The reader, then, cannot always expect to find, in a treatise ostensibly constructed along the lines of a rational philosophic discourse, an application of these rational principles in a consistent and unalterable pattern. If it so pleases the author—and indeed, often without his being aware of it himself—he will lapse into arguments of a completely subjective nature which require acceptance on faith alone, if at all.

Consequently, when the rationalistic and enlightened idea of equal rights for women stands face to face with the biblical (Pauline) teaching requiring subjection of that sex, Hippel is not forced to yield reason to faith: the Pietistic belief in the living presence of Christ in all human relations based on the foundation of love renders inapplicable the cold and dogmatic doctrines of the orthodox church. "Without a doubt it would have been the intention of Christ," Hippel writes in his autobiography,

> that His teachings be transmitted orally, for He well knew that words which have been written down, which have become

permanent and attained a certain respect, are capable of causing a great deal of harm. . . . Since, however, His life and His
teachings, although without His having been consulted, have
in fact been written down, [it follows that] the various exegeses
and explanations, according to which one aligns himself with
Paul, Apollos, or Cephas [Peter], do Christianity far more harm
than good."[20]

Thus in the present work Hippel can even make the bold assertion that
women would make good preachers, and he dismisses the biblical
teaching of Paul, which even in the last quarter of the twentieth century
has proved to be the greatest stumbling block to the granting of clerical
authority to women, in one sentence—and in a parenthetical comment
at that (see Chapter V).

Hippel's first published work of any consequence was his *Rhapsodie*
of 1763, a poetic work giving vent to his sentiments after the unfortunate love affair with his employer's daughter the previous year. This
was followed by two short comedies in the French manner and a series
of discourses on Freemasonry. In 1772 he published a collection of
Christian hymns of a strongly Pietistic bent, a number of which have
become a permanent part of Protestant hymnody in Germany. In 1774,
the year in which Goethe's *The Sorrows of Young Werther* appeared,
another work was published in Germany which in some respects was
hardly less of a literary sensation than *Werther*; four separate editions
had been issued by 1793. This work was Hippel's treatise *Über die Ehe*
[On marriage]. While the first two editions of this book (those of 1774
and 1775) continued to follow tradition in their advocacy of the su-
premacy of the male in the marriage relation, and in fact contain some
censorious comment on the manners and behavior of the female sex, the
third edition of 1792 actively advocates the emancipation of women and
equality in marriage. (The reasons for this striking reversal will be
discussed in detail later in this Introduction.)

Hippel's next work was the long genealogical novel *Lebensläufe nach
aufsteigender Linie* [Biographies in the ascending line], which appeared
over a period of four years, 1778 to 1781, and is the main source of his
reputation as a sentimental novelist. This was followed by a satire on
the relationship between Frederick the Great and Johann Georg Zimmermann, the author of the famous four-volume treatise *Über die Einsamkeit* [Solitude] and one-time personal physician to Frederick. *On
Improving the Status of Women* followed in 1792, close upon the heels of
the completely revised third edition of *Über die Ehe*. That the work did

not sell well is indicated by the complaint of Hippel's former publisher in 1828, upon the publication of his collected works, that there were still too many unsold copies on the shelf to warrant a new edition of the work.[21] Hippel's last work was the humorous novel *Kreuz- und Quer-züge des Ritters A bis Z* [Crusadings of the Knight A to Z], a satirical novel after the manner of *Don Quixote* which takes as its target the lodges and secret societies of the day.

Hippel maintained his anonymity with an almost paranoiac intensity. It was merely a matter of occasional conjecture that the author of *Über die Ehe* was also the author of the *Lebensläufe*, and although Hippel had confessed to a few friends his authorship of certain works, only his friend Scheffner knew all that he had written. Hippel's letters to Scheffner, extending over a period of thirty-one years from 1765 to 1796, are filled with complaints that this or that critic or reader was about to discover his identity, as well as exhortations to Scheffner to find some way to outwit the snooper. His communications with his publisher in Berlin, Voss, were always carried on through two or three intermediaries, and Voss never knew the identity of his best-selling author.[22]

Hippel himself never really explained the reason for this insistence on anonymity. The most he would say was that it would "ruin his whole plan"[23] if he were found out. Even Scheffner, a friend of eighteen years' standing, who may have suffered most, apart from Hippel himself, from trying to protect this anonymity, was only scolded when on one occasion he attempted to ferret out the true reason for this secrecy. "That a man like you," Hippel wrote him, "with so much intelligence and understanding, can still ask after he reads the book [*Lebensläufe*] why the author keeps himself hidden has ever been a puzzle to me, and is an even greater mystery to me now."[24] The reasons for Hippel's secrecy have been the subject of some speculation in the past.[25] The most likely explanation is that he felt that the demands of an author's life (or those of domesticity, for that matter) would interfere with his career as a public official, and that he could allow himself only a minimum of distraction if he was to attain the ambitious goals which he had set up for himself at the beginning of his career. Furthermore, public literary disputes were anathema to him, and throughout his life he was unusually sensitive to criticism.

Hippel discusses the subject of his anonymity at some length at the end of Chapter VI of the present work, and although we must view this passage as an attempt to throw the curious off the track, the anecdote concerning Frederick's annoyance with a public official who insisted on pursuing a literary career while in government service indicates that he had taken his sovereign's sentiments on the matter to apply to his own case. As sorely plagued by "daemon poesy" as his monarch, Hippel could hardly desist from writing. At least his anonymity would preserve him from a public rebuke from the king.

Amid the chaos of papers comprising Hippel's literary estate were found several hundred pages on which he had jotted down personal observations, often entire conversations, and quotations from things he had read or otherwise heard of which caught his fancy or which he felt might be useful. It is clear from these papers and the general format of his writings that part of his method of composition was simply to incorporate such information and observations wholesale into his literary works, often with only slight changes in form and with no acknowledgment of their source. This practice, combined with his almost pathological insistence on anonymity, was the chief cause of two singularly unfortunate incidents which clouded his name for many years after his death and contributed to the controversy concerning the true nature of his character.

In the first instance, Hippel put forth in his *Lebensläufe* many ideas of his good friend Immanuel Kant which would not appear in the latter's major works until years later. To be sure, these ideas had been known for some time through Kant's university lectures, for it was his policy to allow his thoughts to mature for years before submitting them to the public in printed form, but Kant's annoyance at their premature revelation was considerable. Moreover, at Hippel's death, when the authorship of the *Lebensläufe* was finally revealed, Kant, to his even greater vexation, was called upon to defend himself against charges that it was he who had plagiarized from Hippel, since the latter's work had appeared in print before his own.[26]

The second incident was precipitated by Hippel's sudden death. Apparently the notes which he left contained much in the way of uncomplimentary character sketches of his friends, as well as statements made to him in casual conversations whose dissemination their authors would have found embarrassing. Furthermore, upon examination of his published work, his friends found traits possessed by his fictional characters which could only have been drawn from members of his circle—traits which were not always flattering. The natural result was that these characterizations, as well as Hippel's own character, were denounced as ruthlessly and as systematically by his friends as they would have been by lifelong enemies. As his nephew later described it, shortly after his uncle's death, "vermin of every sort descended upon him, as upon every corpse. The dead lion could not defend himself, and there was no protecting hand nearby, for he was cursed with the lot of all those who remain unmarried. No loving hand pressed closed the eyes of the dying man, none spread the veil of goodwill and brotherly love over the deceased and his memory."[27] His friends, even his beloved Scheffner,[28] vied with one another in reviling Hippel; unfortunately some of this meretricious material found its way into the biography of Hippel in Schlichtegroll's *Nekrolog* for the year 1796,[29] and into print elsewhere.

The first attempt at a rehabilitation of Hippel's name was not undertaken for almost forty years,[30] by which time many records had been lost and the facts blurred by the passage of time. His nephew's investigations prior to the editing of Hippel's autobiography for inclusion in his edition of Hippel's collected works also did much to correct the impression given by Schlichtegroll, yet a great deal remains to be discovered regarding Hippel's later life. The autobiography ends with his return from Russia, and he apparently laid the manuscipt aside in 1791 in order to prepare the third edition of *Über die Ehe*. Hippel's letters to Scheffner would provide the most valuable source of information regarding his later life, yet the letters from 1786 to Hippel's death appear nowhere in the collected works. It is possible that the editor grew too ill to continue his work. In any case, it is presumed that these later letters were sold to collectors around the middle of the nineteenth century,[31] and subsequent efforts to trace them have been unsuccessful. Some of Hippel's papers had also vanished by the middle of the century, ostensibly as a consequence of what Emil Brenning refers to as "irresponsible" handling on the part of those involved in editing them for the collected works.[32] The remainder, especially those which found their way into the archives of the city of Königsberg, were probably burned in the fire which swept through the city after the air raids of August 1944.[33] The present volume thus marks only the beginning of scholarly investigation into Hippel's ideas concerning marriage and the position of women in society. More than I would have cared to be, I have been bound by the limitations of the source material. Perhaps scholars may one day be permitted, through the chance rediscovery of material long thought to have vanished forever, to fill some of the *lacunae* which at present necessarily exist in a work such as this.

At the beginning of this work, Hippel conducts a colloquy with his muse on the subject of the form his prospective treatise ought to take.

Two problems seem clear from the outset: he must persuade the male sex of the truth of his argument and the advantages accruing to men were his proposals accepted, and he must discuss in a serious manner a topic which had traditionally been the subject of coarse witticisms and broad humor. He solves these problems, in his own words, by "joining in the laughter" and in his tone avoiding "gravely proffered inanities." The treatise attempts to persuade and instruct through gentle humor, and Hippel is nowhere secretive regarding this intention. It is thus somewhat bewildering to note that several reviewers of the period attempted to dismiss the entire work as an anti-feminist treatise written in an ironic vein.[34]

Yet humor is not the only arrow in Hippel's quiver; he asserts that "our life is ebb tide and flood tide; a continuous alternation of joy and sorrow," and then goes on to demand the whole spectrum of emotions from his readers. He alternately scolds and praises, laments and rejoices; he cajoles us and is indignant with us, upbraids us and laughs with us. According to his self-professed dictum that systems are "lazy servants of understanding,"[35] his treatises, like his novels, are a rambling hodgepodge of facts, anecdotes, quotations, sermonettes, panegyrics, and philosophical musings, held together, in the case of the novels, by the thin thread of a plot, and in the case of the treatises, by a single line of reasoning which, although often stretched to get around these encumbrances, is never dropped from the beginning to the end of the work.

Hippel is the master of emphasis through repetition and the discursive interlude. And if he requires much in the way of emotional participation from his readers, the demands he places on their learning are even greater: a more than cursory knowledge of classical mythology, Roman and Germanic law, and the Bible seem indispensable prerequisites to the understanding of the allusions even in our present text. Although the classically educated upper classes could be counted on to be well versed in mythology and ancient history, Hippel in fact was only able to count upon one single area of universal knowledge among the two social classes, upper and middle, to which he directed his writings: a knowledge of Scripture. In the didactic eighteenth century, however, it was expected that the reader who had at least a modest inclination toward self-improvement would acquire the information necessary to follow the arguments of his author with understanding.

The body of the work—in accordance with the rules of good essay-writing in the eighteenth century—then begins with an explanation of the precise form which the treatise is to take and a cursory reference to the topics to be discussed. The first chapter may therefore be viewed as an operatic overture, in which almost every theme to be later developed is given brief expression. Hippel introduces himself as a latter-day Don Quixote, a knight of "truly merry countenance" ready to do battle with any members of either sex who resist reason by continuing to advocate the oppression of one sex by the other. In the chapters which follow he discovers and jousts with windmill after windmill in the arguments of his opponents. This theme of knight-errantry reaches its climax in Chapter V, when, at the end of a long and exhausting tournament with an imaginary male opponent who is upholding the popular prejudices of the day concerning the character and capabilities of women, he declares himself the victor, and the only one to have spoken the truth, because he "espoused the cause of the oppressed and carried the banner of humanity."

In Chapter II, Hippel addresses himself specifically to the question of the supposed physical, intellectual, and spiritual superiority of the male sex. Guided, as he says, by reason and experience alone, he examines the accounts of primitive tribes brought back by such explorers as Cook, Bougainville, and the Forsters. His method anticipates that employed by modern anthropology, although in this Hippel is neither original nor unique—Rousseau, for example, made extensive use of such accounts in his *Dissertation on the Origin and Foundation of the Inequality of Mankind* of 1755. It is readily apparent that Hippel is influenced by Rousseau's disquisition in this chapter, and even more so in the next two chapters, where he discusses the origin and foundation of the inequality between the sexes. Aside from the obvious thematic similarities, the single all-pervasive idea which Hippel's treatise shares with Rousseau's dissertation is not, as one might assume, the notion that mankind return to a more "natural" state (although he does advocate a rational application of this doctrine) but rather the notion that man is separated from all other animals by virtue of his capacity for improvement—that man alone is a perfectible being.[36]

Yet Rousseau's groundbreaking work uncovered only half the problem, and to answer the question of how some groups of men gained domination over other groups is not to answer the question of how man gained his domination over woman. Hippel is probably the first to attempt, as he does in Chapters III and IV, a detailed analysis of the second question. What is of particular importance here for the history of ideas is the application of reason and empirical data, however primitive and unsophisticated those data may be, to the solution of a problem previously considered (even by Hippel himself) only in the light of Scripture. For example, in Johann Gottfried Herder's *Älteste Urkunde des Menschengeschlechts* [The oldest record of the human race] of 1774 and 1776, Herder attempts to cast light into the dark corners of human history by means of a detailed exegesis of the Book of Genesis. His declared intention is to attack the eighteenth-century exaggeration of and exultation in the power of human reason and to stress the role of Providence in human history, and he attributes the ascendancy of man over woman to the woman's part in the Fall and the resultant punishment set forth in Genesis IV:16. In his own analysis of Genesis in the *Lebensläufe*, Hippel adheres closely to Herder's interpretation, although, as one critic has pointed out, not without sidelong glances at Rousseau.[37]

In his *Dissertation*, Rousseau attempted to justify the introduction of a rationalistic approach and had dismissed the biblical account of man's origins by arguing that although "religion commands us to believe that, God himself having taken men out of a state of nature, they are unequal only because it is his will that they should be so: . . . it does not forbid us to form conjectures from the more natural state of man, and the beings around him, concerning what might have been the state of the human race, if it had been abandoned and left to itself."[38] Hippel pays lip service to the biblical account in the present work by offering an exceedingly modern interpretation of Eve (woman) as "intermediary and herald" for mankind's emancipation from the paradisal yoke of instinct as well as for the development of consciousness, and, later, the power of human reason. He then justifies the use of that faculty in his own disquisition by asking rhetorically whether anything can be an affair of God which contradicts human reason. "Or," he continues, "does God ever desire that His affairs be conducted by means of such things as contradict her [reason]?" The reader is now prepared for an investigation conducted according to the principles of reason—an investigation which arrives at the conclusion in Chapter III that the subjection of woman was less a punishment from God in the biblical sense than a gradual usurpation of natural rights arising out of the formation of social structures which, for various reasons delineated by Hippel in Chapters III and IV, came to assume a patriarchal form. The biblical accounts of the subjection of women are consequently viewed merely as a convenient justification for the continuation of a process of subjection which has been in effect from time immemorial.

In Chapters III and IV Hippel discusses the position which woman enjoyed among the ancient Germanic tribes, with a view to analyzing the influence exerted later by Roman law on the native customs and habits of these tribes. His source for such early customs was the *Germania* of Tacitus, although it is not the content of the work so much as its stance, its literary viewpoint, which Hippel adopts and which becomes most conspicuous in the final two chapters. By the eighteenth century the view had become generally accepted that certain parts of the *Germania*, particularly Section 19, were written with the express intention of bringing Tacitus' fellow Romans to a realization of their own decadence by comparing their corruption to the simple and loving domestic life of the supposedly barbarous Germanic tribes to the north. Adhering to this model, Hippel finds little to reproach in the conduct of the women of his time, but the misbehavior and foolishness of the men, as well as the evil, inefficiency, and incompetence in their governing of the state, are prime targets of his ridicule.

It might seem that Hippel—an emancipator advocating the restoration of natural and inalienable rights based on abstract principles of justice and equality—wastes too much time and ink on the practical rewards to the state of bringing about an end to attitudes and practices which, as he puts it in Chapter I, "leave half of the resources of mankind unknown, unassessed, and unused." The reason is that Hippel desires merely to utilize the most promising approach. The state itself, under the Great Elector, had already set a precedent by invoking the enlightened and high-sounding principles of religious tolerance, while giving at least some thought to the practical consideration that refugees from religious persecution would add significantly to the population of a new state rich in land but without manpower to exploit it.

The criticism that Hippel idealizes women is not so easily dismissed. To a certain extent this idealization can be explained in terms of Hippel's attempt to reform his own sex; to a certain extent it is basic to the nature of the man himself. He doubtless believed that as a bachelor and outsider he could view the institution of marriage from an objective point of view. He probably also considered himself to be in a favorable position to contemplate the true nature of the female sex in his role of "objective" (albeit favorably disposed) male outsider.

Chapter V provides a list of many women who achieved eminence within their fields, drawn up with the intent of forestalling the objections of any who would dispute woman's natural capacity for any human endeavor. He appears to have derived the model for such an approach from Madeleine de Scudéry's *Les femmes illustres*, which he read in 1777;[39] the material itself he gleaned from various classical, biblical, and contemporary literary sources, and from his own experiences (for example, his trip to the Russia of Catherine the Great).

The remainder of the chapter consists of an inventory of biased opinions regarding the intellectual, moral, and physical limitations of the female sex, offered up by an imaginary misogynist of the period, and of Hippel's point-by-point refutation of these statements. In part, many of these attacks on women are similar to those to which Condorcet addressed himself in cursory fashion several years earlier; however, Hippel attempts to counter prejudice with logic and rhetoric, whereas Condorcet, while denying the conclusions categorically, declined to submit either his own or his opponent's statements to any criterion of rational validity.

The concluding chapter is really not the application of the ideas proposed it purports to be in Hippel's title: it consists of a summation of his arguments and a final impassioned plea for the restoration to women of *true* rights, which have their basis in the very nature of things and which have been, in his words, "purified of the dross of capriciousness and Turkish despotism."

Only one study in any language deals with the relationship between Hippel and Mary Wollstonecraft, Emma Rauschenbusch-Clough's *A Study of Mary Wollstonecraft and the Rights of Woman* (London: Longmans, Green, 1898). However, since the author derives the utterly incorrect conclusion that Hippel was indebted to Wollstonecraft's *Vindication* for significant ideas in his *Status of Women*, it is necessary here to discuss briefly the salient differences between the two works. (For a detailed examination of the arguments presented in Rauschenbusch-Clough's study, the reader is referred to the Appendix of the present work.)

The most significant aspect of any question of literary indebtedness is that of content and style. Here it becomes abundantly apparent how different the two works are. Mary Wollstonecraft is a woman addressing herself chiefly to women; Hippel is a man talking to men. Hippel's style is florid, convoluted, and at times pedantic; Wollstonecraft states at the outset that it is her intention to "avoid flowery diction."[40] Hippel's history of the origins of the subjection of women, his catalogue of women who have achieved prominence in their fields, and his analysis of the legal position of women have no parallel in Wollstonecraft.[41] Conversely, Wollstonecraft's "animadversions" upon certain writers of the day whose work, she feels, whether intentionally or not, has been detrimental to the female sex have no counterpart in Hippel. Where the two books *do* treat the same theme in what appears to be somewhat similar fashion—for example, the issue of educational reform—neither puts forth ideas which are wholly original.[42]

Two salient differences in intellectual viewpoint tend, by virtue of their pervasive effect, to color almost every opinion offered by Wollstonecraft and Hippel and must be mentioned here. First, for Wollstonecraft, the emancipation of women is indissolubly associated with, and dependent upon, a social revolution which would abolish all ranks and classes. In her first chapter she attacks the English army, aristocracy, and church. She rails against a society whose tyrannical institutions are perpetuated through inherited wealth or property. In such a society the principles of reason are not applied and the natural order of equality cannot assert itself. In this respect she echoes Rousseau, for whom the institution of property was the root of the evils inherent in civilized society. The fact that Hippel judiciously avoids any such criticism is, however, not to be seen as an attempt to circumvent the ever-watchful censors in a monarchy which, while enlightened in the extreme in matters of religious tolerance, would doubtless have exacted heavy tribute from an author attacking the fundamental assumptions of a social order considered to be divinely ordained. Rather, it would have run counter to Hippel's very nature and fundamental principles to subject such institutions to criticism—he believed in them, he rose to prominence through strict adherence to the doctrines they espoused, and consequently the changes he wished to bring about in the status of women had to be accomplished within the existing structures of these institutions. Wherever he inveighs against political despotism and tyranny, it is the despotism and tyranny caused by man's folly or selfishness. For him, true change can sooner be brought about by the application of right reason to the *act* of governing than to the *institutions* through which human government functions. Hippel's ambivalent attitude toward the French Revolution, which was in full swing at this time, is a case in point. He felt compelled to acknowledge that the French (and, in his opinion, the American) Revolution faithfully represented the practical realization of the principles of liberty, equality, and human brotherhood which had been preached since the beginning of the Enlightenment; yet he deplored the use of violence to solve a problem on which human reason alone should have been brought to bear, and in his supercilious view, the spectacle of a state determined to wreak its own destruction through the systematic execution of its "most noble" citizens was appalling.[43]

The second important difference between Wollstonecraft and Hippel centers around the concept of what one might call "sex-linked" virtues, that is, the notion that the virtues (or traits) of men and women are, in general, different in kind and, where shared between the sexes, different in quantity, males possessing a greater quantity of some traits, females of others. The two opposing viewpoints on this question reflect, in essence, the difference between the Aristotelians and Platonists mentioned above, and it is statements like this from the *Vindication* which place Mary Wollstonecraft indisputably in the Platonic camp on this question: "Where is then the sexual difference, when the education has been the same? All the difference that I can discern, arises from the superior advantage of liberty, which enables the [men] to see more of life."[44] Thus, for example, were conditions equal, Wollstonecraft would expect a modesty in men equal to that of women and a sexual appetite in women equal to that of men—the latter notion in particular constitutes a radical departure from eighteenth-century ideas of female gentility. (This manner of thinking is reflected in the views of certain modern feminists who deny all differences between the sexes except anatomical ones.)

Hippel, like Rousseau, is charmed by what seem to be the feminine virtues of modesty, gentleness, and patience, but unlike Rousseau and the opponents of emancipation who would offer these virtues as evidence for a female need for protection by, and submission to, the male, he wishes to turn them to the advantage of society and of the female sex itself. Patience and gentleness, along with other qualities attributed to woman in generous amounts, he finds admirably suited to the practice of medicine, her wit and common sense useful qualities for the learning and teaching of foreign languages, and so on. In fact, the fifth chapter of *Status of Women* contains a long list of virtues characteristic of the female sex and the professions or occupations which would be most suited to these talents. Earlier, in Chapter II, Hippel attempted to answer the thorny question of sexual differences on the basis of the scientific knowledge available at the time—but to no avail.[45] He later strives for a synthesis of the Aristotelian and Platonic views: he attempts to prove that sexual differences, if they in fact exist, need not imply physical or mental inequality, and that they therefore cannot justify the subjugation of one sex by the other. For him the human race consists of two equal but in many respects different parts, and only when humanity decides to exploit the differences between the sexes, and not the sexes themselves, will the race attain its divinely ordained goal: the perfection of man.

As noted earlier, there seems to have been an abrupt change in Hippel's point of view between the first edition of *Über die Ehe* in 1774 and the third edition of 1792. Without a doubt, the misogyny and disregard for the marriage bond which characterized Frederick the Great exerted a strong influence on Hippel's thinking and played a part in setting the tone of the first edition. Hippel's letters from this period reveal him as a man willing to acknowledge only a few women (the most conspicuous example is his friend Scheffner's wife, Babet) to be entirely free from frivolity and superficiality and to be genuinely capable of true friendship, as the eighteenth century conceived of it. His thoughts on marriage recorded over the twenty years of correspondence with Scheffner reveal, both explicitly and implicitly, a continuous interest in the institution, as well as a growing perception of the benefits accruing to both parties from it. In his practice of law he saw daily evidence of the injustice and prejudice to which women were subjected by the legal system; in his letters he is indignant about the unfair treatment of one widow at the hands of the law,[46] and the numerous references to such unfairness in the present work seem to have been based on first-hand experiences.

Moreover, along with the proclamation of the rights of man by the propagandists Thomas Paine and Wollstonecraft herself, a gradual but inexorable change in the general attitude toward women had taken place. The sort of obscenity in the name of woman represented by the notorious John Wilkes' *Essay on Woman* gave way to the view expressed in the eighties by Johann Georg Zimmermann in his much-discussed treatise *Über die Einsamkeit* [Solitude] of 1784–1785. Passages such as the following from this work, which was doubtless well known to Hippel, could not fail to catch his eye:

> all the twittering of an assembly and all social chit-chat is nothing compared to domestic happiness and the spirited association with a beautiful female soul, who awakens all the slumbering powers of our intellect; who gives us more fire and strength than we alone possess; who overcomes every difficulty in the completion of our plans through her encouragement and approval; who inspires us through the flight of her ideas and through the mobility of her sentiments; who weighs and

examines with critical acumen all that we think, do, and are; who sees all our faults; who always exhorts us in earnest and ever punishes us with love; who continually elevates our taste through her feelings; who, by lovingly communicating all her observations and thoughts, enlightens us more and more, and through the outpouring of her heart into ours makes us receptive to every virtue; who puts the finishing touches on our character by the gentle brushstroke of her love and by the most charming harmony of her sentiments and thoughts [with our own.][47]

Not an emancipatory treatise in any sense of the word, Zimmermann's work nonetheless represented a step in the right direction.[48] Its acknowledgment of the importance of intellectual development in woman beyond that of providing entertainment for man was more enlightened than most of the countless treatises and articles on woman and her education published during the last decades of the eighteenth century. The most significant aspect of the passage for Hippel, however, would have been its emphasis on greater equality for woman within the marriage relationship. Hippel's work indicates that he was abreast of the state of the debate in France as well, and that he had read the work of Voltaire, Rousseau, Helvétius, Montesquieu, D'Holbach, Condorcet, and Talleyrand on the subject.

Finally, the events of the French Revolution led many to hope that the liberty and equality advocated by the Enlightenment would at last attain universal legal sanction. The Constitution of 1791 failed to grant equal rights to women, however, even though it spoke grandiloquently of "universal" suffrage, and Hippel's remarks concerning this document make it clear that the publication of *Status of Women* was in part an attempt to do what he could to correct this fault.[49]

Yet in spite of all of this, it seems clear that the most important single cause of Hippel's change in attitude between 1774 and 1792 is derived from his preoccupation, for the greater part of his life, with the theme of marriage, the most basic social contract which exists between the sexes. He gradually came to realize that this institution—like man himself capable of continual improvement through the instrument of human reason—could not be perfected until equality between the sexes had been achieved. This theme first appears in the third edition of *Über die Ehe*, and *Status of Women* is but the continuation and culmination of a train of reasoning which started almost twenty years earlier.[50]

The history of Wollstonecraft's and Hippel's work could perhaps have been foreseen at the outset. Although the effect of Wollstonecraft's *Vindication* was immediate and sensational, while *Status of Women* seems to have been noticed only in a few reviews and to have created no great stir among the general public,[51] in each case the author was too far ahead of his time for the ideas presented to be translated into action. The political and social climate simply had not kept pace with the intellectual climate which produced the two books. A few other isolated treatises on the subject of the emancipation of women appeared in England, and a group of nonconformist intellectual women in Germany associated chiefly with the Romantic school of literature developed, but England grew more conservative, and there was actual political repression on the Continent following the defeat of Napoleon in 1815. It was not until 1848, the great year of revolution and liberation in Europe, that a feminist movement began to grow. Interestingly enough, English feminists after 1848 did not immediately recognize Wollstonecraft as their intellectual forebear; they were concerned with achieving limited reforms, in many cases focusing on the problems of a particular class of women, and Wollstonecraft's suggestions were still regarded as too radical for the time. Furthermore, her unconventional life severely challenged the morality of the day and had tarnished her reputation for decades. Feminists in England were willing, in the words of one writer, "only to forgive Wollstonecraft, not to accept the implied challenge of her personal life to conventional tenets of sexual morality."[52] Nevertheless the *Vindication* has been reprinted many times—between 1844 and 1892 there were at least six separate English editions—and with each new edition her influence on the women's movement has continued to grow and her standing as the originator of the movement in English-speaking countries has become better established.

Such has not been the case with Hippel. The reasons for this can only be guessed at, yet we possess a great deal of circumstantial evidence. The Germany of 1792 was a conglomeration of small kingdoms, principalities, and duchies, which varied in political atmosphere from quite enlightened (in the case of a few) to exceedingly repressive (in the case of many). Thus it could be predicted that such a work would be favorably received by only a small segment of the population. Many states simply would not have permitted the sale or reprinting of such a work within their borders, especially if the local censors deemed the work in any way inflammatory or seditious. Then too, by publishing the work anonymously, Hippel had to forego much of that particular kinship with or antipathy toward a writer which the reader feels and which, rightly or wrongly, contributes to the sale of books and the dissemination of the author's ideas. In contrast, Mary Wollstonecraft's unconventional personal life did much to bring attention to her work at first, even though in the end her book suffered by being identified so closely in the public mind with its author. Another factor was the tendency of reviewers to see the work as ironic because of Hippel's humorous tone, which would cause many of those interested in a serious and positive treatise on the emancipation of women to look elsewhere. Finally, acceptance of the ideas represented in the book, although in some respects they are less radical in the abstract than those of Wollstonecraft, would have required a greater change in the attitude of German men (and women) than Wollstonecraft demanded of her English readers.

Hippel's work on female education was published after his death.[53] The *Status of Women* was reprinted in 1828 in Volume VI of his collected works. It was reprinted once more in 1842 and has not been reissued in any language until now. It appears to have been overlooked almost entirely by German feminists of the late nineteenth century,[54] who, because of the more advanced state of the movement in English-speaking countries, derived their ideological foundation from English and American feminists—a phenomenon which persists even today.

"The birth of a girl in the eighteenth century is no welcome event for her family. The house holds no holiday at her coming; her parents know no rapture of triumph; she is a blessing accepted as a disappointment."[55] These few introductory lines from the De Goncourts' classic work on the French woman of the eighteenth century summarize succinctly the fate of virtually all the women of the period: to be born into a world whose laws were drafted by men to the sole advantage of men, where women could neither own property nor claim citizenship, and where they could not carry on the family name or honors.

In this work by the Goncourt brothers, the best study on the life of the woman of Hippel's time available in English, every aspect of being, whether spiritual or mundane, is described for the woman of each class, marital status, and time of life. Since the model for *haute culture* throughout the entire period was provided by the French upper class, it becomes not so much a question of what attitudes, manners, and practices would be copied (for virtually any new entertainment or fashion was sure to find acceptance at some court in Germany) but merely of the extent to which these innovations would be adopted. While the upper class of Germany openly and unashamedly aped the French mode, this was less true for the middle class. At a time when Frederick the Great preferred to speak French because he regarded the

German language as coarse and vulgar, German literature was consciously and vigorously trying to free itself from the enervating influence of an overly sentimental and refined French taste which was antithetical, many German writers felt, to its true nature. By 1774, when Hippel's *Über die Ehe* was published, in the same year as Goethe's *The Sorrows of Young Werther*—a work which became the sensation of Europe and which, in the opinion of Madame de Staël, marked the birth of a German national literature[56] —similar movements were under way in other spheres of German cultural life as well.

Consequently, the situation of the German woman in the latter quarter of the century can be described as paradoxical. On the one hand, Hippel apparently quite accurately characterizes the women of Germany as less coquettish, conscious of fashion, and over-refined than their French counterparts—and thus less in need of the world of men for the fulfillment of every want. On the other hand, almost every visitor to Germany from the eighteenth century up to the period of the Weimar Republic has been struck by the great disparity in the roles of the sexes, so that we may well assume the German women of the period to have been even more restricted in their freedom than the French or English women of the day. As late as 1908, it appeared to the English writer Mrs. Sidgwick that the Germans felt that "woman was made for man, and if she has board, lodging and raiment, according to the means of her menfolk, she has all she can possibly ask of life. [German women] do not actually fall on their knees before their lords, but the tone of voice in which a woman of the old school speaks of *Die Herren* is enough to make a French, American, or Englishwoman think there is something to be said for the modern revolt against men."[57]

In great measure the position of women in Hippel's period was a function of their legal status. The legal system which assigned this status was obviously a paternalistic one, and Hippel is correct in attributing the development of such a system to the male's adoption of the sword of battle by virtue of his superior strength. Despite all the legends which have come down to us concerning the Valkyries, and in spite of Tacitus' idealistic praise of the fighting prowess of early Germanic women, it seems that they were in fact regarded as incapable of bearing arms except in cases of dire necessity. Moreover, as the early Germanic tribal community consisted only of those persons who were legally permitted to carry weapons, the result was that women "could not be independent members of the community; they were incapable of serving in the army—and therefore also in the courts, for he who would participate in the popular court had to be able to bear arms, since the procedural contest might at any time be transformed into a war-like combat. Consequently, women were excluded from public life; in a legal sense they were but members of a household community [which] was represented in external relations by its head."[58] Therefore, their capacity for legal action under private law was also prejudiced. They could not own property, for in ancient times, when representation was unknown, whoever held property was also legally bound to administer it. This responsibility, however, required him to be able to perform "juristic acts," which in turn required the capacity to sue and be sued—both of which were denied to women because of their incapacity to participate in the popular court. Moreover, proprietary incapacity meant that women could not legally inherit property.

During the Middle Ages, the sex guardianship described above assumed a different character, as the state and the church took over the protection of the weak. No longer based upon the inability of women to bear arms, guardianship was transformed into protection by a court, and this only in certain judicial proceedings in which women, because of their ignorance in business matters, were forbidden to participate. Yet the equality of women with men in private and procedural law was by no means effected through the gradual de-emphasis of sex guardianship. During the medieval period women became capable of owning land—sometimes even of fiefs—but they remained subordinate to men in the law of inheritance: they were incapable of acting as guardians or of dispositions by will, and in court a lesser value was placed on their testimony than on that of men.

The fact that they played an ever-increasing part in the economic life of the period brought about further changes for a small number of women. In many of the craft guilds—for example, those of the tailors and the wool and linen weavers—women were received into membership with full rights. There were also craft guilds in some towns made up entirely of women. In the later Middle Ages, such women were granted unlimited capacity for legal action—within the scope of their trade, they were free to assume liabilities and to prosecute a case in court.

It might well be expected that the degree of independence attained by women in the medieval period could have been extended gradually to complete equality of the sexes in the later periods, yet at the end of the eighteenth century Hippel is complaining of the loss of rights and privileges which women had possessed three hundred years earlier. This is mainly attributable to a development known to legal historians as the "Reception"—namely, the introduction of Roman law into Germany in the later Middle Ages. The effect was, in Hippel's own indelicate phrase, that "German modes of conduct were emasculated with the tailor's scisssors of Rome" (Chapter IV).

Roman law had always maintained itself as the personal law of the Roman population in Germany and as the law of the church. The Carolingian kings had also declared the legislation of the Roman emperors, whom they felt to be their predecessors, to be binding. Among the circumstances which prepared the way for the actual Reception at the end of the medieval period, Huebner cites these four: (1) the prevailing opinion that the medieval Holy Roman Empire was a continuation of the Roman world dominion of ancient times, which meant that the Corpus Juris of Justinian was entitled, as "imperial law," to claim direct validity in the later period as well; (2) the increasing interest in the study of foreign law at German universities during the Renaissance; (3) the circumstance that the canon law which was used in the ecclesiastical courts could only be thoroughly understood and properly applied with the assistance of Roman law; and (4), most decisive, the disintegrated character of German law and its lack of scientific cultivation because of the fragmented composition and unfortunate political history of Germany.[59] This Reception occurred with rapidity and ease— almost everywhere in Germany the transformation was complete within a few decades.

The result of this development was the restoration of sex guardianship, and in a form far harsher than that of older law. At least one legal scholar places the blame on a general fixation of culture, whereby the collapse of the household regimen caused men to feel misgivings about making women generally independent, particularly at a time when trade was expanding and legal affairs were becoming more difficult and involved.[60] One justification for the renewal of sex guardianship was found, strangely enough, in the alleged "defective mental acumen" of the female sex, whose understanding is described as "somewhat weak and easily taken advantage of"[61] —a view in sharp contrast to both earlier Germanic and to Roman legal thought. Nevertheless, the specific and detailed development of the practice was aided by the Reception, for although Roman law did not acknowledge such an institution and recognized merely the guardianship of *impuberes* (persons below the age of puberty), the rules which were applied to the latter were later transferred to the *cura sexus* (sex guardianship). In the judicial practices of Saxony and Lübeck, which, according to Huebner, became especially influential, "every adult woman, unmarried, widowed, or separated, again received a permanent guardian as the curator of her property; a 'true steward,' whose acquiescence alone gave validity and obligatory force to her processual and business acts."[62] Moreover, the Roman inhibition from the assumption by women of obligations of suretyship also attained common law authority.

The acceptance of this legal institution and others regulating the behavior and status of women gradually diminished as the force of human reason was applied to legal thinking during the period of the Enlightenment. Yet it is clear from Hippel's lament that his contemporaries had "made so bold as to view the Roman code of laws, like the Pillars of Hercules, as an outer limit beyond which no point of reference could possibly be imagined" (Chapter IV)—that the conquest of prejudice by the human mind had not yet been effected. In 1780, Hippel himself had served on the commission to prepare the way for the introduction of the Prussian General (or Territorial) Code. He must have viewed its adoption in 1794 with great satisfaction, for apart from the retention of certain cases of curatorship over adult married women and a legal advisor for adult unmarried women, this code set down as a general principle the legal equality of the sexes in Hippel's own nation. Following the example of the French, the first German state had abolished sex guardianship as early as 1784; it was not abolished in the last of them until 1875.

NOTES TO THE INTRODUCTION

1. [Mary Astell], *An Essay in Defence of the Female Sex*, 3d ed. with additions (London: A. Roper and R. Clavel, 1697), pp. 3–4.

2. *Beyond Good and Evil*, sec. 239 (1886 ed.).

3. An extensive general bibliography of literature from this period dealing with the woman question can be found in Paul Kluckhohn's monumental work *Die Auffassung der Liebe in der Literatur des 18. Jahrhunderts*, 3d ed. (Tübingen: Niemeyer, 1966), esp. chaps. 1–4. The history of the movement in England before 1800 is described in A. R. Humphreys' article "The 'Rights of Woman' in the Age of Reason," *Modern Language Review*, XLI, no. 5 (1946), 256–69; for the situation in France, see David Williams, "The Politics of Feminism in the French Enlightenment," in *The Varied Pattern: Studies in the 18th Century*, ed. Peter Hughes and David Williams (Toronto: A. M. Hakkert, 1971), pp. 333–51.

4. Paul Heinrich Dietrich, Baron d'Holbach, *Le système social, ou principes naturels de la morale et de la politique, avec un examen de l'influence du gouvernement sur les moeurs*, 2 vols. (Paris: Sirviere, 1795), II, 142–58.

5. Pierre Ambroise François Choderlos de Laclos, *Oeuvres complètes* (Paris: Bibliothèque de la Pléiade, 1951), pp. 428–29.

6. *Politics* I. 13.

7. *Republic* V. 3–5. For a more detailed discussion of the controversy between the Platonists and the Aristotelians on this matter, see Humphreys, "Age of Reason," pp. 257–64.

8. Humphreys, "Age of Reason," p. 265.

9. Wollstonecraft had written in the introduction to her work: "I wish to persuade

women to endeavour to acquire strength, both of mind and body, and to convince them that the soft phrases, susceptibility of heart, delicacy of sentiment, and refinement of taste, are almost synonymous with epithets of weakness, and that those beings who are only the objects of pity and that kind of love, which has been termed its sister, will soon become objects of contempt" (*A Vindication of the Rights of Woman*, ed. Carol H. Poston [New York: Norton, 1975], p. 9; hereafter cited as *Vindication*).

10. *The Second Sex*, ed. and trans. H. M. Parshley (New York: Knopf, 1953), p. 128.

11. Marie Jean Antoine Nicholas Caritat, Marquis de Condorcet, *The First Essay on the Political Rights of Women*, trans. Alice Drysdale Vickery (Letchworth: Garden City Press, [1912]), p. 5.

12. Miriam Kramnick suggests this in the introduction to her edition of the *Vindication* (Harmondsworth: Penguin Books, 1975), p. 29.

13. *Biographie des Königl. Preuss. Geheimenkreisraths zu Königsberg, Theodor Gottlieb von Hippel, zum Theil von ihm verfasst* (Gotha: Perthes, 1801), p. 273.

14. *Sämmtliche Werke*, ed. Theodor Gottlieb von Hippel, 14 vols. (Berlin: Reimer, 1827–39), XII, 58. (The editor is Hippel's nephew.)

15. *Ibid.*, pp. 31–32.

16. December 18, 1780, *ibid.*, XIV, 203.

17. *Ibid.*, p. 78.

18. That this attitude prevailed throughout Hippel's life is illustrated by the fact that while he was still a student of theology he chose as the topic for a sermon which he was to deliver at his father's church in Gerdauen "The Peace of God—Greater than Human Reason" (*ibid.*, XII, 106), and by a statement he made near the end of his life: "I have even been cured of [my] enthusiastic devotion to reason; only friendship can now rouse my enthusiasm, and it will continue to do so until I have reached my end" (*ibid.*, XII, 295).

19. See Fritz Werner, *Das Todesproblem in den Werken Theodor Gottlieb von Hippels* (Halle: Niemeyer, 1938).

20. *Werke*, XII, 65.

21. *Ibid.*, VII, 1.

22. Hippel's distrust of Voss was perhaps not unfounded, for he complains to Scheffner in his letter of July 8, 1778, that Voss had mentioned in the literary newspaper which he sponsored that the author of the book on marriage was also the author of the *Lebensläufe*, ostensibly in an attempt to sell more copies of each of these books. This action greatly annoyed Hippel (*ibid.*, XIV, 97–98).

23. Letter to Scheffner, August 17, 1775, *ibid.*, p. 9.

24. Letter of January 27, 1783, *ibid.*, p. 264.

25. See, for example, the introduction by his nephew to Hippel's correspondence in the *Sämmtliche Werke*, XIII, xiii-xiv; and Ferdinand Josef Schneider, "Theodor Gottlieb von Hippels Schriftstellergeheimnis," *Altpreussische Monatsschrift*, LI (1915), 1–35.

26. See Immanuel Kant, *Gesammelte Schriften*, ed. Royal Prussian Academy of Sciences, 24 vols. (Berlin and Leipzig: De Gruyter, 1910–66), XII, 360–61.

27. *Werke*, XII, vi–vii.

28. That Scheffner never was able to overcome his feeling of having been deluded is seen clearly in his treatment of Hippel in his autobiography, written many years after the incident and published posthumously in 1823. For a more detailed account of the entire sequence of events, see Ferdinand Josef Schneider, "Hippel und seine Freunde," *Euphorion*, XIX (1912), 110–22.

29. Adolf Heinrich Friedrich von Schlichtegroll, *Nekrolog 1796* (Gotha: J. Perthes, 1797), II, 171–346; *1797*, I, 123–416.

30. In an article by Theodor Mundt in *Zeitgenossen* (Leipzig: Brockhaus, 1832), 3d ser., bks. 1–2.

31. See Arthur Warda, "Der Anlass zum Bruch der Freundschaft zwischen Hippel und Scheffner," *Altpreussische Monatsschrift*, LII (1916), 276.

32. See the introduction to his edition of *Über die Ehe* (Leipzig: Brockhaus, 1872), p. xxv.

33. It seems unlikely that any of the then extant documents or books of Hippel's were taken elsewhere for safekeeping during the horror and chaos of the last days before the capitulation of Königsberg (now Kaliningrad) to the Russian armies in April 1945. In 1958 a colleague of mine, James C. O'Flaherty, inquired about the existence of Hamann documents in the Soviet archives. The reply from the Soviet Academy of Sciences was negative. If no attempt was made to preserve the papers of the philosopher Hamann, then internationally known, the work of the unknown Hippel presumably also perished.

34. As an example, the following is taken from a review in the *Neue allgemeine deutsche Bibliothek*: "If anyone wishes . . . to come to the conclusion that the entire book is persiflage, we would not object—except [to say] that it is very lengthy and devoid of warmth, and that the author often adopts a very serious tone. On the other hand, it might also be said that whoever could write in such a way about a serious theme must have taken leave of his senses, and [since] we in fact do not quite know how to contradict this argument, we shall leave undecided the question of whether the whole book is to be [viewed as] nonsensical seriousness or a frigid and boring joke" (cited in Warda, "Hippel und Scheffner," pp. 275–76).

35. *Werke*, XII, 46.

36. As an example of Hippel's views on this subject, as well as for the insight it provides into the importance he placed on his writing as an even greater means of bringing about improvement than his office as a high-ranking governmental official, the following excerpt from his letter to Scheffner of April 16, 1780, is reproduced here: "'Whoever can do less, should write etc. . . .' [Hippel is quoting from Scheffner's last letter to him]. Not so, my friend! With the world situation the way it is now? Or the condition of the countries [in it]—who can do any good? Everything lies knee-deep in misery, in corruption. If the world is yet to be raised up, who can save it from affliction, fear, and distress? Who can turn away its misfortune? Is [salvation] not in the hands of the author? If not here, then nowhere. What good does it do even to educate a disciple? If he [then] thinks as we do, is the world made even a hair's breadth better thereby? If man ever comes to anything in the world, it will be through ideas, . . . and it is a good book which brings [us] to ideas, to concepts. . . . Perhaps I can make myself clearer if I say that with the present state of affairs man [simply] cannot act. The only thing left to him is thought" (*ibid.*, XIV, 175).

37. Ferdinand Josef Schneider, "Hippel als Schüler Montaignes, Hamanns, und Herders," *Euphorion*, XXIII (1921), 185.

38. *Miscellaneous Works*, 5 vols (London: T. Becket and P. A. De Hondt, 1767), I, 166.

39. Letter of June 16, 1777, *Werke*, XII, 55.

40. *Vindication*, p. 10.

41. In the advertisement to the *Vindication*, Wollstonecraft states her intention to publish a second volume on a number of topics not treated in the first, "especially the laws relative to women," but this volume never appeared.

42. While Wollstonecraft, by her own admission (*Vindication*, p. 106), was greatly indebted to Catherine Macaulay's *Letters on Education* (1790) for many of her ideas, both Wollstonecraft and Hippel, like every other writer on education in the period, including Macaulay, owed much more to the book which first advocated truly modern educational methods, Rousseau's *Émile, ou de l'education* (1762). It was merely Book V of this work, dealing with the education of women, which justifiably aroused the ire of the feminists.

43. *Werke*, XII, 275.

44. *Vindication*, p. 23.

45. Hippel concludes that "differences of a sexual nature between man and woman may not serve as an answer to the question whether the male sex was endowed with significant physical and intellectual superiority over the female," but he admits that the present state of science is not advanced enough to determine whether there actually exist differences other than those of a distinctly sexual nature. That Hippel himself, in spite of his seeming affection for the talents of the female sex, actually was more in sympathy with the ideas of the Platonists can be seen from his letter to Scheffner of November 21, 1793: "The matter

cannot be set right in an *a priori* way, since nature has created no difference between the sexes. *A posteriori* just as little, since the opposite sex was very early rendered incapable of obtaining experience [in worldly matters]" (cited by Schneider, "Hippels Schriftstellergeheimnis," p. 26).

46. See, for example, his letters of June 28, 1777, and July 17, 1777, *Werke*, XIV, 58 and 63.

47. *Über die Einsamkeit*, 4 vols. (Frankfurt and Leipzig: n.p., 1785), III, 339–40.

48. Although Zimmermann still reflects the tenor of the times when he wries later: "for our good ladies are satisfied even if they only half please [us]," and "love can pass away, but coquetry never" (*ibid*, IV, 165).

49. The first edition of the present work, in contrast to almost all German books of the period, was done in Roman type, not fraktur. It is possible, even probable, that he chose this type to make his text more accessible to foreign readers and thus broaden its effect.

50. It seems, however, that Hippel's ideas on the role of woman in marriage—as reflected in his *Über die Ehe*, the genesis of which Schneider places convincingly at 1765 or earlier (*Theodor Gottlieb von Hippel in den Jahren von 1741 bis 1781 und die erste Epoche seiner literarischen Tätigkeit* [Prague: Taussig & Taussig, 1911], pp. 103–4)—and on the role of woman in society in general did not precisely coincide at that time. Hippel then was less willing to speak of equality in marriage than of a need for reform of the *civil* status of women. As evidence for this assumption, in Hippel's collected works (X, 234–46) there is a remarkable document which clearly places Hippel among the earliest true advocates of such reform. One of his speeches delivered before his Masonic lodge, in his official capacity as Lodge Orator, carries the title "On the Duties of a Mason toward the Fair Sex" and can be accurately dated in 1768 (Schneider, *Hippel*, p. 194). Hippel here considers the duty of the Mason to be that of combating prejudice toward the female sex and of working toward removing restrictions on its rights. Such statements as "Why should we talk away rights to which the fair sex has been appointed by nature? Let us, rather, far removed from the flatteries of this siren [song], speak to and for the fair sex in the way truth and honesty demand, in order to wrest its heart and soul from the house of bondage and tyranny" fall far outside the usual framework of Masonic rhetoric, and more properly belong, in Schneider's words, "at a congress of modern suffragettes than at an assembly of pigtailed Freemasons of the eighteenth century" (p. 195). Thus, an equilibrium between Hippel's views of the role of woman in marriage and in society seems to have been achieved only in 1792.

51. A few later works, however, do acknowledge the influence of Hippel's pioneer work in their very titles: see, for example, Ludwig Wilhelm Weissenborn's *Briefe über die bürgerliche Selbständigkeit der Weiber* (Gotha: Perthes, 1806).

52. Miriam Kramnick makes this statement in her edition of the *Vindication*, p. 67.

53. *Nachlass über weibliche Bildung* (Berlin: Voss, 1801).

54. Clara Zetkin, from 1891 to 1916 editor of the Social Democratic women's newspaper *Die Gleichheit* [Equality], was an exception. In her book *Zur Geschichte der proletarischen Frauenbewegung Deutschlands*, 2d ed. (Berlin: Dietz, 1958), pp. 17–18, she gives Hippel full credit for his contribution to the theoretical background of the feminist movement. It must also be noted that during the period of most intense activity within the movement for women's suffrage in Germany (1909) a pamphlet of thirty-nine pages was published by Felix Dietrich Verlag consisting of short selections from Hippel's *Status of Women* with the added subtitle: *A Contribution to the Woman Question*. This work, edited by Achim Winterfeld, was brought out as part of Dietrich's new series "Culture and Progress," a continuation of the publisher's previous series entitled "Social Progress, Pamphlets on Political Economy, Social Politics, the Woman Question, the Administration of Justice, and Matters of Culture."

55. Edmond and Jules de Goncourt, *The Woman of the Eighteenth Century*, trans. Jacques le Clercq and Ralph Roeder (New York: Minton, Balch, 1927), p. 3.

56. Anne Louise Germaine, Baronne de Staël-Holstein, *De la littérature*, 2 vols. (Paris: Maradan, [1800]), I, 311.

57. Cecily (Ullmann) Sidgwick, *Germany* (London: A. & C. Black, 1909), cited in W. H. Bruford, *Germany in the Eighteenth Century* (Cambridge: Cambridge University Press, 1935), pp. 225–26.

58. Rudolf Huebner, *A History of Germanic Private Law,* trans. Francis S. Philbrick (Boston: Little, Brown, 1918), p. 64. Much of the material which follows concerning the legal status of women has been abstracted from this work.

59. *Ibid.,* pp. 17–20.

60. Eugen Huber, *System und Geschichte des schweizerischen Privatrechts,* 4 vols. (Basel: C. Detleff, 1886–93), IV, 293; cited in Huebner, *Germanic Law,* p. 67.

61. *Ibid.*

62. *Ibid.,* p. 68.

On Improving
the Status
of Women

ÜBER DIE

BÜRGERLICHE VERBESSERUNG

DER WEIBER

BERLIN, 1792.

in der Voſsischen Buchhandlung

I / Form and Substance of the Present Treatise

*T*HE MOST RIGOROUS demonstration of the truth of certain matters is provided, it is said, when such matters resist every effort to make them look ridiculous and to travesty them, and when, in spite of all the absurdity with which they are adorned, they continue to remain worthy of respect. But if the curved line is the line of beauty, then one would hardly find it questionable to entrust to laughter the keys of the heavenly kingdom of truth. This is surely an awkward situation, and one which, as far as the present treatise is concerned, involves me in a dilemma of no small proportions, for I have in mind a matter in which by far the greatest part of the seriousness is so intermingled—not from the beginning and by nature, but through long-established habit—with the absurd, that it is not so easy here to entrust to an exposition such as this a model for their division.

When a knight of truly merry countenance[1] begins to fight, who and what can stand steadfast against him? Which fortress of system and dogma can hold out? Socrates, the wisest, not of kings, but of the wise, that most excellent core in a repulsive outer covering,[2] that angel among men (although he was not conspicuously dressed), became in *The Clouds* an object of farce. And what author is able to count with assurance on a heaven filled with happy critics and readers? Seldom has a person existed who has never gone from the frying-pan into the fire, and never has a light come into the world without finding its Aristophanes, who without further ado straightway blew it out again, or, under the pretext of wanting to extinguish it, merely meddled with it and obscured it. In this respect absurdity almost seems to be the daily bread of mankind, and without question one fares best by joining, with propriety and deference, in the laughter; or, disregarding both the image and superscription of the serious, by giving a tone to his treatise which avoids gravely proffered inanities (which are the most ridiculous of all).

"You will not weep nearly so much over me as you have laughed," said Scarron, the ancestor by marriage of Louis XIV,[3] to those who had gathered around his deathbed and wept. It was this notion which was able to cheer him in his hour of death—and indeed, why not? Now, when even hallowed morality neither desires nor is able to seek her fortune within cloistered walls, and instead moves about in the best of spirits, bidding us to adorn with garlands the goblets which she fills with her heart-warming wine; now, when every repugnant facet of a man's outward appearance sooner betrays the hardness of his heart than its purity; now has mirth become an ingredient of good breeding, and laughter and weeping live united in such happy wedlock that those philosophical charlatans of whom the one was never able to get past laughing and the other past weeping[4] would hardly receive professorships at our academies. Children, who are the closest of all to nature, laugh and cry over one and the same thing, and a gentle bride tears herself weeping from the arms of her abandoned mother only to throw herself, almost at that very moment, laughing into the arms of her beloved.

Our life is ebb tide and flood tide, a continuous alternation of joy and sorrow. And should not all affairs of daily life show traces and impressions of the *comédie larmoyante* of this enchanted castle of a planet[5] on which it is allotted to us to play our human role? It is the most difficult one, perhaps, in God's great universe—but perhaps also the easiest, depending upon how it is played.

Notwithstanding all the memorable endeavors of many a noble knight who has wished to remove the spell from mankind and thereby from the earth as well, the adventure is not yet over. O sin, that accursed sorceress, the ruin of such righteous people! If we were not already slaves our entire life through the remembrance of death, then at least it is thoughts of death and God which bring us, at all events, to a *memento mori*. It was truly a philosophic attitude when king Xerxes in his majesty both rejoiced and lamented over his army.[6] Every pain has its pleasure; and how dull is the amusement which is not spiced with some bitterness! The wise man is allowed merely to dream of happiness; sorrow, as the usual lot of mankind, it is his unremitting duty to bear with composure. And indeed, at all times there exists a middle way, a tempered happiness, a smile which comes forth with warm tears in our eyes. In every span of twenty-four hours there is night and day—a light which rules the day, and one which rules the night. I can be more specific in this introduction if I note that the fair sex, true to nature, possesses from on high the good and perfect gift of so sweetening all the acrimony which it is accustomed to using in its defense and attack, and of so tempering all its seriousness by means of a mitigating smile, that I need take no time for reflection in order to pay homage to this charming example and to recall, with a candor inspired by altruism, the double-faced head of the ancient god Janus.

Moreover, to the individual member of this sex, and also to by far the greatest proportion of its members, their burden seems so light and their yoke so slight that they would prefer to remain in a house of bondage in Egypt and at the flesh-pots of comfortable, tangible every-day existence, not desiring to undertake the difficult journey to Canaan, the land where the milk and honey of nature flows.[7] Even women of standing seem often not to realize that along with their purple robes and fine linen they also bear sorrow, and that their life in joy and serenity is a corporal and capital punishment to which they have been sentenced by a secret court of justice.

Wherever there is much glitter, little good taste is to be found—just as bigotry and immorality are generally accustomed to being the best of neighbors. It is truly the absolute height of sickness when patients look upon feverishness as radiant good health and reject every medication; in like manner it also exceeds the usual degree of human corruption when slaves dismiss their claims to all rights and base their constitution on the favorable disposition of their masters. Who is to blame for this tribunal of obduracy—the other sex? Does anyone wish to pass judgment, when even that prophet of nature, Rousseau himself, who desired to convert the whole world—especially the more beautiful half thereof—to nature, preferred, in spite of this powerful sermon on repentance and belief, the company of elegant ladies? How his vanity could luxuriate when people of station patronized him, even though at the very same time he waxed eloquent at every opportunity on the decay of the upper classes! However, I do not wish to jump ahead to the second part of this chapter.

Let my treatise then accommodate itself to the times, and seek its fortune from every side! Let it not put on airs by invoking the holy number of the Three Sisters[8] thrice multiplied, merely because mere poetic works are accustomed to preparing the way with such an invocation. Above all else in the world, moreover, it is not my desire that the honor be given my treatise of decorating the library of the illustrious republic of Plato.[9] But to the point.

When a sort of paroxysm of the conscience actually befell Louis XIV because of the new burdens which he had intended for his already oppressed people, he found in the poor consolation of his father confessor Tellier "that the riches of his people were his own possession" such a soft cushion for his awakened conscience[10] that he would have had no misgivings about doubling, on the spur of the moment, the levy which had previously troubled him; and without doubt it was his implicit faith in this belief which formed the basis for his assertion: "I am the state."

Habit so easily becomes second nature that the French, who were enduring the oppression of a Terray and the harshness of a Maupou,[11] considered themselves sufficiently fortunate when a small, perhaps even the most despicable, segment of society was able to gulp down the cup of joy of the state, filled by the tithes of widows and the savings of the wretched, while the larger working part, languishing under the yoke of the arbitrary rule of despotism and poverty, nevertheless always had the good humor to sing, dance, romp, and whistle, as well as circumstances would allow. For such a carefree group of people, who worried about nothing and relieved the greatest distress with a song, this scourging, partly with whips, partly with scorpions, was all the less noticeable, inasmuch as by means of a complimentary ticket they could be spectators at the gala events and state festivals of the distinguished among them. And the longer this scourging continued, the better this segment of the population learned to accept the fact that the others kept the cup of joy for themselves alone and acted as if they did it in the best interests of all. The crumbs which fell to the artist and the milliner from the tables of the rich were an abundant harvest for them, and the dogs of the great licked their sores.

This wretchedness and misery has come to its blessed end, and lampposts appear to have dispersed in France the light of nature and of an equality among men[12] so widely that at times one does not seem, because of all this light, to see the light at all. There are people who do not see the forest for the trees, and too much brightness is blinding. One can find people dazzled by morality, as well, who have the fortune or misfortune of seeing something glitter where the healthy eye of the intellect perceives nothing. How would it be if I, without war cry and alarm bell, were to seek with a lantern, as once did Diogenes of old, real human beings in the fashionable world, where such a superabundance of thousands upon thousands of objects is to be had either for love or money? Would I find any?

Effervescence is associated with some chemical reactions; in some heat is produced; in others, cold. Let your Excellency please not become too excited; rather let her reserve her acrimony for her unfaithful admirer No. 30![13] One swallow does not make a summer, and my light has been blown out by a single breath of your passion. If it would please Your Excellency to deign to enter, with propriety and honor, into a well-intended disputation with me, You would, as I affectionately hope, change your mind, and perhaps come to the conviction that I deserve less reproach than all your admirers down to this No. 30, who, to be sure, is not behaving as he should—for which I and my treatise are in no way to blame.

If I am not a gallant admirer, then at least I am a devotee of a sex among which You and many others of Your peers are so incorrectly addressed as Excellency, while on the other hand other excellent women, who deserve this title of honor ten times over, are not given this title for reasons of courtly etiquette.

"It would never occur to anyone else but a German to write such a book as this!"

Also among the French there existed genuine individuals, who, even though they did not leap immediately into the foray and consider improving the status of the fair sex, nevertheless allotted a different condition to it. I myself have always believed that one should strike at the heart of the trouble and not leave the state out of the picture.

"France, where everything is now considered equal, left our sex untouched."

Unforgivable! How could a people which exists *by* and *for* the fair sex (as the late Voltaire lived *by* and *for* the comedians and comediennes) neglect, in their proclamation of general equality which has been acclaimed throughout the world, a sex possessing a queen with doubtless few equals in the world?[14]

If I only knew how I should go about interceding here, in order to arrive honorably at the end of this excellent disputation. But of course! I shall follow the course currently favored by the ladies themselves, who defy and plead, bless and curse all in the same breath.

Perhaps it was merely because the world of women was not taken into account that the human race has been exposed to so great a fluctuation between light and darkness, ennoblement and degradation, paradise and fall. The race waxed and waned, depending upon whether it took notice of this other half, and whether this half was viewed as something essential to humanity, or as an extraneous segment which ought to feel privileged to follow along behind. Often the fair sex, like rhyme in poetry, was viewed as hardly more than a crutch to help the thinking process along; and in messiads[15] and other works of poetry where such a crutch was not used, the other sex had to be content with receiving short shrift. The Roman legal proverb: "Measure yourself by the same standard which you use for others" seems utterly to have lost its validity here, when it really belongs to those commandments which it is a sin against the Holy Spirit to violate.[16] How is material to be organized, if it is not planned with the intention of simplifying the complicated? How is the human race to be aided and advised, when it acts in such an awfully one-sided way? The heaven of the ancient world had its goddesses as well as its gods; only among mankind here on earth are there to be, by the grace of God, no other gods in addition to the men!

If it brings joy to the soul when the most radically different viewpoints meet at a point of mutual contact where their original relationship again becomes apparent; when distant objects which have become utterly estranged from each other meet once more in the realm of the spirits; when these same objects give one another their hands and wedding-rings, and a voice is heard from heaven: "What therefore God hath joined together, let no man put asunder"; if it is unspeakable joy when friends, after long journeys on land and sea, embrace each other and recall the delightful years of their youth, when they were still of one heart and mind; how much more splendid will it be, when the other sex stands in the same relationship to ours as Eve did to Adam, and not as Your Excellency to Your No. 30!

Let us relinquish this work of the past; even though it does, by virtue of some incomprehensible generosity, occasionally produce periods of cooperation, nevertheless, according to the usual course of things, one has neither been able to count on this cooperation nor seek it out. Let us look forward to the time when the day of redemption for the fair sex will arrive; when people will no longer hinder others who are qualified for equal rights from exercising those rights; and when no discrimination is made between things which are obviously equal to each other. But I would be a woman-sympathizer of the first rank if I wished to maintain that this golden age will fall from the sky. Merit and worth are the stipulations for human happiness, and man, his own sculptor, can form a god or a beast out of the marble block which Nature has thrown to him. I am limiting myself merely to the assumption that the material from which a Venus was produced can be formed just as well into a Mercury; that to women is due the right to grace and mercy; and that, when

Nature began to shape the human race, she left the greater portion of this work to us, so as to share with us the honor of the creation. Activity is the spice of enjoyment, and enjoyment is the spice of activity.

It is an inborn tendency of man, says Cicero in more or less these words, that when he thinks himself to be a god, it is his own human nature which is hovering before him. People have defined man, as once did the most excellent Plato of old, as a two-legged animal without feathers,[17] or as a creature which carries himself upright like a dancing instructor, or as a god, or an animal. Nowhere are women excluded from these definitions; only they must also not exclude themselves, and do they want to and will they continue to do that? Wesley, the founder of Methodism, held to the maxim that it was impossible to grow in grace without fasting and arising early in the morning. Of what use is the most noble right, if one makes oneself unworthy of it? The female sex must grow in its sense of justification, and not in grace; in the meantime, I can offer no better prescription than this one of the Methodists: vigilance and temperance.

What ruler, even if he were the richest and mightiest, is happy without a feeling of personal merit? Thomas Paine, who vehemently denied the reproach of being an enemy of the ruling class, and in protesting asserted that none could desire more staunchly than he to raise rulers to the fortunate position of private persons, failed to bear in mind that every sovereign leads not only a political but also a private life as well. He further failed to note that sovereigns must display more personal merit than other people if they wish to be loved and admired, and that it is possible for them to distinguish themselves personally and still to remain sovereigns. That is, with Your Excellency's gracious permission, the case with Your sex. "When fashion arrives, good sense will depart."

A *garde-fou*; a danger sign for the benefit of the thickheaded: I have not been conducting this colloquy with a real "Excellency" at all (had that been the case I could hardly have spoken my mind but would have had to coat my few words with sugar). If an artist is limited merely to painting portraits and is not allowed to attempt anything in its ideal form, then his art suffers and his genius, too, approaches extinction; nevertheless, among one's ideal forms one must also make a selection of portraits, if the former are ever to deserve the designation "ideal." In the figure of a Venus is to be found a distillation of five hundred beautiful girls. My Excellency is also in the world of ideas; I hope she will nonetheless remain recognizable enough, and without doubt her reflected image can be discovered more than five hundred times. It was actually my intention, by means of this magic mirror, to vent my anger on the complaisant injustice which our own sex shows to the fair sex—to vent my anger, however, without bringing about a desire in the members of this sex to free themselves from their kings or abolish sovereign rule completely, as in ancient Rome after Tarquinius the Proud was driven from the throne on account of his tyrannical rule and this action was designated as the exercise of a basic right. In reality our dominion is not very much more than a "monarchy of the log," familiar to us from an old fable;[18] and our system of moral values brings about in us a certain impotence, by reason of which (to the true good fortune of the whole) only a few men attain actual domination.

However, in order to draw in the reins on this first chapter, which has become similar to a speech in parliament or even the National Assembly,[19] I trust it would not be in violation of the book *On Marriage*, that catechism of matrimony both acclaimed and censured with which I wish neither to side nor to quarrel, if I conduct business with only a single plan of operation for the destruction of the *bastilles* of the fashionable world, the fortresses of the domestic, and the dungeons of the civil world wherein the fair sex finds itself: if I recommend improvement of the status of women as a practical means of reaching this objective. And I herewith faithfully affirm that this new standing within the state, which will require more of the sweat of our brows to maintain than to attain, will be beneficial to both hemispheres of the human race, both now and for all time to come.

Reason proceeds calmly and with conviction; and only in the case where people shamefully desire to do battle with her using unequal weapons, where prejudice throws down the gauntlet and brute force blocks her way, is she accustomed to giving up her initial well-conceived plan and substituting another for it. In such cases progress is not furthered; rather, the bad is exchanged for the worse; the blind is exchanged for the lame; the affair is merely altered without being improved. This is an infallible sign of weakheadedness, from the throne down to the last minor official.

Thank heavens there always have been, and still are, women for whom this position of degradation is too severe a trial; women who despair not over the fact that they are women, but over the way they are treated by our sex, and who look forward to their deliverance from this treatment. My treatise is not intended to provide ammunition for their attack. One can learn by teaching, and instruct oneself in the art of giving commands by obeying them. I have little intention of freeing the other sex this very moment from its slavery; rather, I would content myself with encouraging it to earn this deliverance. "To become worthy of heaven" is hardly different from saying: "To be an active citizen of heaven."

If even this modest intention finds rocky soil and hearts of stone—no matter! It is really nothing more than a book which I am perpetrating; truly an insignificant thing. Has one ever had an effect? At the very time it was read? Right then and there? Experiences and perceptions of such a tangible evil as to contradict human nature—*these* have an effect; and if it has been precisely a majority of hands which have many times gained a decision and will continue to do so, the superiority resulting from a larger number of workers does not hold true for the plurality of readers, who exist in a proportion to the thinkers of about a hundred to one. And upon my word, even the thinkers! Are they not such an invisible church that only the Lord knows those who are his own? It has truly no influence on the effect of a book whether it has ten printings, five, or only one printing; and the author who wishes to reckon, according to the number of copies sold, on an army of like-thinking individuals recruited with the "bounty" of his book, would seem to know neither people nor books, and ought to be sent back to school.

Every piece of writing, regardless of its rank or reputation, has in store for itself the usual fate of all writings: to be read and then forgotten—forgotten, that is, if it confines itself to the presentation of opinions (the most harmless, ineffectual things in the world, unless the censor has the unkind kindness to attribute to them a semblance of significance). If I succeed, however, in putting life and experience into my little book, and in breathing some spirit into lifeless letters, then at least I can count on a portion of the respect which oral communication has over the written; for it is said of the former: "From the sermon proceedeth faith."

Under such circumstances my objective, admittedly, is a journey around the world—without once leaving my room. Whether this is the most comfortable way to travel is a moot question; at all events it is not the least fruitful way. Newton measured the earth while sitting in his easy chair, and determined its shape without having climbed the Chimborazo or frozen in Tornio[20] —long years before the gentlemen Condamine and Maupertuis;[21] so I, too, am not the first to travel in such a way.

What if I were fortunate enough to show the present passive existence of the fair sex in its true perspective, in order to render suspect the alleged merit in the idea that inactivity is a sign of strength? What if I could teach a pleasure-seeking people—which squanders, by niggardly saving it for emergencies, even the luxury of morality in pursuing the luxury of sensuous pleasure—more economical basic principles, and could bring this people to record *credit* and *debit* over body and soul, and then to keep books on them? What if my well-intended ideas had the effect of causing woman not to become masculine to the extent that men have become feminine, but rather of causing both men and women to make the effort to become *true* men and women. At the present, because of the confusion which has prevailed for years and should be regarded as obsolete, nobody knows with respect to the sexes just who is the goose and who the gander! What if I were not to meet with the usual fate of reformers, who wish to bring forth everything out of season; who lack the intelligence and vigor to bring the new epoch about any sooner, and what is even worse, who understand so little of the pulse of the times that they usually have the honor of coming too early—or, if luck is with us, too late? O, the feeling of intoxication which hope gives the writer!

Improving the status of the Jews has, in our times, been much recommended;[22] should a *genuine people of God* (the other sex) less deserve this attention than one which has been *so named*? Does not the seed of Original Sin lie with the mother? And do not the obstacles to a moral reform of the human race—which reform the best people on earth, and among these Frederick the Great, so energetically proposed in the beginning, but sadly abandoned in the end—arise chiefly from the fact that we have desired to erect this temple of reform from our own sex alone, while the fair sex has been left to lie in ruins? Is it not inexcusable to leave half of the resources of mankind unknown, unassessed, and unused?

Society as a concept presupposes equality among its members, an equality which the creator of man, who made him an upright being, also has ordained for him; unfortunately, however, he seeks many artifices in order to evade this equality. In all social gatherings in which women take part, propriety is proclaimed; and should this not also be the case with the state, into whose affairs a different light and life would enter if women were permitted access to it, so as to let their light shine therein and impart a different energy and animation?

We have no regulations for our social groups governing the duty of each individual within a group; and yet people conduct themselves in such an exemplary manner without a civil code that frequently uncivil persons, for whom society has lost all hope, have gone to this school with obvious profit, and were brought from it to the university of the state as reformed individuals.

I am so bold as to assert (without rendering evidence to the contrary invalid) that beyond a doubt certain refined traits of good breeding could be detected in all governments headed by women—traits which have more effect on a great part of mankind than a well-appointed codex filled with elegantly stated expletives of rebuke. That sweet aroma of the compliment; that spice of agreeableness—how charming! The legislation of Catherine the Great is replete with examples of it.

The very presence of the woman of the house makes necessary a moderation in speaking on the part of the men, even though she cannot, to be sure, maintain the authority of the house with the utmost severity. If anyone should care to reply to the above that ears have become the more chaste in the proportion that the heart has become less so, then he is forgetting that a certain pretense, a certain hypocrisy which people call "manners" is necessary among human beings. Without manners people would not greet each other with a smile, like a pair of soothsayers of yore upon meeting each other, or a pair of more recent ones upon holding a consultation regarding extreme unction for a patient; rather, they would show their detestation for each other. Purity of speech reflects credit on the speaker, and "out of the abundance of the heart the mouth speaketh."[23]

II / Are There Other Differences between Man and Woman besides Those of a Sexual Nature?

*A*T THE TIME when God, after having taken counsel with Himself on the work of Creation, set upon carrying out His plan, He created the first and foremost pair of human beings from the beginning as mature and marriageable adults, in order that their nuptials would not be delayed even an hour. They came into the world with the requisite number of years behind them, in the same manner that sovereigns bestow illustrious forebears upon a new aristocracy which previously had no tradition of nobility. To be sure, Master Adam, the male, had the honor of being the firstborn; on the other hand Miss Eve was thoroughly compensated for this through her birth from a rib of Adam, whereas the latter had been brought into the world from a mere clump of earth!

"A creation, then, at second hand?"

Why not even at third hand! Did not the very same hand which created Adam also create Eve? And does not this "rib hieroglyph"[1] serve in more than one respect to the advantage of the woman? Neither of the two raised the other; neither of them thought to place himself above the other and to assert patriarchal authority. Instead it was parental authority, the finest and most sacred right known to humanity, the fountainhead of the most beneficent virtues, which produced (who would have thought it!) this inequality among human beings. Good parents, and yet such a depraved, degenerate daughter!

If, however, many of our vices are nothing more than ill-bred virtues; and if, according to the declaration of a certain saintly person, our virtues are merely beautiful vices,[2] then one would be committing a crime against mankind if he did not desire to display fairness to evil as well, and to its ideal form, the devil. Indeed, if one wished to go by the testimony of the oldest documents concerning the human race in giving preference to one half of this couple over the other, then Eve would receive the apple of discord from any and every Paris.[3]

"Because she was more beautiful than Helen of Troy? And because every Paris, no matter how naïve in perceptual matters, remains a male nonetheless?"

No! Rather it was because Adam was brought to his fall through her; or (as this noble and profound, lofty and beautiful hieroglyph can perhaps correctly be interpreted) because through her influence he allowed himself to be put in the proper frame of mind to be used and employed, and thus to become receptive to the breakthrough of reason. O blessed receptivity!

It was Eve who acted as the Children's Bureau[4] for the minor Adam; after he ostensibly had been under the guardianship of this good woman for a time, it was she, having already emancipated herself in certain respects beforehand, who then issued the declaration of majority for him; it was she who shattered the bonds of instinct which had prevented human reason from rising up, and it was she who triumphed thereby. In memory of her the words *Eve* and *Reason* ought to be regarded as synonymous.

This first revolution, like every revolution, could not take place without anxiety and affliction. Both of these are, considering the nature of man, so necessary that I know of nothing, be it either of a theoretical or practical nature, which, if it distinguishes itself as new and different in any way, was not conceived and born in disorder and passion. But this riotous condition cannot continue to prevail indefinitely. The waves must finally die down, and Reason must at last gain the victory. So it was with the first revolution, and this is the way it must be with all others if they wish to be worthy of the name.

My panegyric in praise of Eve, which is, after all, fitting and proper in view of the Revolution of Reason which has taken place, would perhaps afford opportunities galore for a theological, legal, medical, or philosophical disputation, or for an essay in some entertaining journal, if one only knew how to get that unwelcome guest of a counselor, the snake, out of the picture. Not much, unfortunately, can be done with this devilish disturber of matrimonial bliss. "In short," says the believer Thomas Paine, "I am an enemy of the whole devil of a monarchy."[5] Since, however—and with due respect for Mr. Paine's opinion—such devilish disturbers of *republican* bliss can and do exist as well, it is best to send all of these little devils straight to hell. Perhaps this is the best kind of justice which can be shown to them.

The story of Creation does not, in its lucid relation of events, speak of any other differences between man and woman than those of a sexual nature. "And God said, let us make man in our own image, after our likeness. . . . So God created man in his own image, in the image of God created he him; male and female created he them." It is only in a much later epoch that we find the words: "And thy desire shall be to thy husband, and he shall rule over thee." [6] And if one imagines with regard to the story of the Fall of Man a portrait of the emancipation of man from the paradisal yoke of instinct, and of the origin of the social condition, for which the wise woman Eve was the intermediary and herald, then these prophetic words seem to proclaim that sad condition which Eve brought upon her sex as a result of this heroic deed.

But would the true nature of the matter confirm those primal documents and their exegesis? Such old and venerable things are not to be convicted by the mere Testimony of the Seven;[7] and of what value is this hazardous method of proof anyway? Of what value, since we can call up Experience and Reason to serve as witnesses for the everlasting recollection of the Creation. From the mouths of these two witnesses proceeds all manner of truth.

In the formation of the two sexes, nature does not appear to have intended to establish a noteworthy difference or to have favored one sex at the expense of the other. Differences of a sexual nature between man and woman may not serve as an answer to the question whether the male sex was endowed with significant physical and intellectual superiority over the female. Differences other than those of a sexual nature have until now eluded the anatomist's knife; nevertheless this instrument has continued to hold fast to the golden rule: Know Thyself—an undeniable influence. On the whole, noble iron has served the human race to a far greater extent than that exhibitionist, gold. Whoever first gave the magnet the name Bride of Iron showed to both the magnet and iron a respect which they fully deserve.[8]

What could have prompted Nature to bestow honor and fortune on one half of her greatest masterpiece, while allowing the other to decay through neglect—and this precisely to the extent that she favors the first? In fulfilling that great purpose of Nature in which human beings display the divine image of God, the female sex plays a disproportionately more significant role than the male with respect to both matter and form.[9] So in order to work quite reasonably toward the aforementioned end, Nature is supposed to have wanted to make women weaker or even to leave them half finished?

"*Not necessarily weaker,*" said a woman-hater as he read this part of my manuscript, "*but not such a commonplace thing. Let women be steel, and let the men be iron.*"

Not so! And why this ambiguous comparison, since pure and un- adulterated right stands on the side of the women! People think that we men, thank the Lord, were created as complete as possible; after our creation the Master broke the mold of clay and the second sex, repre- sented in the figure of Eve, was simply a chance undertaking; was made as an afterthought; was sooner abandoned than carried through to completion; was begun and never completed!

Is woman, to whom the actual business of the humanization of the divine creation was entrusted, thought to bear upon her breast the mark of feebleness and insufficiency? Is Almighty Nature supposed to have allowed her own representative to remain in a feeble state, so that woman could bring into the world not only *feeble* individuals of *her own* sex, but *strong* ones of *our* kind as well? Such would seem to be the case; and surely when experience speaks, then it is up to sophistry to be silent, to genuflect and worship her. Experience is the only artifice Nature has left—but then what does it teach us here? If we were to trust in its conclusions, then the other sex is, on the whole, of a smaller and weaker constitution, possesses less physical strength, and is subject to various disabilities. Is further evidence necessary to accommodate Rea- son in her conclusion that these are imperfections of their sex from which women, according to the order of things, can never be liberated? Everything is good which cannot be otherwise, and in the word *must* there lies a treasure-house of grounds for complacency, grounds by means of which anyone, with a little philosophical legerdemain, can so reconcile the words *I must* with the words *I want to* that in such an instance every curse is transformed into a blessing, and the wicked, evil world into the best of all possible worlds.[10] Let us be at peace with Nature and with the fair sex; let us all be at peace with one another!

But what if there existed such things as illusory experiences and illusory conclusions? If appearances were deceiving? Reason is afraid of the senses; and even if we have fully resolved in our mind to allow surgery to be performed on our body, we still turn our eyes away at the hour of truth. Reason, the heart, and the senses all play into one another's hands; and not only the heart of man, but also his reason and his senses are in turn both defiant and discouraged—who can deny it? No sooner does man consider himself a god than it occurs to him that he is hardly less an animal. Naked and unprotected he comes into the world, and if other animals are armed or protected, then His Majesty the human being cannot be expected to refrain from exercising his kingly right over the animals in order to feed and clothe himself. This regulation of his treasure is often carried out so painfully by means of the rod, however, that the animals could very well file at nature's court of justice the bitterest of complaints against their most illustrious rulers—and without doubt they do file such complaints, if indeed the apostle Paul has observed correctly.[11] For in truth nature conducts a terrible, secret court of justice—the most terrible which can be imagined! Necessity teaches one to pray, to beg, and to take; nevertheless, she is also a wise teacher of moderation and restraint, and whoever fails to recognize this, in him is not the love of the Father of us all, the Father whose child is everything having life and breath. Without his teacher man can do nothing more than weep—as a sign that he is far from having drawn the longest straw in the lottery. For inasmuch as man has not proven able to settle accounts with himself, his gains have often turned out to be worse than his losses.

My dear fellow! That sort of complaint is overcome through the mighty word *Reason*. Without his weaknesses man ceases to be man, and whoever strives toward something higher in this earthly life runs the risk of being something less and upsetting the plans of the Creator. Do we know of a more noble creature than man which also possesses the power to conceive of God or a virtue in its abstract form? And even the most depraved among us has still not given up this privilege. Man can renounce the image of God for a moment, but not forever. Is Reason not greater than all else; and does she deserve her name at all if she is not able to set a limit to our appetites? Is it not possible for us to exalt the beast in man to a rank just below that of the gods, and thereby to intimidate his passions, which are like the great surges of the sea? Wherever *she* is to be found, there resides humanity, and to undervalue this dignity in the other sex deliberately, amidst the radiance of her divinity, is equivalent to leaving no stone unturned in the determination of our own importance. Not a mere code of laws written on clay tablets would be shattered here; rather, we would be sinning against the divine spirit which resides within ourselves. Can anything be an affair of God which contradicts Reason; or does God ever desire that His affairs be conducted by means of such things as contradict her? By means of Reason, the very echo of His voice, He remains ever close to each of us who through her have become like Him, and in Him "live and move, and have our being."[12]

The standard which I bear is no empty pronouncement by some authority, but truth and justice. Is the female sex actually smaller, as a rule, than the male? Is not the size of a person altogether a relative matter—a matter in which we find more significant influences from climate, nourishment, and other factors unknown to us, than from sexual differences? On the other sides of the Tropics of Cancer and Capricorn, as well as below the equator, the human race is much smaller than in the area between these two parallels of latitude. Past the twentieth and the sixtieth degrees of latitude our recruiting officers would experience about as much success as would a stopover by pirates at the caves of the Alacaluf Indians on Tierra del Fuego. Travelers report that men and women there maintain the very same pace, and were they not aided by the difference in the clothing and the beards of the men, they declare that they would not be able to tell one sex from the other. Nevertheless, one might say, perhaps the climate there is more favorable to the development of the female body. Not at all; their premature withering away contradicts this conjecture, for already in their fortieth year they are covered with wrinkles. Even in more temperate climates variations exist with respect to size; and within these climates there are also individual races which differ from the norm, just as the inhabitants of the lowlands are, as a rule, larger than those of the mountains—as if nature when creating these people had compensated for the great size of the mountain. And in the final analysis, what does size matter?

"But surely one cannot deny the frailty of the female body in comparison with the sinewy, angular male body?"

Certainly this ought to prove more; nevertheless, I fear that in this case as well, experience actually tells us less than we are accustomed to letting her say.

Before we begin battle, however, it is necessary to muster our troops. If we dismiss from our own side the elegant and fun-loving groups and the other sex lets the fashionable women of the higher classes return, together with their ladies-in-waiting, to their beloved menfolk of these same groups—on whom do you want to bet? Indeed, even if these elegant and fashionable ladies were to enter into warfare with our elegant young men—on which side ought we to place our hopes?

Among peoples who stand at the lowest level of culture, the lot of the female sex is a hard one. For hunting peoples, to whom domestic animals are unknown, the women are the beasts of burden which accompany the men on the hunt and carry the captured game back to the hut; among pastoral and agricultural tribes their lot, if it were possible, is even harder: they cultivate the fields; they run mills and produce manufactured goods by preparing for consumption that which the field and the herd offers them in the way of food and clothing; in addition to this they must also manage a household (although a very simple one) while the man of the house devotes his own time to the pursuit of leisure.

Even among peoples who have achieved a certain degree of culture, the part played by the other sex among the members of the working class is not of the kind which would allow us to infer a greater frailty in this sex. Those tasks performed in the cultivation of the soil and at the harvest—are they not divided more or less equally between both sexes? It would in fact be difficult to say which share of the labor is more often overlooked here. Indeed upon examining *all* the occupations which employ the hands and the energy of mankind—does not the portion of work allotted to women invariably entail a greater expenditure of energy? With happy heart the harvester returns home to his hut to rest after his exhausting labor, while even in the simplest country household there still remain manifold tasks for the woman to perform—for the woman, who, by the sweat of her brow, has already bound the sheaves, a task for which no lesser expenditure of energy is required. The radiantly healthy country girl, her face rouged with the unfading hue of summer, is a living refutation of the above unfavorable comparison, and she would be a match for anyone who would care to tempt the strength of her muscles. Female illnesses are the scourge merely of that class of women who bear the honorable title *women* only for the sake of the state and the purpose of ostentation, in the same way that the devoted *valets de chambre* in their employ deserve the title *men*.

Can and should Nature be held responsible for the evils which manners, morals, and conventions—whose name is legion—have brought upon her? The companions of our folly and the accomplices in our arrogance should not be added to the account of Nature, who created man in such simplicity and, regardless of where he took up his abode, provided shelter, food, and clothing—daily and in abundance. Was it ever her wish that he should fetch spices from India, which do nothing more than poison his blood? Or exotic foods which merely weaken his nerves? Did she offer ice to the people of India, or place wine before the inhabitants of the Arctic Circle? Did she not rather give to each that portion which was both allotted and suited to him? And how, O Nature perfect in thy goodness, the degenerate multitude of thy children doth accuse thee because of their own sicknesses—the cause of which they gathered, with unflagging greed, from the East and the South—while the little band of thy contented children, following the precepts of its dear mother, walks before thee amidst these wild, degenerate ones and still remains devout, knowing nothing of the hysterical torment or of the countless host of convulsions against which neither the *materia medica*, nor perhaps the whole of Nature herself has any remedy at her disposal! Do not call Nature unjust, when it is you who travel unnatural paths. Nature, it appears, possesses remedies only for natural diseases; for ailments which are a consequence of our unnatural culture she has neither herb nor plaster, and her single remedy is merely: Do penance and believe in the Gospel of Nature!

O, that you would do penance and believe! If we do not become as little children, and return home once more to philanthropic Nature, on whom we have turned our backs, then we are a betrayed people sold into bondage, to whom now and then the well-intentioned utterance reverberates: "Adam, where art thou?" and who try meanwhile to hide from our own image as well as we can.[13]

The fifth and final act is the ruin of most women, just as it is for a large number of playwrights. Love, the fortune of her life, becomes her misfortune; her heart has been trained to love virtue, and it is not fate which transforms it into a transgressor, but her own negligence. The working class knows of no distinctly female diseases. Pregnancies and births are impeded only by secondary circumstances which have their origins in manners, morals, and dress, and are so little to be considered illnesses that physicians could forthwith—and occasionally already do—prescribe them as medication. In the case of some of the so-called primitive tribes it is not the woman but the man who holds a celebration at the time of parturition. Hardly is the woman delivered of her burden, when she bathes it in the nearest river, offers the new arrival her breast—thereby saving herself from lacteal fever and the vexation of enlisting a wet-nurse—and performs her household duties just as before; while the man, stretched out on his bed, lets himself be ministered to and receives visits as well as congratulations from his neighbors because he—just think of the effort—has borne a child by his wife![14] And yet there are also heroes upon whose memory history has bestowed glory and praise because they had deigned, by their good grace, to allow battles to be won and victories gained while they themselves, without exposing their person in the slightest to any combat whatsoever or feeling the least inclination to lie at rest upon the bed of honor, observed very comfortably from a position at best far beyond the range of the cannon just how many arms and legs a couple of laurel sprigs cost. Inasmuch as such individuals do exist, then, let us not be too critical of the childbed behavior of the men mentioned above.

All of you who consider women to be weaker than you because of their pregnancies and childbearing, tell me: how could Nature have brought her greatest masterpiece, the propagation of the human race, into association with such evils on purpose; how could she have poured wormwood into a goblet filled with the most exquisite nectar; how could she have accompanied an action, upon which she bestowed her greatest blessings, with such a terrible curse by allotting to the one side unalloyed joy, to the other unmitigated sorrow? To be sure, pregnancies, childbearing, and the suckling of an infant require the expenditure of a certain amount of energy; nonetheless the female body, if it is not impaired, possesses sufficient substance not only to sustain this expenditure of energy, but also to compensate for the expenditure with no loss of time in the process. The objection which derives from observing so many women of fashion is not valid, for the latter appear already to be so lacking in strength that every pregnancy shakes their flimsy edifice to its very foundations, and every birth threatens to destroy it entirely.

O you inventors, abounding with ideas, who have thought up calculating machines, who have taught an automaton to play chess,[15] have undertaken voyages by air,[16] and who even in your confusion help people more than if they had been graduated *in gradum doctoris utruisque medicinae;*[17] you, who have the spirits under your command just as the centurion at Capernaum his servants,[18] come down a step or two and condescend to a mere trifle. Invent a contrivance by means of which our ladies of fashion may be freed from the burden of bearing children. Let sons and daughters grow like apples and pears; cause them to be planted like cabbages. Even if the political census-taker should, due to this invention, register a minus in the first few years (for no man is born a master of his craft), nevertheless even in these years of lean-fleshed kine[19] the true mettle of the human race will set things aright, and—wonder of wonders!—there would result even more so an undeniable plus, inasmuch as the state would be made up not of small coin, but of individuals worth their weight in gold! What is a Persian army measured in parasangs[20] compared to a Macedonian phalanx?

But no! you must remove your shoes, for this place is sacrosanct. The most legitimate, the most sacred claims of the human race to a disclosure of the truth which were ever based on reason shall not here be offended through mockery, which, like malicious slander, always leaves a bitter aftertaste. Let only human kindness approach this burning bush![21] The power of inertia, which is said to act mischievously on every body so as to keep it continuously in its present state—a state which resists motionlessness when the body is in motion, and movement when the body is at rest—does not have the honor of being to my liking. A power which only resists and yet is not able to be effective in and of itself is not a power about which one is able to do very much bragging. The noblest nation must accede upon occasion to a war of aggression through which we demand our rights and that which is owed to us, and call to account that person who has trespassed against us. He is neither great nor small who is able to possess and to express greatness or smallness merely to the degree to which he is resisted in their attainment. Let both sexes return once more to their original integrity and to their true nature and we shall find that the longer such a happy state prevails, the more we shall find that man and woman are of one body in this instance as well.

But are they also of one soul? Up to now, psychologists have not been successful in advancing far enough into the realm of the intellect to determine whether a significant difference actually exists; at least no Linnaeus of the mind has yet come to classify the mental powers.[22] Let Rorario account for the fact that he finds a greater use of reason among animals than among men; and Helvétius for putting those souls on which a body with hoofs has been bestowed in the same class with those which have received hands; and let both of them settle their accounts with Descartes for bringing about the destruction of his world of machines.[23]

But there are philosophical heretics too, and heretics of reason, simply because the basis for every assertion is taken from nature—from a document which has in common with all documents the quality of allowing everyone who searches therein to find what he is looking for. All history and every fact must submit itself to our governance, and even the most objective man conveys at the very outset something of himself to the whole of history and every fact, to the extent that everything touched by man receives something of his ego, something of his Self. The best water has no taste—and so it is with most facts as well, although we seldom obtain them unseasoned. And even if the seasoner were to add only salt, that basest and best of the spices, our friends and our foes take on so much from one another that one discovers unmistakable features of similarity among them.

"Our foes?"

By all means; I maintain that they are able to make their imprint upon us more easily than are our friends. A friend who is but the echo of ourself has little appeal for us; precisely those traits which single out our *enemies* most of all from all others, which interest us most about them, and which speak best for them tend to receive our imitation. "Learn even from an enemy," runs the old proverb.

A whole host of commentators and collectors of variant texts will impart their sense and nonsense to this document of nature until the day when an authentic document appears and may determine, if it be God's will, the significance or lack of significance of the difference between the souls of man and of the animals—if only we ourselves in the meantime do not venture to set up an order of precedence among human souls; an order which would have no more or less validity than our dreams and their interpretation. Are there, then, differences of a sexual nature between human souls? Do souls exist which are exclusively intended to inhabit female bodies? And where is the bold Argonaut who has navigated this unknown sea? With what has this apostle of the invisible world confirmed his gospel? Where statement and counterstatement are so close to each other as to be able to work in unity and harmony, there it is every man's duty to demonstrate his thesis with the utmost vigor, and then to yield up the power of decision to his public. We are now faced with experience which contradicts other experience—before it has yet been determined whether the soul is indeed capable of experiencing its own being or not. The soul can only perceive itself with the aid of a mirror; and who is not aware of the fact that this mirror reflects images only very imperfectly and often quite inaccurately? Mirrors portray us in reverse, and when the portrait painter is told that he has achieved a likeness which could have been "stolen from a mirror," the expression is in reality a rather unsuitable one.

To be sure, experiences of a specific nature can serve well in generating a subjective conviction; but for the construction of a general truth on this foundation, only experiences will suffice which are as general as the truth for which they are to serve as the basis. How long have we been gathering experiences in this realm? What methods have we adopted? Were these so carefully chosen that we could expect correct results from them? Do we actually possess so large a storehouse of experiences already that we can venture to construct a system whereby such a prejudicial line of demarcation can be drawn for an entire half of the human race? Or would it not be for us as it was for His Infallible Holiness on the other side of the Alps with his own infamous line of demarcation?[24] In general, a system is like an instrument which we know how to play with skill. Have we calculated irrefutably the assured advantages of the system under consideration, or is it merely one like many another of its brothers wherein linguistic disorder reigns supreme, as in the tower of Babel, whose spire was to reach to the heavens? If one removes this jumble of languages from most of these systems, what is left? Empirical psychology still occupies a rather precarious position among the sciences; yet whether she stands or falls, truth, which existed before her and will continue to exist after she has vanished, loses nothing thereby.

Greatness of soul, courage, a superiority of understanding, a larger measure of the power of discernment, firmness of will, a greater intensity of feeling and other excellent qualities are those which men have appropriated for themselves as the right of primogeniture, and at the cost of the female sex. They have been invested by God with the entire world, with the whole globe as their fief—O what noble feudal lords they are!

Inasmuch as they, however, are both plaintiff and judge in one and the same person, they appear to be acting quite charitably in allowing women the legal right to possess a human soul. Now whether (after the male sex has had glorious success in placing the other half of the human creation, which according to its designated purpose was to form a complete whole with his own sex, under his yoke and allows it now only by way of request, only insofar as it does not offend his sovereign prerogative, to take a generous part in the rights of the individual, either human or civil)—now whether all those above-mentioned instances represent truth or illusion is a question suited for an essay-writing competition—a question which is similar to so many others in that the answer thereto halts between the two opinions.[25]

Nevertheless, to deny the fair sex all such intellectual capabilities on the basis of physical appearance and to wrest its rank from it through foul play is to behave in precisely the same way as people have toward the American Indians, when, upon the testimony of a few observers who had seen no beards among these tribes, they not only refused to acknowledge the existence of this utterly masculine, and moreover very cumbersome, badge of honor, but in addition drew the very obvious conclusion from the lack of the latter appendage that nature had refused to grant them the germ cells necessary for it, and thus that they belonged to a much lower class of human beings—and what is not less significant, that it was not possible that both we and they could have descended from the same patriarch. What kind of a role can the beard play anyway, for according to the well-known proverb, "the beard does not make the philosopher." It surely would have been better if people had taken the trouble to determine whether the descendants of Manco Capac[26] had not found this masculine characteristic—may it ever, by the way, remain useful and worthy of reverence—just as uncomfortable as the sons of Japheth,[27] and whether they, because they lacked the metal of enlightenment, iron, did not take refuge in some other means of ridding themselves of this burdensome guest. After more precise observations, however, a beard was indeed discovered, and the preadamites[28] forfeited once again the victory which, with the help of such an imposing argument, they believed was already in their hands.

To say that the female sex does not manifest the above intellectual capabilities is far from saying that nature has denied to it the potentiality for such capabilities, and therefore—O, the beardlessness of the conclusion!—that it stands a step lower on the Jacob's ladder of the creation.[29] Are *we* the ones who are similar to God, while the other sex merely possesses the honor, by the grace of God, of being similar to *us*? What an absurd idea!

It is not through our bodies, or our senses, or our powers of imagination that we draw near to the primeval spirit, rather it is through our own spirit; and what do we wish to maintain at this point—that women lack the intelligence and the will thereto? That they lack the fullness of spirit? Do we not often excel only through them? Do they not in countless instances season more than we with that salt of the earth without which nothing is of value—with reason? And their virtue—is it not abundantly purer than our own which we esteem so highly? Does our own vanity not exceed that of the feminine everywhere and in all places? Was not that Pharisee and his whole Order of Jesuits[30] of our own sex? Can a good woman (and there are many of them) think without fear and trembling of that Pharisee of more recent times who, armed with his creeds, wishes to step before the throne of God, face the Last Judgment and say: "Whoever is better, let him cast the first stone"? Would not Theresa[31] herself have been able to raise up more than one stone if she had not been corrupted by this "righteous" one? Can germ cells germinate and potentialities be developed if no beneficent hand is present to cultivate them, or, what is more, if all things join together with the purpose of subjugating them, and where possible, of bringing about their extermination? Have there not arisen from time to time within the other sex great and noble souls who possessed in large measure all those intellectual characteristics of which they are thought to have been deprived? From where do all these—in reality not so very infrequent—manifestations come, if such potentialities do not actually exist within the souls of women; if nothing more is required to bring them forth than a concurrence of propitious circumstances or a helping hand to aid in the development of these characteristics, whereby is added to their own powers that dynamic force without which they never will divert from their narrow path? Or would we rather charge Nature with having blundered, merely in order to save our own system? Would we rather trespass so crudely against the Fourth Commandment as it refers to this good mother of ours, than give up the alleged rights of our class?

Without awakening the great names of the world of mythology from the dead—individuals for whom no one would gainsay the least claim to reality—which of us would dare to deny to Zenobia[32] or an Anna Comnena[33] an understanding and power of discernment which towered far above that of their masculine contemporaries; an Elizabeth the qualities of a head of state; or Maria Theresa courage and steadfastness? Or, if one wishes that we situate our point of observation on more familiar ground, let us consider two world-famous names: Catherine the Great and Voltaire. Let not the autocratic deeds of the former; let not the laurels of war which she braided into her diadem; and not the superadded nimbus which encircles those who are the gods of the earth—no, merely let her *correspondence with him* determine whether she emerges clothed in imperial splendor with the palm branches of the world conquerer in her hand. And behold! she remains great just as she is. And Voltaire? Small, as small as he became as soon as truth held up her magic mirror before him. His highly esteemed self is always the first person; the great lady has to be content with the second person. Is she supposed to conquer—just imagine!—Constantinople, or at least remove her residence to Taganrog,[34] so that he can come and kiss her feet, because it is too cold in St. Petersburg for the old hermit of Ferney? Not yet satisfied that the empress takes clocks off the hands of his watchmakers to the tune of 8,000 rubles, he even requests that she undertake a traffic in clocks with China in order to provide food for his factory workers. Either he truly did not understand her judicious silence in these matters, or, what is more credible, he had no desire to understand it until she finally referred him, along with his mercantile speculations so unworthy of an empress and a poetic philosopher, to an excellent commercial establishment. The most prosaic of all passions, an abominable greed, brought Voltaire down from the heights of Parnassus to the depths of the stock exchange.

King Frederick William the First was wont to characterize his portraits with the motto: *in tormentis pinxit*.[35] And indeed, this was precisely the spiritual state in which Voltaire was writing at this point. At other times his genius was accustomed to elevating the poet above himself and above all restraints; to inspiring thoughts in him which were greater than their creator and which he himself could not help but behold with respect and admiration. Where do we find the slightest indication that the same is true here? We are all the more willing to bestow honor on others because we are covetous of honor ourselves; Voltaire was both of these a thousand times over—only not in this case. His instrument, which at times he played with consummate mastery, is, in this particular instance, completely out of tune; and is it a wonder that under these circumstances his flatteries turned into mere Gallicisms, such as one can hear by the thousands among his people? The letters of the empress are couched in the language of nature; only in cases where she desired to make a sacrifice for the vainglorious Voltaire did she pay him back in his own coin, just as the other monarch[36] paid back the verses of a shameless poet with verses of his own. Only facetiously does she speak of her own person, while the whole world cannot refrain from mentioning her name with reverence; she calls so little attention to her deeds that it is as if she would have them speak for themselves. Continuously preoccupied with making her boundless empire richer in population and in noble disposition, she drew up—at the same time she was routing the Osmanlis,[37] dispersing the confederation in Poland, controlling the plague, and resisting the depredations of Pugachev[38] —a code of laws for her people, a people which was then gathered together by her under this law from among all languages and tongues, so that she might be able, in the same manner as at the first Pentecost, to pour forth a single spirit over them and to ennoble them in their striving toward a single goal for all. Equally adept at the greatest and the smallest administrative duty, she introduced inoculation against smallpox; devoted her time to matters of education; reaped a thousandfold harvest from the institutions founded by her; thought up and put into effect gay celebrations for Prince Henry;[39] and still had sufficient leisure time, and without the slightest trace of vanity, to write to the conceited Voltaire. These two souls weighed against each other with the scales, if possible, in the hands of a superior being—which pan of the scale would fall, and which would rise?

Mankind has not yet fallen so far as not to be able to give honor where honor is due. And why a complete inventory of such famous women as have been called to their crowns by fate, and who then bore them with great dignity? It is sufficient merely to utter the name of a Margaret of Denmark,[40] a Christina of Sweden,[41] a Sophia Charlotta of Prussia;[42] and of those who, had they been men, would have obtained much honor for their sex, do not a Cornelia, the noble mother of the Gracchi,[43] an Arria,[44] and the figure who has been the subject of so many rumors,

Joan of Arc—do they not deserve our admiration? In view of these examples, one will undoubtedly absolve me from proving further that the female soul is not lacking in rich natural talents and abilities. Autumn and winter rob even the noble oak of its leaves; only the roots remain. Why is the manifestation of the above-mentioned potentialities not more often the rule, rather than the exception? Why are they not more frequently developed to the fullest extent?

But then are these justifiable questions? Does *our own* sex possess such a great superfluity of noble souls? That honor with which Ulysses and Aeneas were canonized—not by the impartial goddess of justice, but by the often very partial god Apollo—occurs but infrequently. Without doubt Homer took his Penelope, Andromache, Nausicaa, and Arete from nature; and I shall always believe that the greater equality which existed at that time between the servant class and the ruling class; the tasks performed in common by both high-born women and their slaves; the intimacy which resulted from their having grown up together; the manner of work required of women at that time as well as the profit which it yielded; that all these factors served to make that period in man's history infinitely more tolerable than the present Leaden Age into which the female sex has had the seeming good fortune to plunge, and from which it unfortunately has not yet been extracted.

In the Heroic Age social custom and the manner of expressing love (from the beginning love and social custom have remained in close association) were cruder and more barbarous—and yet the female sex still kept up the pace! The evils attributed to the opposite sex in those times were merely those of spoiled children of Dame Fortune whom we, in the face of so many of hers who were well brought up, can easily forgive; the evils of the following and the present time are inbred, and have their basis in error and inconsequential casuistry!

It would truly be an unheard-of, and in terms of the accepted basic precepts of psychology, inexplicable phenomenon, if under the ironlike weight of despotism one's feeling of freedom did not in the end lose its elasticity; if through lack of cultivation and maintenance the richest piece of land did not become a wilderness and finally suffocate every sprout of any profitable crop; if, in the face of rights withdrawn and the possibility that these rights have been irrevocably lost, the remembrance of such rights and the feelings which correspond to them, as well as the belief in one's own self and individual worth, should not finally disappear. If the original rights of human beings are not preserved, respected, and cultivated; if careful cultivation and maintenance of all the great and noble seeds planted in the soul of woman by Nature never come to pass—what can be expected in the end? A boat which leans too much toward any one side must tip over—and our own sex? What if it were subjected to the chemical processes of humid and dry analysis or to an ordeal by fire or water; if these Job's sufferings which we inflict upon woman were imposed upon us—what would have become of us? Would we still retain as much of the ingenuousness and originality as the other sex? What a great example the other sex has set—not with pomp and ceremony at the time of death, like the Stoics and their arch-martyr Peregrinus Proteus;[45] rather quite naturally, not merely by loving their enemies, but what is more, by forgiving their friends! That great tribute to the women, that they "possess all the weaknesses of humans and at the same time the contentment of a god," that tribute is everywhere manifest in them.

As long as women have only *privileges* and not *rights*; as long as the state treats them as mere parasitic plants, which are indebted for their existence and worth as citizens only to that man with whom they have been united by fate, will not the woman fulfill only very incompletely (and the longer it takes, the more incompletely) that great calling of her nature: to be the wife of her husband, the mother of her children, and, by virtue of these noble designations, a member, a citizen—and not merely a denizen—of the state? Light burdens, borne long, grow heavy. But let one give them their rights back, and he will soon discover just what this sex truly is, and what it can become!

Why this criticism of the examples I have chosen? Why the reproach that there are so few exceptions? According to the plain truth of our philosophers, virtue, unlike the fine arts, cannot be imitated or fashioned according to examples, even if they were the finest which could be found. It must flow from the first principle of self-legislation if it is to be pure and genuine. Only when the artist creates from within himself is there energy to be found in the soul; and what is the value of multiplicity without overall unity? Of fine individual features without ordering and clarifying principles?

The French princes who abandoned their country declared publicly that they wished to make their appeal to God, to the king, and to their swords; three courts of judicature, and yet the good Lord had to be content with being the first—that is, in a legal sense the lowest. The other sex has but a single court of appeals: that of God. And everywhere members of the male sex are to be found for whom it is not the importance of the reasons which matters, but their plurality; and what kinds of reasons? Reasons of state?

But I am getting ahead of myself; yet who could hold me back? Truly, the laws of the state as they apply to women are almost more contradictory than a frivolous love affair! As much as they restrict the civil rights of women with respect to person and possessions because they pronounce them to be feeble and not sufficiently competent to perceive what lies in their own best interests, as much as they feel duty-bound to banish the entire sex to an everlasting guardianship, just as quickly does this feebleness cease to be feebleness as soon as there is talk of crime and punishment. Then both sexes are measured by one and the same standard—and in the church, in the courts of justice (one hopes, also in heaven) there exists no respect of persons between male and female; then they are of a single body and a single soul. All honor to the Code of the deified Justinian which, with more coherence than our own lawmakers, did not allow women to be charged with crimes, and placed them above all punishment—even in face of the most flagrant transgression.[46] In its opinion the woman was so good as to be useful for nothing, whereas with us she is at least acknowledged to be worthy of punishment—what an advantage! With us the woman stands under the law; at that time she stood only under the rule of grace.

And indeed, none can deny that with us she has taken a step toward improvement even though her completion, which is still a long way off, still possesses in our eyes the aura of a miracle. Yes, indeed—a miracle! There are even those who would now gainsay the everlastingness of the punishments of hell; and I predict this infernal riddle will finally be answered in our own epoch of unravelment in which a frigid philosophy has already cooled off so many things—answered for us by eternal consequences which in the final analysis will prove to be inseparable from any evil action. And the enslavement of the female sex remains a worm which dies not and a fire which is never quenched.[47]

Justice! Thy blindfold has been removed, and yet thou seest not that, although all actions which have to do with the person and possessions of the other sex are invalid without legal support and remain therefore utterly without effect in civil matters, thy poor underage children are bound by all moral and civil laws to precisely the same extent as are the men! Not even in laws dealing with contraband is a question raised concerning the customs agent, and whether with regard to his person those things are rendered unto the emperor which belong to the emperor[48]—and yet a woman is only related to the state through the person of the man; only *he* is to pay homage to the state and to its laws. Is it any wonder if women observe the law the way a nun sings the Psalter? If they overlay the solemn regulations of the state with a veneer of the comical and take the liberty of making their own interpretations of these laws in cases where blind devotion is required? Has any group ever enjoyed being lionized more than we men; and has the point ever been made more clearly that smaller thieves are bound to be hanged, while bigger ones still run free? States which have arisen for the protection of human rights remove this protection from half their populace! But then it is only quite natural for the will to feel reluctant in situations where reason encounters so many vexing hindrances and stumbling blocks of aggravation.

The sufferings of individual people (providing they themselves are not the cause of them) exert a perfecting effect, and nothing which was great ever came to fulfillment without such suffering. But suffering which has been inflicted upon a people not by nature or fate, but in a purely arbitrary fashion, dampens any spirit; it enervates and enfeebles the noblest of peoples, so that there is no longer a place for them in heaven.[49] What an everlasting pity about all the progress which is being obstructed through this masculine cruelty! What inner strength the other sex must truly possess, inasmuch as it has so majestically resisted all these obstacles until now!

Nevertheless, it would be impossible for women to be what they are, and to maintain their present state, if they had not been subsidized by their own charms and the mutual inclination of each sex toward the other. Thus, up until now, Nature has never completely abandoned mankind, even if the latter has thanklessly turned its back on her! A certain happy state of affairs in which there is little to be desired—and precisely for this reason much to be feared—makes people unhappy: they aspire to nothing, and their spirit loses its vitality, their mind the keenness of its intellect. Just as this happy-unhappy state of affairs turns out to be the fate of so many rulers, who, knowing their profession only from the stanpoint of its grandeur and power, descend to the level of triviality and to the pursuit of matters secondary to the business of ruling—or even devote the major portion of their concern to affairs which have nothing to do with their office whatsoever; so also has this condition befallen, according to all appearances, the whole royal male sex in general. They seek to deal with danger more through evasion than courage and wisdom; they play more at being lord and master than they actually are; accustomed to acting capriciously, they no longer bother to reflect on the proper way to rule; born and raised to a position of leadership, they give no thought to earning this position; they neglect their person, since they have no incentive and are not even allowed to exert themselves in dignified competition within their own houses. The whole sex is collapsing, because it does not take the trouble to hold itself upright. Let nobody say that one man can bring about the birth of light in another man—tyrants are faint-hearted, and wherever they are not permitted to give orders, they grovel. In truth, it is not only the women, but also we who have lost through this degradation of the other sex—and who the most? Is it a surprise, for example, when the female sex exchanges base coin for base coin, and when women repay the tyranny of their honorable husbands with lip service? Is it a wonder that each of them makes the life of the other bitter, and at the blessed departure of the honorable husband—may he rest in peace—the small winged spirits opportunely placed on the stately catafalque are the only ones who, unceasingly and without any purpose whatsoever, weep bitter tears of remorse, tears with which they extinguish the last embers of the inverted funeral torches, while behind a cloak of respectability his widow plays her role masterfully, walking about in the gayest of spirits? In the beginning it was not like this.

III / *Whence Arose the Superiority of the Man over the Woman? A Retrospective of the Earliest Period*

IF WOMEN are called by nature to the same rights as men; if they once possessed and for the most part still do possess equal physical and intellectual faculties; *where, when,* and *how* did the superiority of the man over the woman come about? What was it that placed the sword into the hand of the man and relegated the woman to the spindle? If we were closer to the *when* and *where,* the time and the place of the matter, we would probably have no need of the likes of an Oedipus to win the prize of thirty pieces of silver for the answer to this question of questions, and that concerning the *how,* to everyone's satisfaction as well.[1] Yet in no chronicle or topography is here to be found a single dead word, not to mention a living one, concerning this *when* or *where;* thus until such time as the hieroglyphs on the pyramids are revealed to us, or a previously hidden monument no longer withholds its secrets concerning these questions, the answers "somewhere" and "at some time or other" must serve as a foundation, and the question as to *how,* in the absence of historical evidence, must be resolved by a conjecture of human reason. All that we have in the way of facts can only be traced to a certain point in history. At that point where the sun of recorded history goes down and even the moon of legend withdraws its borrowed light, there is nothing left to guide human reason, and it floats aimlessly on the limitless sea of possibility. The human condition that preceded history and legend (since even the earliest sagas speak of it as of something which already existed) is that in which each individual lived in the most complete state of independence without associations of any kind, nourishing himself merely from the fruits of the soil on which he walked and simply taking these fruits as he found them, without any further preparation than Nature herself provided. In short, man lived from the soil and nothing more. Yet did such a condition ever really exist? Did man (the most social of all known animals, notwithstanding those pious orangutans in the Theban desert[2] and their more recent brothers who have found it more comfortable to change themselves from hermits into monks) ever live in such a state? Let our friend Hans-Jakob,[3] on whose grave is written: "Here lies a man who dedicated himself to nature and to truth," give us the answer to that question. Neither Columbus nor his martyred successor, Captain Cook, saw any such children of nature. Wherever these two went, they found the first broad outlines of society already drawn, family relationships established (even if incompletely), and traces (although often weak ones) of culture and artistic production. Rude huts and a form of food preparation were encountered even among the most primitive peoples, most of whom also were beginning to clothe their bodies. If the travelers were able to remain long enough at one place and were fortunate enough to make themselves understood by means of sign language, they became convinced that the inhabitants—who appeared to exist at a level so near to man's natural state—had lived so long in that place that according to their own traditions the race had known no other home. They had not the slightest inkling that outside the region which they inhabited others could exist alongside them. But no matter how simple and slight the affairs of the family, the house, and the search for food may have been because their needs hardly rose above the level of animals; no matter how few their wants, for a love of art had not spoiled them as yet, nevertheless between the two sexes *castes* had already been established, causing a separation into two parts of that which God had created whole. The more unequal this social disposition was, and the more difficult it was to fulfill basic needs, since nature had provided the soil, the forests (the royal residences of these people), and the rivers and seas with but meager resources, the harder was the lot which fell to the female part of this half-tamed race of men. If the man was not otherwise urgently called upon to hunt or to fish, his life was divided chiefly between pleasure and repose. Only seldom did the woman accompany him as a helpmate, for while the male of the species was stretching his limbs in the sun, it remained the woman's duty to prepare the food.

To be sure, such evidence is too weak and inconclusive to serve as an answer to our question; yet, it is enough to lead us further in our search for an answer as to how this superiority came about—this superiority which cast all that is *burdensome* onto one half of the human race and kept all the advantages for itself. Has not Nature herself through the means of pregnancy and birth given us our first clue to the disproportionate loss suffered by the female sex in the division of human dignity and worth into parts? And no matter how comfortable and delightful we make this share which fell to womankind—can it truly ever be classified under another heading than that of toil and need? The man seems called to a life of pleasure; the woman to grief and misery.

In any case, in the relationships within the family; in the manner in which the first germs of social behavior in man began to develop—to which he was perhaps initially brought by the business of reproduction—lie half-hidden clues and hieroglyphs as to why the development of human society, which gave the human race as a whole such an astounding impetus, was nevertheless so disadvantageous to one half of this same race.

Even in the earliest documented reports concerning the social origins of man there are traces of inequality between the sexes and a debasement of the female sex—of which a conspicuous example is provided by the practice of polygamy. How despotic is the idea that a man could feel himself justified in possessing more than one wife, when a single calculation on the fingers of one's hand yields the conclusion that such wastefulness must bring about want in others! Truly, polygamy is a condition which neither body nor soul can long endure and which contradicts both reason and that passion which (like the children of the wealthy and refined classes) has been educated in the school of human reason. Wherever a man has more than one wife, the advice of tyrants is fulfilled: divide and rule. Through this masculine indulgence in luxury women were made to feel their dependence to the highest degree, and if the sultana of the day was able temporarily to assume a sort of precedence over her colleagues, the airs which she gave herself thereby did not last very long and she was soon brought to the conviction that in fact there exists no order of priority among slaves.

The story of Sarah and Hagar[4] seems to show that concubinage was initially not merely subject to the whims of the man, and that at first he was obliged to ask the permission of his wife before he could take a concubine. This story of concubinage also appears to yield the conclusion that such contracts were not entered into for life, and that often before the contracted period of time had run out the angel of conscience and that guardian spirit which serves to warn us of dangerous situations called out to the husband to "Cast out the bondwoman and her son."

By this time I must have expressed to the reader my conviction that the first reason for the masculine assumption of priority over the woman is to be found in the particular form which human society took at its inception. The question whether the manner in which the germs of society developed was the single possible one, or whether among several other possible courses the one along which man was led by nature was the narrow path which alone leads to life—these are side issues which, like our original question, may remain unanswered for a long time, perhaps forever.

This much seems established, then—that these germs must have developed everywhere through similar causes, for in each case (and this is a conclusion of which I would gladly be disburdened) similar disadvantageous consequences for the female sex arose. Society is the source of all fortune and misfortune which ever fell to the lot of the human race, and it is not yet apparent what mankind can be or become through its influence. We do know, hoever, that when it does become apparent, when we come to observe the laws of heaven and learn to love, rather than fear, both them and their Author, we shall become more like God and be worthy of the crown of life. This is a hope which Plato would not need to call the "dream of a man awake,"[5] and which has for its basis a *faith* in the human race—and, if I might be allowed to add, a *true and living* faith! But none such as this has yet been found in Israel.[6] This belief is world-patriotism.[7]

But may I be allowed to procure for myself, once and for all, permission to cast a backward glance into time, without fearing the fate of Lot's wife[8] from the pen of one of my critics? Man has always shown a special propensity for catching fish and snaring birds, to the point that now both rhymed and unrhymed warning signs have had to be posted in order to divert people from this earliest of human preoccupations and to accustom them to other necessary and more artificial sources of food. The noted St. Évremond[9] was, up until his last days, duly appointed keeper of the ducks at St. James. That Swiss gentleman in France requested for himself the reversion of the position of the rhinoceros at court, and that scholar at the court of Frederick the Great the newly vacant post of atheist-in-residence; and how many more times must human beings condescend to the rank of rhinoceros or atheist-in-residence in order to earn their daily bread according to the methods in vogue today—methods which the bird-snarers and fishermen never knew and would never have been able to imagine in their wildest dreams![10]

The question arises at this point as to why the female sex did not claim for itself the relatively bloodless task of fishing, in order to leave the hunting of wild game to the bloodthirsty male. But perhaps the female *did* have a hand in everything and *was* nowhere inferior to the male; perhaps only the last hours of pregnancy and the six hours after delivery afforded any hindrance to taking immediate part in the affairs of her husband, the chief ranger and master of the hounds. The goddess of the hunt, Diana, was, after all, of the feminine gender to the later ancients.

Yet this cessation of activity caused by pregnancy and childbirth, as short as it may have been, was without doubt the reason for the subordinate status of the female. It was perhaps in these short intermissions of indolence that the woman herself, because of that instinct to save which is unique to her sex and which perhaps is also directly related to her destiny as the bearer of offspring, paved the way for her fate as a slave. Why did she not follow the divine teaching to "take no thought for the morrow; for sufficient unto the day is the evil thereof"? It had never occurred to the man to store up his food as long as the sources of nourishment were abundant; his hunting grounds were his larder, to which everything belonged that had life and breath. This living larder kept him quite secure from that corrupted taste for game which has become lazy and fat, a taste man has developed for everything—filthy lucre not excepted—which is gathered together in barns, and to which moreover the reproach is directed: "Thou fool, this night thy soul shall be required of thee: then whose shall those things be, which thou hast provided?"[11]

But even the miser, even the devil must be accorded an advocate, and in fact man's concern for the morrow, if of the right kind and exercised within limits, is no mean expression of the power of human reason. The thought: "To hunt without hunger today is to feast without want tomorrow" reveals—the above-mentioned divine teaching notwithstanding—more mental deliberation than is to be found in a whole tribe of savages. Thus in this instance, too, the woman was called upon to aid the man, and in fact whenever it was a question of using the powers of reason, the woman always seems to have led the way. The indisposition caused by the last hours of pregnancy and the first hours after childbirth led the female of the species, on the strength of an almost instinctual drive toward self-preservation which becomes all the greater during the period when the infant must be cared for, and wisely and powerfully guided by the hand of human reason, to think of storing up food so as to do without something one day, in order not to be deprived utterly the next. This storing of provisions, which at first occurred only occasionally and only as long as conditions demanded it, was later repeated more often and after a time became a permanent practice, depending upon whether the population multiplied or decreased and whether the sources of food grew more meager or more plentiful.

If it is indeed true that in many cases the animals were the teachers of man, then without doubt the storing of provisions is a part of that catalogue of lectures which make up this course of instruction. Instinct (which stands in the same relation to human reason as the trainer of a dancing bear to the tutor) has always brought her children more quickly and safely to their goal than cold and meticulous reason her own dear ones. Most certainly the bee and the ant gathered before man; perhaps the ancients were disguising this truth in the fable of the Myrmidons.[12] Yet it was not mere curiosity, as some wish to assert, which first guided the woman to learning through experimentation, but her powers of observation. Food which was stored demanded continuous supervision and more precise arrangement and preparation, and for this reason household furniture and utensils were developed. Some chance happening, most certainly the attraction and attachment of certain wild animals to mankind, taught them (probably first the woman) to tame some of these animal species for their continuous use and service, and thus the household was increased through these domestic beasts, which in case of need also served as sources of food. At this point the work had to be divided; the man chose the hunt, the woman the household. Thus the woman gradually became mistress of the domestics, and before she realized it, the chief domestic animal herself. The poor woman—what could be more astonishing? By virtue of the very same revolution in which she brought freedom into the light of day, she herself became a slave!

Gradually those advantages and disadvantages so closely related to the two different ways of life became more and more apparent. The body of the man, made hard, firm, agile, and strong by the toil of hunting and fishing, began to exert an influence over his soul. Acquainted with danger, he became through this very familiarity courageous, intrepid, and steadfast. He began to feel his superiority over everything that was not a man, and consequently over his wife as well, whose physical strength remained undeveloped through lack of opportunity and who, being unacquainted with danger, began to fear what the man had learned to avoid or overcome. Surrounded by small objects and by animals which tolerated reins and the bit, the woman gradually sank to a lower level in body and soul, and learned to be content with the place of the foremost slave in the presence of her despotic master. That is right, a slave! Doubtless man was brought to this inhuman idea by those animals he had tamed, and such a terrible notion so deeply devalued the honor of mankind that when recalled, this coin no longer showed any trace of the image and superscription which it possessed in former times. As surely as the woman had invented and introduced animal husbandry through the possession of tamed animals, just as surely this same sex, more bound to a single location, was able to devote more time to the pursuit of agriculture. Unquestionably it was the woman who produced the first salad for the roast venison of the man. A root or some seeds, which in absence of an alderman's feast remained from an antipythagorean meal of beans,[13] and which were not noticed because of the choicer morsels present— these took hold and multiplied around the hut until it occurred to the woman to sow and plant intentionally. Thus from the hand of the woman the first garden arose, the English[14] garden of Eden excepted, and the care of the garden has for the most part remained in the hands of the women ever since. In all probability the woman tasted everything before the man in order to test it—partly to determine whether it was harmful and partly to see whether it was fit to eat, and thus she also served to protect the man in these two matters as well. Even now the highest attainments in the art of cooking are a prerogative of the women.

The changes which the woman perceived in her own body accustomed her to observing changes in atmospheric conditions, and taught her to pay close attention to the passing of the seasons, so that the instability of the weather might in some way be overcome. Was then the woman perhaps the inventor or developer of both animal husbandry and agriculture? What a marvelous subject for conjecture! Even today the lowly farmer or gardener concedes that that faithful vassal of the earth, the moon, exerts a great influence over his crops—he plants his cabbages and other leafy vegetables by the full moon, and his tuberous vegetables when the moon is on the wane. Its phases are still clearly marked in his almanac, and what else could have brought him to this knowledge of moon lore besides the ways and habits of the woman? But with a good eye for the important, the more mobile man was soon able to divert the woman from these two chief sources of food, animal husbandry and agriculture, in order to bind her once again to the household, to which His Lordship had previously sentenced her.

"Sentenced?"

A poor choice of words—rather, to which he, by a peremptory decree and in a travesty of justice, banished her forever!

Only the hunt, the earliest manifestation of the work of the soldier caste, appears to be the invention of the man; and since he often was compelled to search far and wide for his prey, this became the first cause for the woman's abasement. She would surely have been able to remain with honor and dignity at her tasks of agriculture and animal husbandry if the hunt had not armed the man and carried with itself all the advantages and disadvantages of the soldier caste. The wife of the man then did nothing more than look after his quarters. Even now I am no friend of the hunt, for it bars the woman's every step to a higher level of culture, and fosters all those evils to which the male sex is subject in wars or in the pursuit of other human beings.

To be sure, it is said that war is often a path to culture and will continue to be so in the future. If this is true, it would also not be the first time that good has come from evil. But is not war now and will it not remain in the future—and I say this without prejudice to the abovementioned transformation of metals from the base into the noble—a manifestation of Original Sin? In the kingdom of God, whose sunrise and morning blessing we await daily with thanksgiving, people are as little likely to be slaughtered or exposed to the angel of destruction as they marry or are given in marriage there. [15] Sunspots, which we look upon more or less in the way we view those spots with which even the most careful housewife bespatters her sleeves in the kitchen or the ink spots of the businessman at his desk—sunspots are not what they seem to be. In the physical world everything is good, in fact, very good! And should this not give us grounds for hope that the moral world as well will come to that level of culture where evil is not needed in order for us to learn some good from it?

The family feuds which arose had their origin in the increase in the human population and the decrease in the number of wild animals (the single and most available food source for primitive man). Two families which previously had been compelled to flee singly before the might of a third joined forces, perhaps by chance or perhaps intentionally, against this third family and forced the latter to give over its hunting grounds to the stronger power. As long as the danger lasted, this circumstance formed a social bond between the two families, even though it never went as far as a formal agreement or constitution. Through error and folly man found his way to truth, and through toil and quarrels to unity and social organization.

The life of the shepherd and the farmer (the New Testament to which man became enlightened after the Old Testament of his existence as a hunter) was no less inclined to lead to quarrels than the former one. The shepherd did not spare the cultivated areas of the husbandman, and before the latter could lay hold of him, he and his herds had completely disappeared. When called upon for restitution, the shepherd was often able to avoid such payment by means of deceit and cunning. This forced the farmer to pay more attention to his own defense; and since he felt himself compelled to lay on more hands to take care of the land (hands which were required to remain together for longer periods of time to wait for the seasons and utilize good weather), there arose one house after another on the same piece of land. In this way the farmers were better able to combat the roaming of the shepherd and his wilder counterpart, the hunter. These farmers gradually became lords of estates—a title accorded to them by the conquered hordes of hunters and shepherds—and only very recently have the tables been turned so that once more we find princes and lords doing the hunting, while slaves are compelled to till the soil.

At the time when bourgeois society was developing from the ruins of familial social structures, the fate of the woman, it seems, was irrevocably decided. The weapons which the men found it necessary to carry under almost all circumstances and which therefore almost never left their hands, while the women busied themselves with the daily needs of their men and children, these weapons gave the former a decisive superiority over the latter, who, because they did not know how to handle these instruments of war, became afraid of them. The women were terrified by dangers which the men, who were more accustomed to them, treated with contempt. In body and soul the man had, if I may put it this way, underhandedly made himself superior to the woman, and since he found himself in sole possession of the weapons of defense and offense, he was called upon to defend not only his own person, but his possessions as well, among which he classified his family, and within that group his wife, whom from this point on he viewed as completely dependent on him.

Then, while understanding and the powers of judgment in the man began to increase through his enlarged sphere of influence; while his dealings with bourgeois society took on a higher form through the generalization of his concepts, the soul of the woman shrank more and more into the limits of her household. In heroic times, according to Homer, even in royal households the management of the household consisted, because of the simplicity of the needs and wants, merely in weaving and other crafts of this sort. By and by the vigor of the female sex disappeared entirely. Because the business of the state was taken away from the women, and because upon the foundation of bourgeois society they were banished to the household, they failed to become true citizens of the state, and remained simply aliens enjoying certain citizen's rights. Having shown very quickly that they were quite happy with this kindness which the state had bestowed on them, they were satisfied with but a few privileges more than were granted to slaves, privileges which it seemed society was "generously granting" to them.

Thus it was a whole series of factors (to which nature, although for the most part misunderstood, gave the first inducement) which caused an entire half of the human race gradually to lose its original human rights and to enjoy at present—*nota bene*, only as long as it pleases the other half to continue this arrangement—a mere vestige of those rights under the title of "privileges." And to add insult to injury, every other word of this oppressing half of mankind has always been: rights and justice, legislation and the administration of laws!

Behold then! Neither superiority of body nor mind placed the sword into the hand of the man—mere circumstance favored this step. In the battle with his equal over support of the family the man won the day. Madam, it is true, at first remained at home to protect and care for her children, enjoying the honor of having command over this particular fortress and providing provisions and clothing for her husband during his campaigns. Yet in this as well she was very soon replaced by her firstborn son who, although still too young and defenseless to follow the army of his father, nonetheless proclaimed himself commandant until at a later time, bypassing the mother once again, he was able to entrust this position to the second brother.

It is clear what kind of change such circumstances have gradually brought about during a period of several centuries or millennia in the character, the mode of thinking, and even in the physical characteristics of both sexes. It would have been nothing short of miraculous if relationships other than those based on the superiority of power could have resulted from such beginnings; indeed, not a single miracle but rather a confluence of miracles would have been necessary to produce a different conclusion from all these obvious external causes. It often lies within our power to alter the course of events at the beginning, but seldom at the halfway point, and never at the end.

But why should I try to hide the fact that we, who are men by the grace of God, so love to gloss over the manner in which we came to this superiority? Above all else in the world, we would like to convince the other half of the human race that it was not *we* but *nature* who pushed them into the background and subjected their will to ours. And yet it is also we who stimulate their wants and who make certain opinions fashionable by means of which, just as through their desires, we play the master over the fair sex. The clubs and secret societies[16] which surreptitiously procure power, authority, and dominion without ever drawing the sword are but copies of the course taken by the men in their rise to power. And the Bible? Up to now every philosophical sect, the oppressed, the quarrelsome, and the triumphant, as well as every new reform in the state right down to the French Constitution, has found its justification in this book.

It is with the most artificial web of arguments that we sentence the female sex to an eternal guardianship; and even in the most solemn of marriage vows, uttered before God and in the presence of witnesses (bribed, it must be admitted, by the prospect of the Lucullan feast which awaits them), the ecclesiastical formula requires, although both parties are called upon to honor each other, that the honored female of the species obey the male and swear allegiance to him as her lord and master. Is it a wonder, then, if the most holy of promises, that of faithfulness in marriage, is so despicably dishonored, since so many secondary promises weaken this principal article? And how does one reply to the well-put question as to why in many states, where oaths are the daily fare of the courts, the marriage vow (the most important contract which humans can make between one another)[17] is uttered without the aid of an oath? Do we reply perhaps that the matter is as important as the crime of patricide, which in the wise law books of wise peoples always remained an unpunishable offense? Or that there exists no formula strong enough to seal the marriage vows? Or that we have had to return to the nature of the matter, to a simple "yes" or "no," to express ourselves in the most significant way? Or do we not require an oath during the marriage ceremony for the simple reason that we cannot keep such promises, and that we think it impossible for anyone to keep them, except in such special cases as he is helped along by nature? Ah, yes, my dear fellow! Who keeps his oath of office? Able to withstand the greatest temptation to bear false witness, the judge, or what is even worse, the legislator, experiences not the slightest scruple when it comes to evading an oath. And is then the promise of fidelity in marriage, on which the dignity, security, and welfare of the state, the happiness of domestic life (the most pleasant and comforting state of human existence), as well as all human industry and endeavor rest—is this promise beyond the capability of the human race? Have you never known true and loyal marriage partners?

I seek the basis for this remarkable custom—passed down from our oath-rich ancestors to their equally oath-hungry descendants—in the fear that we would be exposing all oaths to the charge of sheer absurdity if we were to profane them through the unnatural circumstance of requiring from the women that they submit themselves willingly to the unconceded authority of the men. This question of homage caused the removal of the oath in many Protestant states, and the chosen implements for change who were the reformers were not wrong in dismissing the oath from the marriage ceremony. But should masculine power and authority, utterly discredited by both nature and experience, maintain itself merely through loathsome artifice? Will we continue to carry the day at the time when nature and truth reclaim those of their rights which are not subject to limitation? We have long been mere titular rulers in any case, owners *in partibus infidelium*.[18]

You Germans, whose ancestors respected their women because their advice was important and their judgments holy, especially if the latter inserted in them prophecies of the future—perhaps in such a manner that they were able to guide the men according to the dictates of their own will (a prophetic art not unworthy of respect). . . . You Germans, who, even if it is said of you that you will do much for money,[19] have never sold your women (as if they were household goods) as the Romans did. . . . Germans! are your ancestors so unworthy? What is more respectable, to keep step with the other sex or to let ourselves be led by this sex without knowing it? Only the *outward signs* of rule are of value to us—*rule itself* we sell for a despicable mess of pottage;[20] and many a clever wife lets herself be elected to the position of governmental representative by her husband, who would never suspect high treason, and who (for pride goeth before a fall) places his wife on the throne himself, fully convinced that everything is being dispatched under his name, under the formula: "We, by the grace of God . . . etc."

But even if such a duped husband, who lowers his wife to the use of cunning and trickery, debases his children to the same mode of thought, and publicly lets himself be trifled with, even if such a man is not unhappy because of this; even if he finds at present in his wife a very human judge in household matters, a faithful advisor in those situations where he wavers indecisively, how much more would she be to him if she were by law his full and complete equal? How infinitely freer and easier would the state of domestic and national life become, if we learned to acknowledge and protect such an alliance? Selfishness, indolence, and pride—three idols which also go by the names *covetousness, carnal desire*, and *arrogance*—chain us to old ideas and customs. Women have long enough been tested through suffering and have adequately proved themselves worthy of the glory which nature would make manifest in them.

The first period of our life is as obscure to us as the genesis of the world itself, of which we know nothing, for the reason that it remained yet beneath the heart of its mother. During the period of our infancy (when we are utterly without will, and live, breathe, and exist according to instinct and the guidance of the parents who brought us into the world)—are we not similar to that period in the history of the world which we have designated as the State of Innocence? And perhaps this title is all the more deserved, since at this period of our lives we are held accountable for nothing. Man perceives himself; that is, he emancipates himself, frequently awards himself prematurely privilege by virtue of his age,[21] believes with his powers of reason to be in possession of a god, and behold! in the midst of this self-deification he sinks, often so far beneath his fellow beings that he can hardly be recognized. His passions cause him to plunge, and he falls deeper and deeper. At first these passions are but unwelcome guests, which one would usually rather see go than come, but in a short time they become brothers to our reason, bosom friends and pampered darlings whose association with us we justify and defend to the death when our conscience reproaches us, so that this usually composed and objective organ begins to deceive itself, shortly thereafter becomes contaminated, and finally turns into passion itself.

Only much later, when the day that is our life leans toward evening, does man come again, through the voice of his recuperated conscience, to reflect upon himself. "Adam, where art thou? What has become of thee?" The fever of self-deception abates, the power of human reason has brief interludes where its influence is felt, it returns gradually to strength, and finally drafts laws which the race, as a whole at least, accepts and obeys. Yet man will never completely stop being man—and how can he expect to play to perfection a role which is utterly foreign to him? In the mistakes of old age he remembers the sins of his youth, sinks, falls, stands up again, and in the end finally realizes that he will never attain perfection. But pursue it he will, striving ever to reach that goal which is the crown of life.

Woman—is like man; there is no difference here. They are both human beings and lack the honor they should have. The relationship between the sexes? Certainly the main point of this entire chapter, and the true basis for the development of all large and small societies. Adam and Eve first lived in a state of innocence—then Adam became Eve's subordinate, obedient to the point of intemperance. Thereupon he made himself her lord and master, which he has long remained, until in the end when both will live together once again in peace, harmony, and equality, and return to that first state of innocence, this time with far more happiness and understanding than before.

Enough—I do not wish to color or to add more detail to this little sketch of the relationship between men and women. Each of us will be able to recognize himself in the strokes already visible, and through this self-knowledge the course of the human race and that of each of the sexes. May one day these two sexes become one shepherd and one fold.[22] Yet such a wish in the third chapter is premature; for who would rush headlong into such a purchase? Who would marry before the fifth and final act?

IV/ *Further Declarations Concerning the Question: "Whence Arose the Superiority of the Man over the Woman?" A Look at More Recent Times*

*T*HE SWORD gave the male sex the advantage of power over the female, but its possession was no more able to add even a hair's breadth to his natural allotment of physical and moral strength than the lack of it was able to detract from this allotment. This is not to say that its absence did not have for a consequence a certain faintheartedness and lack of confidence in their powers of which the women were not aware. When the Greeks and Romans in their wars with the Indians[1] first caught sight of elephants, they were terrified of these colossi and their courage deserted them; yet it returned as they came to see more of this military scarecrow and learned to scorn it. They convinced themselves of how little these helpless masses could avail against the mobility of an experienced army, and if they did not exactly gain in physical strength thereby, nevertheless this experience doubtless increased their confidence in their own military might.

In point of fact, we have gained so little over our ancestors in terms of physical strength and the traits which result from it, courage and bravery, that we find it the better part of wisdom to fight in their armor and with their weapons. But would not our ancestors, with all their physical superiority and with all their courage and bravery, be forced to quit the field when faced with the best of our armies of today? By means of luck and ingenuity we have equipped ourselves with powers which they would not be able to withstand. But do all these things actually strengthen our bodies or our minds? Have we become mightier than our ancestors through their use? Have we thereby attained the right to tread our ancestors beneath our feet, to dishonor and degrade them? It is just the same with our presumptions *vis-à-vis* the opposite sex. The fact that social groups eventually became more lasting and stable; that they took on certain forms which caused them to become more similar externally; that within these forms the individual gradually developed a relationship with the masses; in short, the fact that bourgeois society attained its present form did nothing whatsoever to benefit the rights of women. Once these original rights had been lost, nothing changed from that time on. Women were counted with the household goods belonging to the head of the family, of which some had been granted a dearth, others a superfluity. They were only valuable to the man insofar as they served to enlarge his possessions and increase his inventory through clever bartering.

Man became a citizen; nevertheless, he did not begin by endowing his system of government with a sense of order, permanence, or uniformity. Even now he is still learning how to become a social being, and nothing is so little understood as the theory behind this art. The first societies expanded simply through the power of weapons and were not interested in making fellow-citizens or friends out of their free neighbors, only slaves. Thus the Roman state arose, expanded, and developed, and that it was the very first of all great bourgeois societies is illustrated by its history, from its darkest beginnings to its supposedly enlightened end. The men always kept their weapons at their side—these proved useful in dictating laws to their friends and foes, in suggesting regulations for the good of the state, or in aiding in the decision of questions concerning citizen's rights. In this way the men possessed and maintained the advantage of authority over their women, bestowing grace and mercy upon them in the place of rights, if, indeed, they granted them any crumbs from their plenteous larders at all—that is, if they would even admit that the women had any right to precedence over the slaves. Yet in spite of this the Greeks, and particularly the Romans, found it more just (or more politic) to include the female sex in the executive and legislative systems of government.

Little has come down to us concerning the status of women in the Orient, aside from what the Hebrew lawgiver decrees concerning them;[2] nevertheless, it would not seem that their earlier status in this homeland of despotism and polygamy differed much from that of the present, since Asia and Africa have been rather more backward than advanced culturally since the time of the Greeks and Romans. Man is born to freedom—it is the sun whose influence supports all human growth. Where freedom is suppressed, nothing worthy of the appellation "human" can flourish. Without freedom the sacrament of marriage—the holiest and most important contract in society—becomes nothing more or less than the buying and bartering of goods. To be sure, women are considered luxury goods in such cases, because the Zenana (harem) forms an essential part of an Indian palace and takes the place of those areas where the European displays his love of splendor. Instead of exhibiting masterpieces of painting and sculpture, instead of veiling nature through art, they exhibit it naked and unadorned, and instead of leading us into a temple of good taste, they lead us into a bordello. For the Indian, women are the mere object and instrument of his pleasure and pastime. Of the highest pinnacle of human worth, love, he knows nothing, for in a relationship such as this the sexes do not share that emotion. Brutish desire is the sacred relic on his altar of love, and extravagant voluptuousness the goal of his domestic bliss. O, what an animal of a man, rich only in his utter poverty!

Yet, whatever civil rights the Greeks and Romans granted to the female sex through legislation were only a meager part of that which was due them and had actually been given them by nature, and which could be taken from them neither by fire nor the sword, neither by well-meaning nor malicious courts of law. The latter represent truly a special type of thievery, whereby one is divested not only of his body but also of his soul, a thievery of which the Romans, famous throughout the world for their justice, were also quite guilty. Can we put any trust at all in a system of justice which showed no shame or hesitation in asserting that slaves were to be considered as nonentities[3] and was capable of observation, harmful as it was droll, that there were human beings who were only to be valued as goods? All humanity lost in this legal assessment, yet who was more dishonored by it, the master or the slave?

And the unheard-of ingratitude of these Romans, who were raised by Sabine maidens and turned into men by the opposite sex, and who doubtless brought into all aspects of Roman life those traces of humanity which they learned from their governesses, in order to purge it of the bitter taste of crudeness and brutality—which of us can recall this Roman ingratitude without becoming ill-humored? What a humiliating honor was bestowed upon the women in placing them under a state of permanent guardianship, in removing the legal responsibility for their behavior, and in rendering them by formal decree a mere shadow of the man in the eyes of the state. All the laws which pertain to the opposite sex give the appearance of having been decreed amid thunder and lightning; even if they try to give themselves legal airs by assuming the guise of true gospel, one sees upon closer examination so much of the legality based on this thunder and lightning as to be convinced that no woman was allowed a vote in the affair.

It is itself a supreme insult to state that someone *cannot* suffer insult from any other person; and the legal immunity from *being able* to do wrong has not given those who are so privileged any greater advantage of security than the mentally incompetent. Female persons of the lowest moral character wish to be flattered for honoring outwardly that virtue which most of all graces their sex, and do we not degrade an entire sex to the level of slaves by taking from its midst a select few—and far from the most admirable—and worshipping them as goddesses in heaven?[4]

Can it be denied that it was the Roman legal system and its adoption in Germany which more than anything else accorded the female sex those odious privileges, thereby doing it the greatest disservice possible? It is true that both regulations pertaining to the legal adoption of a child or grandchild; namely, that the process of adoption use nature as its guide, and that it function as a means for serving the needs of those who neither have children nor any hope of having any,[5] that these regulations did not stem from the introduction of Roman law into Germany. Nevertheless, due to the fact that knowledge, artistic skills, and customs spread to the north and west from Rome, and the fact that our entire so praiseworthy culture still today clearly reveals its Roman paternity, our constitution and system of government, and above all our civil laws have borne on their forehead and breast the stamp of their Roman origin since the time of the rediscovery of the Code of Justinian at Amalfi.[6] But allow me just a few more observations before I quit this field entirely.

It is inexplicable how anyone ever came to the idea that not only the male but also the female sex is accorded privileges under Roman law. I find none of the latter type whatsoever; rather, the so-called privileges of women seem like secret wounds from the dagger of an assassin, which do more damage than if the law declared itself openly against women. What further proof do we need than the fact that women are not allowed to hold public office; that they (mothers and grandmothers excepted) are not permitted to serve as legal guardians; that even in legal proceedings where the law requires two witnesses in order to impart a greater degree of solemnity to the occasion, neither of them may be a woman; that they also cannot be used as witnesses in the drawing up of a will; that there is still much argument and strife among the learned concerning whether and to what extent the honor of serving as a witness can be granted to them in cases involving codicils; that women have no share in the rights of paternal authority in Roman law (which in this case, as everywhere else, tended to favor the interests of the children over the mother); and finally, that they have been declared incapable of legally adopting children, for it is here that this paternal authority reveals itself in all its uprightness and dignity! Moreover, a woman may not be charged under a suretyship obligation. Truly, in the face of robbery of this sort one becomes curious as to the supposed advantages with which Roman law has so generously indemnified the opposed sex. And what is more, ignorance of the law cannot be attributed to the women if they attempt to make use of even *this* miserable excuse in such cases where they seek safety through some lightning rod from the thunderbolts of pain and punishment. In a word, they have the right to remain perpetual children up to their blessed end.

The Decree of Claudius[7] was given the merciful interpretation that in cases in which a free woman acknowledged a slave to be a human being in the eyes of the law and became somewhat too free in her association with him, she was to be declared a slave of that slave's master, providing the latter had prohibited her this association the sacred number of three times beforehand. This was to occur immediately upon receipt of his petition by the court, and thereupon—let it be noted—the entire possessions of the woman were consigned to him as well. All this to the surely well-meaning gentleman merely for taking the great trouble to warn her three times! Justinian abolished such severe punishments as unworthy of his age, and yet today we still shake our heads in indecision over whether this should be considered worthy of praise and thanks, or as a reproach to his Golden Age of law!

In this and other circumstances we bestowed citizenship not merely on the spirit of Roman law-giving, but upon its crudities as well, raising high the portals to its acceptance in our own land. Our manner of life and our customs, it is true, took on another form, but not a Roman one, and the uniqueness of the German folk character made the difference between the two all the more obvious—German modes of conduct were emasculated with the tailor's scissors of Rome.

If the citizens of a state have a proper concept of their rights and duties and willingly conduct themselves accordingly, they are certainly more enlightened than when they possess great learning which does not contribute to the happiness of the populace and has only the appearance of authority. How distressing was the fate of the Germans under their Roman laws! No attempt whatsoever was made to fit these laws to the national character of the Germans and their ancestral customs. It occurred to no one to bring these laws and customs as much as possible into harmony, or in cases where neither custom nor law would submit to transformation, to dispense with the latter and to devise a set of regulations for the former. We have made so bold as to view the Roman code of laws, like the Pillars of Hercules, as an outer limit beyond which no further point of reference for human reason could possibly be imagined. No one even entertained the suspicion that what was wise and just in the Roman state and for Romans could be very unwise and unjust in Germany and for Germans. The unsophisticated spirit of German customs relied more on a virtuous, straightforward way of thinking than on certain turns of phrase which could be interpreted this way or that, depending upon whether one was in or out of favor. The Germans would have known nothing of the hundred kinds of desire if Roman law had not ordained: "Thou shalt not covet." Is it not possible to propagate vices just by painting a true picture of them? Are there not sins which one cannot reveal without running the risk of seducing others to them? And if it is difficult enough for the *writer* to give a true picture of the morals of his time without endangering public morality thereby, with what wisdom must the *legislator* proceed in order not to do more harm than good? Can the writer, at least nowadays, depict things as they truly are, or is he not sooner compelled to veil his portrait with a mask of conventionality and consequently to represent humanity as more moral than it presently is? And the legislator, prosaist that he is—must he not follow the same path? The sheer quantity of Roman law would perhaps have been frightening enough; nevertheless, it was the legal system in which these laws were formulated—a system which not only the legal scholar, but, let it be noted, also the simple citizen was required to study carefully if he was not at every turn to stumble on pretense or sophistry—which brought the Roman art of lawmaking into general circulation. The great masses only learned these laws halfway, and it was just such a half-acquaintance which endowed them with an almost mystical reverence, so that all genuflected and paid homage to the law of the Romans. The non-Roman German women came under Roman law as well, and thus the German men became entangled in the snare with which they had thought to catch the women.

History has left us too little information concerning our forefathers, may they rest in peace. They were more concerned with performing deeds worthy of posterity than in recording and preserving them. That which friend and neighbor Tacitus recorded of their customs and folk-ways[8] is far too little for us to obtain a correct, let alone complete, idea of their domestic and civil affairs. According to his report, adultery among the ancient Germans—among whom custom was capable of more than laws in Rome—was punishable by death. Are greater proofs needed to show that marriage was not a matter of indifference to them? They guarded carefully a matter which concerns the state so deeply that every case of negligence sooner or later directly brings suffering upon the state itself. Moreover, they guarded it with such jealousy and severity that even though transgressions of this sort could, as a rule, only occur very infrequently in a clime such as theirs, given their simple and frugal way of life and their unfamiliarity with indolence and the life of pleasure, the two companions of luxury, they still saw fit to assign a harsh penalty to this transgression.

The influence of German women in matters of state was considerable, for priestesses were chosen from their midst who, in addition to their duties in the performance of the sacred rites, also asserted their influence in the affairs of state, gave guidance in their councils, and inspired their warriors in battle with disdain for danger, love of the fatherland, and courage in the face of the enemy. Women served their men not as a right or left hand, as is the case with great statesmen and their greater princes, but as heart and soul. History has preserved one famous name for us, that of Vellede.[9] But whether they took active part as citizens in the assemblies of the people or whether they possessed in every case the same rights as the men is a question which history leaves unanswered. It is to be presumed, however, that even among our forefathers women played these roles more as a concession from the men than on the strength of a formal authorization; for such an authorization, which was not the rule among any other people known at the time, certainly would have been transmitted to posterity.

Even if slavery is tolerated and practiced on but a small scale, in the short or the long run it makes slaves of us all. Under a lenient, moderate governmental system whose powers are not unlimited, the woman has from time immemorial counted for more than in despotic states, where the slavery of the woman is politically necessary. Without a doubt we have the women to thank for that leniency, moderation, and limitation of power in government. Where they have a word to speak, all is in keeping with the concept of justifiable and lawful civil liberty—I say justifiable and lawful, and add that neither in body nor in soul are women disposed to despotic rule. If they show signs of being so inclined, then it was the men who seduced them to it.

Which relationship is more delightful than that between friends of both sexes? *Friendship* can exist between members of a single sex—a *relationship* cannot. Friendship, genuine friendship, is like a rare coin—to be used only in the direst emergency; a relationship is the circulated money with which we buy our daily bread. Where would we be without it? How many people are there who, although they do not feel called to that elevated state of mind required in true friendship, would nevertheless be counted among the living dead if deprived of all relationships with the opposite sex? Friendship does not ask, it demands. It does not lend, no matter how propitious the circumstances; it only calls in debts. Friends are joint possessors of the blessings of life; their emblem, to use Aristotle's phrase, consists of two bodies with but a single soul.[10] Damon and Pythias, or Orestes and Pylades, whose friendship transcended life and death, may serve as historical examples. One epoch of history considered any man to be extremely fortunate who had encountered the mere *shadow* of a friend. A relationship, when *both* sexes have a part in it, can be a similar realm of shadows, an Elysium this side of the grave.

The Latin language seems to be very poorly suited for use in relationships with women, and even in relationships of any sort, for the Romans simply did not understand that salt of the earth of which we have been speaking, namely the women. It is true that every nation has traces of its favorite virtues and vices in its language—thus technical terms of navigation come from the Dutch language; military expressions from the French; architecture, painting, and sculpture reveal their Italian homeland through their terminology; and the sport of hunting acknowledges Germany as its preserve. On the other hand, all of the modern languages, German not excepted, have retained something unique by virtue of our relationship with the opposite sex, something which the ancient world lacked. If the eternal fire maintained by the vestal virgins served to ignite the flames which provided light for all, just as a public fountain distributes its water, so this furnishes a fitting image of the service which the fair sex has performed for the world through the refinement of relationships within society—we have all received light from them. Women are often called upon to endure the advances of men and then to defend themselves; in both they combine such fine breeding and manners that if these qualities do not have the honor of being designated modesty themselves, modesty certainly cannot exist without them. And physical pleasure of whatever kind is of short duration, sooner smothering the enchanting soft glow of a relationship than contributing to its endurance.

In addition, the right to put away one's spouse,[11] assumed by the men without granting the same right to the women, further degraded the female sex. Why was this right not given to the members of both sexes?

The woman would certainly have made use of it only seldom, for most of her charms, like those of the rose, soon wither and fade. After having lain for but a few weeks in the arms of her Adam, her worth is infinitely reduced,[12] whereas her Adam remains undefiled. In cases where separation was not desired by both parties (for otherwise it would have come to a divorce), this putting away of one's wife has to be viewed as an unprecedented and undisguised show of force. Yet, in spite of all these remarkable laws and customs which so degraded the opposite sex, some of its members were able to distinguish themselves to such an extent that the entire sex gained greatly through them, and it is most often because of these women—to the everlasting praise of the fair sex—that men did not universally exercise a right which could have brought about a hard and unnatural law. In this respect such customs[13] are the most honorable things I know, and reveal, where present in unusually large number, that great and noble desire of human beings for right, justice, and liberty, as well as the fact that man did not lose his own identity when he established his social institutions. For what shall it profit a man if he shall gain the whole world, and lose his own soul?[14]

In conformity with the diversity of laws pertaining to women there also exist, it is said, diverse motives for granting them—and it is within each law itself that we would seek with the greatest certainty the reason why it was made. To be sure, it is not always that reason which Their Majesties the legislators would have us believe it is; and indeed, we need not bother ourselves here with the flourishes and flowery language of the alleged reason. Thus, for example, the inherent weakness of the sex is the reason given as to why the latter are not legally permitted to act as bondsman or surety in a contract. However, since, in the words of the law itself, this weakness does not imply a deficiency in the woman's powers of deliberation, it appears sooner to have its basis in that goodheartedness in women which has not yet lost its belief in the words and promises of others—and is this belief in mankind a weakness? If it is, then it can most certainly be said of it: "When I am weak, then I am strong." [15] In fact, a well-chosen punishment for the swindler would perhaps be far more effective than the Velleian Decree,[16] since it would be capable of extricating good-hearted men out of similar embarrassing situations as well. And if lying, the root of all evil, were punished with the severity it deserves, or in some other fine fashion were banished from the face of the earth—what a gain!

The bearing of children, generally considered among the main proofs of weakness to which the law has condescended to assign an extraordinarily high value, is none other than an example of the strength of this sex from the realm of nature. I should not like to see this business handed over to the men. How pitiable would be our vast array of fops and dandies, these hybrid creatures, and how much more pitiable the state itself! What a debit we would experience in the number of children born even the first year, and what a credit in fathers lost in childbrith! Count the days when each sex is incapacitated by sickness, and I wager the accounts would balance. . . .

Modesty is also given—*nota bene*, by the law itself—as an authentic reason for the repression of women's rights. Are we really to understand that the fair sex is denied due process of law simply for reasons of feminine modesty? How generous the laws are—as if one's modesty were in danger, or could even be lost entirely in a court of justice! What is it here that could lead to illicit passions and inflame a heart which is so far removed from such things? Before either sex decides upon adopting this virtue of modesty and demanding from every seductive word in the language that it give account of itself, we must ask the question: is there such a thing as modesty? And what is its value as a unilateral virtue? Modesty is a virtue, if I may be permitted to say so, which lives in a state of matrimony; that is, if it is not practiced by both men and women equally, it degenerates into affectation and feminine legerdemain. Is not everything pure to the pure in heart? A noble ingenuousness, an unaffected demeanor, clothes a married woman far better than the hypocrisy bred of the cloister. Man is not defiled by eating with dirty hands, but to honor a virtue with our lips while our hearts are far away—is that not an abomination?

If a pure mouth means more to us than a pure heart, however, then that section of the law[17] will have an easy time of it which maintains that feminine modesty would be led into the labyrinths of temptation if the fair sex were permitted to meddle in legal affairs. O, what an overly refined sense of apprehension this betrays! Does not the kingdom of God lie within us? Virtues which never have the good fortune to be led into temptation are, like our coin of small denomination, of questionable weight and alloy, even if they do generally possess the advantage of remaining in continuous circulation. The right to resist, by means of which we oppose those things which would do us harm—when this right is never put to use, does it not sooner or later bring about a loss of self-discipline, so that in the end men begin to flee before their own shadows? Are the most horrible crimes conceived and born in the open or behind closed doors? And that which in plain language we call a *right*, that is, the capacity to perform an action or to abstain from it—is it our wish to deny in the finest legal language that the female sex possesses the ability and the moral strength to make use of this right? Has it not occurred to us that rights arise out of assumed obligations, and that there can be no rights without obligations?

As a logical conclusion from Roman legal principles, the Justinian Code decreed that no woman could be imprisoned for any offense.[18] Even on account of the most heinous crimes she was only to be punished with the cloister and entrusted to the supervision of other women. We, in the plenitude of our power, have dispensed with this law—without, however, having released the opposite sex from the other "benefits" of Roman law. Who would have thought that people could ever be so besieged, overwhelmed, and plagued by their benefits? Who would have thought that the Roman woman herself, overburdened as she was with such benefits, would not have been permitted to attend the national assemblies? Or that she was not considered worthy of the honor of being a citizen of the nation, and that out of precisely this state of degradation arose her privilege of remaining, with the full consent of the law, utterly ignorant of that law, and of adorning herself with this ignorance as if it were a precious jewel? This benefit of eternal childhood was not merely harmless, it was actually laudable—a benefit which enabled her to live, breathe, and have her being in the realm of Saturn in a season of eternal springtime. She gave away everything she owned in order to live on charity; she exchanged gold for baubles and tinsel, coins of rare value for polished tokens. But none of this can be compared with the exchange of rights for goods, the exchange of the masculine "I demand" for the feminine "I request."

And how could one then do otherwise than to bestow mercy and benefits on a woman under the legal dominion of her husband, on a slave subjected to the power of another human being? The children were not hers, but her husband's. She had renounced her own family in order to be joined with that of her husband. Had we forgotten already that marriage is an institution of equals, that authority in marriage is distributed equally, and that the man can only claim his wife as his own by means of an *express* agreement?

"Not through tacit consent?" you ask?

Ah, indeed—I had nearly forgotten this most silent of sins. Nevertheless, should it not be possible to bring all of these exorbitant benefits and privileges together under a single rubric? While we cannot know precisely, yet in view of that which has happened in other cases, we can presume what official and unofficial motives and objectives, both primary and secondary, are behind this enthusiasm for retaining the old laws. If I am not sadly deceived, it was the *fear* on the men's part *of being subjugated* by the women which brought the former to overwhelm the women with benefits and privileges. Just like the judges of the courts, who tolerate no moral equinox where good and evil counterbalance each other, so the men, who already count among their number so many enemies and detractors, seem to want to protect themselves against attack from the rear by the women as well. Would it be the first time that we have tried to protect our dominion with the home remedy of depriving—albeit very discreetly—those whom we have ruled and wish to rule forever of their hopes for self-improvement and recognition? Has no voice cried in the wilderness[19] showing this masculine conceit for what it is, and calling the attention of all to this state within a state?

At one time there were gods and goddesses who could be bought with gifts and sacrifices. Thus it was with the opposite sex, which also was compelled to accept gifts at the cost of its rights, and which, no matter how much its humanity served to ornament its being, was nonetheless forced to give up this humanity in exchange for divinity. To show a person kindness by taking away his rights is tantamount to treading on a natural law and pluming ourselves with a human one; to selling one's birthright for a mess of pottage; to straining at a gnat and swallowing a camel. O, you blind guides,[20] who with pharisaical hypocrisy lulled the opposite sex to sleep, fished in troubled waters, and through the appearance of justice sought to extinguish natural rights which were written in the heart! Nature cannot be forced.

Fear! Does the word strike home? It is meant to do just that. Behold, I shall lay open my heart and confess to the honor of the masculine sex that no more evil intention lay behind our dominion over the opposite sex than the fear that they would become our masters. Perhaps we, for our own part, did not think to become a burden to the women because of this plan, or to cause them injury or suffering—rather that it would be useful and advantageous both to them and to us. Perhaps it was a plan of this supposedly useful sort which was the beginning of many another now degenerate dominion. Fear created the gods, said the ancients; but did not *love* have a hand in it as well? "We should fear God and love Him"; thus Luther begins his exposition of the Ten Commandments— and yet it is love which drives away fear.

Look around you! Even nowadays you will find that men who *worship* their wives keep especially clear of anything which would contribute to the improvement of the status of the opposite sex. And why this odd resistance? The awareness of the value of his splendid wife strengthens the fear in the heart of her spouse. The honor which he bestows on her person suppresses any thought of showing justice to her sex as a whole. Even the best of men is jealous of the truly great qualities in his wife—qualities which can threaten him. With his beneficence he desires to keep her from speaking, to set limits in order to check and channel her use of reason and desire for it—a remarkable way of bending the law with gifts and of not paying a debt, rather of making the creditor a present of greater value than the debt! Such men take extraordinary pains to show their best side to their wives; and since they well realize how far their wives have outdistanced them in everything, they place inordinate value on their civic duties and official functions merely in order to maintain the respect of their wives! That poor sex! How we keep it in the dark! The story is told of a Turkish ambassador who, when questioned regarding his opinion of the lady from ———, replied that he really knew very little about the art of painting. Is not every official of the state made up in a way similar to this? Take away the red and the white[21] in which the state has draped him for the sake of honor and we would find in him neither beauty nor form.

We do not wish to have to exert ourselves trying to keep step with the opposite sex, and if they were our equals we would often be forced to do so to a greater extent than we can either imagine or are capable of. Consequently, we give them riddles which are not worth solving; we require that they interpret our dreams without knowing what we have dreamed; we seek to involve them in the workings of the world and at the same time to remove them as far as possible from all that is serious or requires contemplation. And yet this idleness—and what woman is not sentenced to it in both crass and subtle ways?—is the very basis for all those evils from which true and meaningful activity would free all mankind. Activity has for its daughters the three Graces: Virtue, Knowledge, and Riches. But, we may ask, what kind of activity? That to which men, in the plenitude of their power, have sentenced the women, or that which one applies to work which one has chosen oneself? That in which one's song and dance are rewarded by payment, or that in which the work we ourselves have chosen is its own reward? Work which has been commissioned can, it is true, lead to other, freely chosen, work which is infinitely more noble; nonetheless, the work which one is commissioned to do must never be as monotonous as that of the women if the soul, when it finally begins to soar, is to become a truly effective force. When will activity of one's own choosing ever cease to be the royal prerogative of the men! When will women attain that human right to perform work not for bread, not in the hope of selling something, but wholeheartedly and as a labor of love! When, O when! How we could shorten the explanation of the seventh petition of the Lord's Prayer[22] by improving the relationship between women and the state!

We prohibit—and are correct in doing so—not only immorality, but also the appearance of it; for shamelessness, when it becomes public, brings about a general corruption of the state and is a very visible sign of its impending collapse. But we do not take into account that the exclusion of the opposite sex from all serious public business must needs bring about in that sex the idea of dethroning all that is sacred, of degrading it, and of so spoiling the solemnity of life for the impertinent world of youth that when the young men finally begin to devote themselves to the affairs of the world, they will everywhere apply the maxim of absurdity which they learned at the feet of the fair sex. Few things will be able to withstand the blight of our pettiness and pedantry unless the women, the single possible preventive against the evil of our sex, are woven into the fabric of the state.

Man is inclined to imitation, and it is a well-known observation that people introduce into their domestic life what is traditional and fashionable in the state at large. Despotism reigns in the private residences of despotic states and attempts, in order to soothe its conscience, to give itself the air of necessity, since greater freedom for the women would be accompanied by insurmountable disadvantages for the state, and this sex, born to be true to nature, would relegate the entire unnatural phenomenon of despotism to its proper place. But it is also a fact that the fair sex has never attained the possession of its rights to any respectable degree in republics, either. To be sure, in a republic women gain more through less outward display; but this gain has also had the effect of teaching the gentlemen who represent the state to choose their words more carefully. The women play a somewhat more serious game here than in despotic states and monarchies, but they are not permitted to overstep certain bounds—their supposed advantages are at stake. Whatever they do remains forever a game. Every imagination of the thoughts of their hearts[23] is from their youth on a mere trifle and remains so. What is worse, their artificially arranged cosmetics so disfigure their natural beauty that the query of the wife of the Sultan of Morocco to the heavily made-up wife of the Dutch Consul, "Is all of that you?" is not entirely undeserving of an answer.

In an aristocracy the good gentlemen aristocrats are by nature so inclined to envy and jealousy that they fear to lose much if they grant their wives the upper hand; and since even the French Revolution has not changed their status—although the women carried its banner high[24]—it appears that the differences in governmental systems are not destined to bring about a healing of these tribulations of Joseph.[25] At best, the women's status has remained more or less the same.

"It defies the laws of reason and nature," says a certain worldly philosopher, "for women to *rule in families*, but not that they should rule *kingdoms*. In the former case their natural weakness does not allow them this privilege; in the latter this very weakness disposes them to kindness and moderation."[26] Methinks this observation is but sophistry. Whose intention is it that women should rule in the family? According to the old rhyme of a certain German reformer, only where each does his own lesson will all be well with the household.[27]

Considering that one half of the human race is concerned with nothing else than getting itself married off honorably anyway, it is surprising that there is so much control and surveillance in this most important of matters, and, since the woman is damned to a state of eternal guardianship, that she is content merely to take her revenge at first hand on her husband, all the while remaining upright and philanthropic in the world at large. Strict concentration on a matter we have set before ourselves can enable us to suppress our cares and sorrows; and even the most severe illness loses a good part of its discomfort through conversation with a good friend—who, it should be noted, must nevertheless entertain the patient in such a way as to keep him from becoming excited. Are the marriages of today really much more than such an entertainment of the sick, whereby we try as much to avoid boredom as excitement, and above all attempt to divert the opposite sex from experiencing terrible feelings of dependence and oppression? If the men were to express the opinion more often that they know better than nature herself how the relationship between the sexes should be structured, then those of the higher classes, at least, would long since have had war declared on them by their enlightened spouses. At present, however, since the men hardly ever strike this chord, or at most express themselves concerning this matter in the same way Machiavelli talked of tyrants, peace remains as yet in the upper classes, and in the lower classes the difference between male and female worth or lack of worth is too insignificant to mention, or else they think too seldom about their destiny to know other than in an animal-like way that the human race is composed of two separate sexes.

Let us be honest! Every means by which human beings can distinguish themselves has been taken from the women. A conspiracy among their enemies debases this sex as deeply as an unavenged insult does a husband, expelling it to the class of servants and menials by means of the bugbear that the limits of its feminine modesty might otherwise be transgressed—when in truth it is only so that we may remain secure from their challenge to a duel.

Not physical resemblance but the law determines paternity through the institution of marriage; it alone designates the father, and tolerates no contradiction.[28] How is it possible then, since it is nature alone which directly determines who is to be called the mother of a child, and since this determination is as unquestionably certain as our own existence and death, how is it possible that her children have degenerated to such a point of ingratitude? How is it possible that those among them who are still well disposed to her do not unite in snatching their mother from the humiliation in which she languishes because of her sex? Up to now the male sex has been playing its hand with extraordinarily good luck! If, because of the sex drive, the fathers were not so favorably inclined to their daughters as is usually the case, perhaps the daughters would long since have formed a conspiracy against them for the purpose of making human beings out of young ladies who at present are allowed neither to see, to hear, nor to think because propriety forbids it; who have the right to be impertinent and audacious only when alone; and who are able only in their own company to escape that enforced monastic life which condemns them to the most terrible loneliness in society. What can be expected of such an upbringing directed by hypocrisy—hypocrisy in accordance with which even the plan to induce a couple to marry has to be carried out so secretly that often the loudest "no" signifies the most heartfelt "yes!"

All those laws for the propagation of the human race—the encouragement to marry, the three-child marriage—are nothing other than unnatural remedies which would all cease to be important if men and women were guided back onto the path of nature. How obvious everything would then be! Let us first seek the kingdom of God and His righteousness,[29] and truly, all else will come of itself.

For the state to honor people because they are married, because they have precisely three children, or because they have children at all; or to allow the man with the most children to cast his vote first in the council, is no less ridiculous than to measure the size of a person's soul from the size of his body.[30] Perhaps the time will yet come when we will be paid for eating, drinking, or sleeping! The state is not served by the sheer numbers of its people alone, but rather by citizens who stand in proper relationship to their natural state and acknowledge its importance; who are free, industrious, right-thinking, and prosperous. And the number of citizens itself! Would it not be increased by half again if we decided to raise the other sex to the level of citizens and make them colonists within the state? We are compelled to resort to the most wretched of artifices if we choose to ignore the hints provided by nature; it is remarkable to note that even the women of Rome in one certain period were actually permitted to "bear" themselves out of their eternal guardianship by having children—the freeborn woman was required to have three, the woman who had been set free needed four.

Should women not someday sooner or later prove the worth of their existence to the men, just as Alcibiades of old proved his to the Athenians, who had condemned him to death?[31] Should they not likewise find their Sparta, from which they may declare war on their Athenian men? They, who already now during their five-year Pythagorean silence[32] have given such a clear indication of how much they deserve to come of age? They, who see more with two eyes than Argus[33] with his hundred? They, who already, before it has become apparent what they shall become, are required to produce exceptional souls from among their ranks who are a match for our own sex—exceptional souls who break out of the limited sphere of their contemporaries and, burning their bridges behind them, soar on wings of the spirit, or, if this is not possible, take flight by means of their imagination, in order, like Felix, to await a more convenient season?[34] Or does pleasure consist in knowing no pleasure; is fasting the feast of the gods? Is mere striving a virtue and hope alone our fortune? Do not a large number of women demonstrate that noble souls are free whether in chains or not, just as a despotic ruler of the opposite turn of mind often finds himself captive to a slavery of his own making? Thus Alexander served, and Diogenes was free. Diogenes, who, as Alexander gave him the opportunity of requesting a pension for himself (a greater one, it might be added, then Frederick the Great ever gave to his personal philosophers and poets), asked merely if His Supreme Alexandrian Highness would mind standing a little to the side so that he who was worth being warmed by the rays of sun would no longer be deprived of this prerogative. Diogenes dismissed Alexander; the rich beggar the poor conqueror of the world who sought his favor. If continuous improvement of the human race and true, not sham, enlightenment are grounded on an objective understanding of nature and on the ability to use her gifts correctly, then no political force in the world can prevent people from the pursuit of happiness or keep them from realizing the value of justice and its true relation to all mankind.

A man will seldom deny or even question what is generally accepted by all; a woman, however, considers it her privilege to make exceptions of this sort every day. She often does it before she has examined the circumstances, and when she then finds herself compelled to make a virtue out of necessity, it is pleasant to see how she seeks and finds justification for what she does, thus retaining her honor in this hazardous enterprise of questioning generally held truths, or if not, then at least gaining the advantage of appearing to be unique. It is a good thing that in such cases of need there is still enough reserve in the women's mental faculties to show what they would be capable of it they did not have so many obstacles to overcome. We men are more for habit and custom, women for novelty. Both of these propensities can be fairly accurately explained by the particular situations of the two sexes. What else must the opposite sex give up in order to be considered worthy of being completely restored to its former condition?[35] Women's tears are not merely a proof of weakness, but also proof of a certain strength which is in them. Are not tears in everyday life more a sign of resolve than remorse? And do not both guilt and innocence have their tears? The fact, by the way, that not only women and children weep—if we are speaking of the feigning of one's feelings by means of tears—but also men, should be obvious even to the most unobservant. As a matter of fact we pay too little attention to the moods of women; even with regard to the smaller inundations we would often find that the causes are profound, even though these moods soon flee from us on the wings of the dawn and cannot be captured again by any means. Women themselves are the last to know what to make of them, and they should thank me for making here what is no small discovery. They should ponder many things in their hearts[36] which are a part of that true peace, of the peace of God, so that they may learn to appreciate a strength which is solidly founded in this supposed weakness of theirs.

All declarations of devotion from lovers are odious to us if *we* are not the true object of that devotion. Men! Have you more than just the appearance of love from your women? And do you deserve more? Do you not deserve for them to love you only to the extent that slaves serve tyrants? Eyes can speak in love as well as in respect. If we had excluded women merely from a few affairs that are utterly masculine by origin and by nature, who among this gentle sex would have complained? They would simply have chanted their old "Marlborough Goes Off to War,"[37] and with that everything would have been forgiven and forgotten.

Power can in every instance accomplish less than wisdom. Whoever conceives of God as almighty is His slave, but whoever looks upon Him as all-knowing deserves to be called His child.

V/ *Suggestions for Improvement*

JS THE OPPOSITE SEX always to remain as it has been and is? Are the
human rights so basely taken away from the women, the civil
rights so indecently withheld from them to be lost forever? Are the
women never to attain an absolute value *in* and *for* the state, but always
to possess mere relative worth? Are they never to take a direct part in the
founding and preservation of the state? Are they never to think and act
for and *by* themselves? Will we seek the answers to these questions in a
subtle and sophisticated Roman legal fiction or in ancient and traditional property rights and statutes of limitation, so that we may again
reject such questions and force them into a state of distasteful silence?
Will we even soothe our masculine consciences with misgivings concerning the possible consequences, with further abuses, or with whatever other bugbears people use to frighten children and thus put off and
put off again this concern of the entire human race? If so, then the
glorious morning of redemption is not yet at hand. Will we be able to
refrain from still calling ourselves Vandals and Goths[1] —the names of
our forefathers of old—if we do not seek to rectify this injustice, and the
sooner the better?

Abuse of a right does not cause its disappearance. Human rights can
never be lost; civil rights only through a felony. This latter term, derived
from feudal law (not a particularly exotic ancestry), designates all sins of
omission or commission in the relationship between a vassal and his
liege lord, according to their particular contract. Since both the vassal
and the lord possess certain rights and duties in relation to each other,

not only the former but also the latter is capable of committing a felony. And is the fief itself lost merely because of a sin of omission or commission? Rather, is not the feudal lord, since he is nothing more or less than a human being, bound to hold the vassal to the performance of the deeds required by the contract and to the avoidance of those which run contrary to the contract, as well as to petition for damages if the contract is broken? Are contracts weakened when penalties for contravention are added to them, or are they not rather strengthened? Can the actions of one person ever be ascribed to another? And if the vassal loses his fief because of a felony, is the feudal lord not duty-bound to return it after his death to whomever inherits it from the vassal guilty of the felony and declared unworthy of holding a fief? Can a fief ever cease to exist because of a felony? And who made the man a feudal lord and the woman a vassal? Do they not both hold their fiefs from God? The earth could perhaps sooner be called a woman's fief than a man's, and is a very mixed fief at best. Let us put this felony against woman—of which neither nature nor history has the slightest comprehension—back in its place and not forget that God entrusted the fief of the world to the first human couple, whom He (O, the worth of mankind) himself created, and that between His feudal law and the shoddiness of human law no comparison is imaginable. So much for *civil* rights! In matters of *human* rights only God can act as judge; and to fall into His hands—how comforting that is when compared to our own petty concerns here on earth!

Is it perhaps fear, or merely a grimace of the same, which we pretend to in order to evade in a dignified way this well-founded and legally valid demand? "Become as little children"[2] is a well-intentioned piece of advice, for it is only a childlike fear which is not unmanly. It consists in taking care to avoid that which is contrary to the eternal laws of the True and the Good. That servile fear of punishment which arises when we do what these laws require and avoid what they prohibit is the truly unmanly one. Do we wish to fear a sex which was created to love, and which, even when it becomes angry, seldom lets the sun set on its anger? A sex which, except in one particular point (and here we are speaking of a sin against the Holy Spirit of the sex itself)[3] comes to meet its accuser even three-quarters of the way in order to offer him reconciliation! How much more cause do we have to fear ourselves than a sex which, if we were to restore it to its rights, would owe us good will, if not gratitude, and would strive with the very nature of its being to pay this debt gladly!

It is said that we can hardly hope that the human race, which has had the impertinence to have removed itself so far from nature, which will not allow itself be guided by religious sentiments of any sort, and which will not let itself be blinded by the deceptions of the state—that we can hardly hope it will conform its behavior to eternal laws either, and that consequently our fears and apprehensions are not so completely out of the question as one might generally think. My dear fellow! How can you require that the human race remain forever content to be led about as if on a leash? Do not both the deceptions of the state and religious sentiments, whenever the latter are not founded on fundamental principles, give rise all by themselves to disbelief and skepticism with regard to these laws? Is man never to be brought to a respect for duty? Is he never to attain to the main principle of life: "be reasonable"? Does sensuality mean more to him than moral reason and moral law? Will he never raise himself high enough to be worthy of his spiritual nature and to render respect and esteem also unto that which he cannot see? Should mere meekness of temperament determine our inclinations? Or is there such a thing, besides inclination of temperament, which, if it were to be distilled and refined, could be called an inclination of the heart? And is there not also, besides these two, an inclination of the mind, just as there are pleasures of the mind? Proud man does not long honor what he can perceive with his senses—he familiarizes himself with it, and it becomes a part of him. The single means which great heroes and scholars possess to survive in the face of extraordinary honor (and what is it really worth?) is to withdraw into themselves. As soon as we reveal ourselves for inspection, we sell ourselves more cheaply. The greater the tension, the faster the recoil. Man must learn everything except dying. He can accustom himself to anything, good or bad. One leads a shy horse back to the object which has frightened it. And here, where the highest goal of his honor and dignity is at stake—is he to renounce his vigor and force? By no means! We can and shall come to the point where we will honor the divinity of the laws in their sanctuary, in our soul, and win our heart over by means of the beliefs of our mind. To be sure, at the present any legislator would be guilty of the grossest miscalculation if he formulated his laws on the basis of a firm confidence in the reasoning power and wisdom of his constituents. But will humanity never grow up? If not, then everything remains but a patch job on the old edifice of injustice, and man ought to be ashamed to call himself human.

If, however, mankind is capable of rising to that degree of perfection which it imagines is possible for itself; of exercising those virtues which in their ideal form give it pleasure, then let us do away with the mist of deception by means of which people were taken in who sooner or later will come to use their powers of reason and find themselves deceived. Men, would you not consider that fear to be barbarous and inhuman which took away all your liberty merely because it could be misused in part? What kind of name will you give to that fear which keeps you from giving the opposite sex back its honor? The times have passed for convincing the opposite sex that a state of guardianship like the one which has existed up to now is advantageous to them, and that this guardianship allows them to be more comfortable and carefree than emancipation, wherein they would be burdened with responsibilities, cares, anxiety, and a thousand other unpleasantries of civic life which they now hardly have the good fortune to be able to call by name. This is truly a shabby piece of trickery from that inhuman despot of whom we have been speaking, whereby he wishes to lighten the heavy chains of his cowardly slaves. As if liberty, with all her discomfort, were not to be preferred to the most comfortable slavery! "Do not think that the land of Württemberg was created merely on your account," wrote Frederick the Great to the present Duke of Württemberg. "But understand that Providence had you born in order to make your people happy." And men! do you wish to believe that half the world exists for your *bon plaisir,* at your behest—that is, translated, for your own self-interest? Animals behave; people act. Why should the woman not be able to express her own *ego?*—truly a gentle word to those who understand ungrudging *nature.* Whoever understands only *art* is jealous and does not betray in himself the hand of the Master.

Is it not the greatest of human prerogatives that we are able to understand ourselves? Our price is our own matter; our value is the concern of God and righteous men. Did God make a mistake with the opposite sex? Or was it the men who sinned against the will of the Creator with regard to this sex? Why should women not be considered as persons? Why do we not know the difference between: "that is good," and "that is good for me"; or "that is right," and "that works to my advantage"?

Even now France is terrorizing with liberty those powers which threaten to restrict the excessive decrees of the National Assembly.[4] God help us! At the end of the eighteenth century, where no specter, even one of some considerable stature, a poltergeist for example, any longer has an effect, can people terrorize with *liberty*? Has it come to that? Why, even those who were raised in chains are now illuminated by the radiance from this word! Liberty, this divine spark by means of which we are what we are, and which renders us not so much unbridled and unrestrained as it binds us more firmly than anything else to the holy sanctuary of the eternal laws. The female sex was deprived of its *human* rights through no fault of its own, but merely through the great strides forward taken by all human activity and affairs in their advancement toward civilization. Moreover, it has not made any effort to regain, either by negotiation or by force, the *civil* rights which it lost at the time of the formation of smaller family-states and still awaits today, with complete self-abnegation, from our sense of justice and magnanimity. Do we wish to let it wait in vain? Will we reject the petition which nature submits on behalf of the female sex with a clear and straightforward "nay" at a time when human rights are being preached loudly from the housetops?[5]

The new French constitution deserves a repetition of my reproaches, because it has considered it sufficient not to make mention of an entire half of a nation, even though it did grant the rights of active citizenship to a smaller part of this nation—that is, to those who already enjoyed the right to religious toleration.[6] All human beings have the same rights—all the French, men and women alike, should be free and enjoy citizens' rights. Proposals for a *degradation civique*, a public ceremony in which men are declared unworthy of citizenship in the French state because of criminal acts, have not been extended to include the female sex. In such cases, women are merely to have the following curse spoken over them: "Your fatherland has found you guilty of an infamous act."

Mirabeau, who perhaps had lost confidence in the present generation, finally came, like all great men of action, to place his hope for the future in education. In his posthumous work *Travail sur l'education publique*, published by his friend and physician, Cabanis, he assigns to the woman domesticity and the quiet and gentle virtues (is not every virtue quiet and gentle?) on which in the final analysis the happiness of the state is so dependent. Without getting involved myself in the dispute which has been conducted among his friends and enemies with such gross exaggeration concerning count or "no count" Mirabeau, may I be permitted at this point to contradict the assertion that a person who is a miserable wretch in his private life is capable of being the most virtuous citizen in public life, let alone the highest example of public life, a competent state official? An individual who is capable of indifference toward all that is good or bad, just or unjust, simply cannot be an upright citizen. And since the opposite sex is accustomed to drawing conclusions about a man's public life from his private life and very quickly learns to size up role players who do not act according to basic principles, but merely as the situation and circumstances seem to require, is it any wonder that these fortune and misfortune hunters seek to cast away the opposite sex as they do?

We err if we let ourselves be convinced that women have no feeling for humanity's affair of honor, for the fight for freedom against absolute authority. Not only by their vociferous approval have they shown that they understand the value of liberty and that its flame is still able to blaze brightly among them, they have even worked themselves to break the fetters in which the nation lay, and probably are not to be held altogether responsible for the fact that they have only been allowed to play supporting roles in this drama.

That famous author of the history of Queen Elizabeth, Madame Kéralio,[7] has been defending the rights of humanity with candor, truth, and vigor ever since the Revolution in her *Journal d'État et du citoyen.* Women felt that snub, that profound silence on so glorious an occasion, that rejection when it came to serving the state. One among them dared to allow her indignation to become vocal. In a letter addressed to the National Assembly she made the observation that there was not a single word in the Constitution concerning women, although mothers would logically have had to be considered citizens of the state.[8] She then requested that mothers be allowed in the presence of the proper civil authorities to take the ceremonious oath of citizenship. This sacred ceremony certainly would have made it worthwhile to be a mother. History has not recorded what the representatives of the nation decided to do concerning this request from a noble Frenchwoman. It is with sadness that today, the 18th of March, 1792, I celebrate her memory, for I read in the newspapers that the French, unmoved by this suggestion, have let it come to pass that the opposite sex is now more urgently demanding these rights. It would have been much better if the men had come first with their offer of citizenship and given women no cause for the embarrassment of appearing ridiculous in this very serious matter. And would all those lamppost spectacles have taken place if women had been legal voters in France?

Nevertheless, the question remains whether the fashionable ladies of Paris can overcome themselves and return far enough back to nature to be able to ponder the matter in humane and homely fashion. Surely we can have more faith in the women of Germany. Does not God, who gives us our strength, also give us the right to use it? Should a woman wrap her talent in a handkerchief and bury it in the ground, thus deriving no interest from it—interest which would bring the state fruits, some perhaps of a thousandfold?[9]

It is up to human reason and its masterpiece, human society, to determine whether this strength should be given freer rein, or whether it is to be curtailed; however, the state may at no time take steps to suppress it completely. Could the state dare rob us of our liberty when the safeguarding of this very entity constitutes the chief reason for its existence? If members of a certain social class can only be represented by their peers; if even our ancestors had justice meted out to them and laws interpreted for them by those of equal rank, how can we exclude women from service to the state, insofar as legislation and the administration of laws is concerned? Do we wish to deny women initiation into these mysteries to keep them from seeing that our true weakness lies precisely at that point where we pretend our greatest strength by means of hieroglyphic rituals and incantations? Most officials of the state are nothing more than midwives to a mountain giving birth to a mouse, a mouse which nevertheless is baptized with the most glorious names and brought before the public with almost more fanfare than if a writer were to review his own books. Whoever has had the good fortune to have lived in close proximity to those who govern the state will readily grasp my meaning. What sweat of the brow!—councils and boards, assemblies and committees, tribunals and commissions! What great quantities of paper are carried about, written upon, and read! Stockbrokers of merely another sort—paper dealers of a higher dignity! And yet it seems as if everything is against everyone, because everyone is warring against everyone else.[10]

Are these the high and mighty committees and organizations from which the fair sex is excluded? One really ought to take the women in, just as in the Free Imperial cities political tub-thumpers and outright agitators were made members of the council in order to keep them quiet. And perhaps this little stratagem would already have been put into practice if we had been able to rely on the women a little more to keep their silence. Truly, in order for us to get our bearings once more we ought to allow women a voice in the matters of the state, to which they have an indisputable divine calling—which is more than can be said for most of the ne'er-do-wells whom we now call our high-ranking public officials.

Can it be denied that in every code of laws one can and must proceed from the basic premise of a natural equality and begin with the Garden of Eden—provided, of course, that one does not forget thereby the Fall of Man? Yet, such a promise of natural equality will and must, when applied to the state, have as a consequence political inequality among its citizens.[11] The opposite sex stands to gain from this natural equality, of course; nonetheless, it is simply not possible for the resulting political inequality to proclaim an entire sex—in which there are perhaps more who are of age than in our own—as unworthy for perhaps no other reason than the fact that the business of making laws rests entirely in the hands of the men. Should I add that I am not speaking here merely of using mouth and tongue to vote, but of using soul and heart as well? As soon as the time comes when physical strength, the notion of male superiority, and outmoded tradition play no part in the making of laws—and woe to the state which lays such cornerstones into its foundation!—as soon as every normal society exists for the express purpose of bringing such natural preponderances into equilibrium once again, the women will have a right to demand of the state that it show them justice and not lose sight of their strength of soul in the face of their physical weakness, which for the most part is a result of blind prejudice. For is not the soul the chief part of man?

Natural equality necessitates political inequality, for the elevation of the natural worth of the human race is only possible through a reciprocal political contract between its members, and because outstanding men must be held in check by laws, just as genius must be subject to rules. But can this fundamental principle, not contradictory in and of itself, be applied to an entire sex? Is it just, reasonable, advisable, or even humane that our entire sex be elevated and viewed as the center point around which the other is to revolve?

There are but two entities of which we can truly have any notion: nature and liberty—and for both natural science and ethics women have undeniable talent. And if we wished to have a visual representation of nature or liberty, both would have to assume the form of a woman. So what is it that stands in their way? Civil law? No book of laws, even if it were to speak with the tongues of angels, can become a Formula of Concord or an Augsburg Confession.[12] Laws educate men, but when men come of age, the laws must be educated by them. Assuming women are in fact physically weak—assuming!—what in that case would be the duty of the law? To be mighty on the side of the weak! It is not the strong who have need of the physician, but the weak.

Am I not aware that many women are still perfectly content with their relationship to their husbands? Nevertheless, whatever is based on personal sentiment must by its very nature be subject to change; and it is therefore necessary that, even in the face of the most tolerant of sentiments within the state, no intolerant passages remain in the law books. Who will stand up for those who come after us? Women know how to convince their men that they have no will of their own. But it is precisely when they seem to be denying their will in the most convincing way that they become the most autocratic—without mitigating in any way the belief of the men that these alone rule the roost. Women rule not by force (*vi*), but clandestinely and by way of request (*clam et precario*).[13]

The admirer of a woman believes himself to be in the service of a goddess who has the power to confer divinity the way university faculties confer doctoral degrees. The happy loved one believes himself to be at least half god himself, because he is so fortunate as to serve such a goddess. But if he wakes from this dream after a short while, behold! The caterpillar is transformed not into a butterfly, but into a harsh taskmaster, and his wife, deprived of all her divine attributes, becomes his slave. The bridegroom becomes not a husband, but a marital steward.[14] In like manner, our monarchs have given up their status as gods and condescended to descend to the level of men—but in order to maintain their superiority over the rest of humanity they relegated the rest of humanity to a step below their former standing as human beings. Half-truth is more dangerous than total lie; the latter is more easily recognized than the former, which is accustomed to disguising itself with appearances in order to deceive doubly. Men, let us call mankind what God created as mankind! "Let us make man in our own image," it is written, and "in the image of God created he him; male and female created he them." They are bone of our bones, flesh of our flesh[15] —and why not citizens like us? Why not, for they lack neither the mind nor the strength for the virtues of citizenship, and it is but a matter of educating them to this role! True, as they are now—moulded to be playthings for men—if they were suddenly to leave the gynaeceum[16] for the great marketplace of everyday life, which is such very unfamiliar soil for them in body and soul, and where they would be expected to play roles now filled by men, they would hardly make a tolerable debut. But who is asking this either of their heads or their hands? They should tread the paths we have trod, cross the deserts which were so difficult for us on our own way to Canaan; only through education, instruction, and experience are they to reach that goal of which they are so worthy. It takes light nearly eight minutes to come from the sun to us, and thus we see any changes which occur in that body eight minutes after the fact. Pythagoras required silence from all his pupils before their philosophical tongues could be loosened. Let the following serve as a rule of thumb for both men and women: for the *latter*, not to lay claim to the privileges of the master craftsman before they have the requisite years of apprenticeship behind them; for the *former*, not to demand fruits before their time from a sex which has been neglected for so long. Nature and the human mind very easily enter into proper harmony; and if the means appear insignificant—if, indeed, they are in fact so—who would judge them on their own merit and not rather on the magnitude of the ends which can be attained through them? An oak of no mean age can still be considered young when a shrub of the same age or a flowering plant at the base of its great trunk are at the end of their years. Not in individual cases, but in every case; not in individuals, but in the entire sex the dignity and the purpose of humanity are revealed.

Why the difference now in the upbringing of the two sexes, which begins at the cradle and ends at the bier? Why such a significant difference, as if the two sexes had not but one origin, were not made of the same stuff, were not born to a single destiny? Let the wall which divides us be broken apart—let us raise citizens for the state without regard to sex and leave that which women must know as housewives and mothers to separate instruction, and all will return to the order of nature. Child rearing is still far from what it could and should be. Only at a very late stage did it occur to us how we should have begun—that is, by determining first the purpose of child rearing, and then seeking out our goals and turning our course in their direction. Instead of straying far afield without plan or purpose like lost sheep, it should be our first concern to return home to nature and not seek the answers outside ourselves. For what is a man profited, if he shall gain the whole world, and lose his own soul? If child rearing has no purpose the bond which holds each of its individual phases together will loosen—and in our children lies the kingdom of God.[17]

To be sure, we have of late begun to take this important need of the state to heart—but we have hardly just begun. The nations as a whole and even their representatives, whose primary and most important concern ought to be the education of the people, seem either not to perceive this need sufficiently, or in fact believe it their duty to place obstacles in the way of attempts to educate their citizens. If the leaders of the people would consider the fact that nothing but a proper education can safeguard forever their possession of legal privileges based on contract, they would at the same time be reflecting upon what it is that insures their peace of mind. Formal instruction and child rearing, so different in form and purpose, have long been considered as one. For a long time we encouraged teachers, who as a rule had not been raised properly themselves, to bring our children up as well as teach them— and we then professed not to understand how a person could be educated and yet deficient in manners and morals. We firmly believed the golden proverb that art and morality are sister and brother, and it never occurred to anybody to investigate whether the two were instead related to each other in terms of cause and effect.

If we add to these deficiencies the fact that half of the human race was educated incorrectly or remained without any education whatsoever, and that precisely this half was entrusted with the most important phases of child rearing, then it is almost a miracle that we are human beings at all. Nevertheless, there can be no doubt that nature destined the opposite sex for the noble business of education and endowed it with all the talents and faculties necessary to fulfill this great calling: with the most receptive senses; with the most refined sensibilities for distinguishing, even in trivial matters and chance occurrences, between the true and the false, the genuine and that which is merely pretense.

The Socratic method, which Socrates learned from his mother, a midwife (*sage femme*), whereby he aimed at the delivery of souls[18] and became a philosopher (*homme sage*) in the process, is doubtless peculiar to the opposite sex, which never, even when dealing with voracious intellectual appetites in their children, overstuffs their bellies with facts, but supplies them with each new concept singly, transforming it as much as possible into a sense perception. Women give to each mental concept a body; they seek to clothe it and lend it perceptible form. Robinet[19] is of the opinion that Mother Nature endowed women with talkativeness so that they might be enabled all the better to pre-digest for their children that verbal fare which is too highly seasoned for them. Thus when we speak derisively of this tendency to talkativeness—is that not tantamount to giving a wonderful gift of Nature a bad name? Rousseau once said to Grétry,[20] who offered him his hand to help him over a pile of stones: "Let me use my own strength." And for whom is the development of those ideas which lie hidden in the souls of children more natural than for this sex? It spins them out like webs, and binds the sensual and perceptible to mental concepts by means of images and parables. We ourselves prefer more heroic methods—yet does not in every case a feeling of emptiness follow the *aria di bravura*,[21] because a single impression which is too vivid tends to destroy the effect of the whole? It is not simply a matter of inducing accurate perception, but of extracting the sum and then concentrating one's efforts upon this sum. And how important here is the matter of *when* and *how*! The wanderer's every path leads him but to a single destination; every stream wends its way to the sea.[22]

But how is it possible that women will be able to do justice to this

profession, when these talents and capabilities are being so little developed? When we not only ignore them, but actually suppress them
intentionally? The child is sexless; why, then, do we seek to get the
jump on Nature, who is wiser than we are? Why have we begun to
separate the sexes earlier than Nature tells us we should? A child is
sociable not because it is compelled to be so by a particular drive, but
out of need and a desire to be active. It is certainly not moral sensibil-
ity—that capacity for feeling which bonds the adult to his peers so that
he may communicate with them, so that he may grind off the sharp
corners of his character and fulfill himself through others—which
causes the child to be sociable. What does it know other than its own
needs? It wishes but to be fed and amused—it is sociable out of a desire
to pass the time pleasantly. Whenever this goal is attained, it is happy;
differences in sex or in moral or intellectual capacity do not play any role
whatsoever in its choice of a companion.

In European countries, it is not until around the age of twelve that the
sex drive begins to develop in the female and bring about the awakening of an unaccustomed unrest, presentiments previously unnoticed,
and yearnings of a gentle nature. Up to this time everything, excepting
clothing, should remain the same, for this is the way Nature would have
it. Upbringing, instruction, and pastimes can be the same for both
sexes, for during this period education should concern itself merely
with the human being and the development of his capabilities, disregarding all further vocations except this first and most important one: to
be a human being according to the original and authentic interpretation
given him by Nature. This single purpose should be the aim of all
pedagogical endeavors; by serving in the role of midwife to young
children, they should seek to extend the latitude for the first efforts of the
child's awakening powers, and only gradually and with great care
attempt to control the luxuriant outgrowth of these powers, thus giving
proper but unobtrusive direction to the natural drives. During this
period of time, instruction need not take differences in sex into account
any more than it would acknowledge future relationships within the
state. Has the child of this age even the slightest inkling of what is to
come, not to mention a hard and fast notion of this? And does not all
such instruction remain knowledge of the most useless sort, until in the
course of nature an awareness develops for such teachings? All instruction during this period must be limited to that which we must believe,
know, and do as *human beings.*

Why this difference between male and female instruction, since man
and woman have not yet been born? Are children's games what they

could and should be? Only recently, now that people are taking greater interest in the art of child rearing, have we begun to perceive the great influence of this facet of life; yet have we not, as usual, made poor use of these games by raising play to the level of a general technique of instruction? Games must never become teaching methods, although they can serve very well as incentives for enriching the memory and training the powers of reason. Yet, whenever they are used to facilitate instruction, their value is and will remain purely subjective. With children's games we must always keep the goal in mind of preoccupying children in a way which is commensurate with their capabilities and their age. The children themselves, however, must never guess this intention, for otherwise the game loses its meaning. Children must become accustomed from an early age to differentiating between play and business in order that they may come to respect and love the latter, while learning to renounce the former—if they are not to remain children forever. Yet why should I go on about a matter which is the object of every other word of our writers and which is preached from every housetop? I shall return to my point with the suggestion that until the child becomes a young man or woman it should remain in the hands and under the supervision of the female sex. Both the state and the women would gain thereby. All children's schools should have women as teachers and supervisors, for nature has richly endowed this sex with excellent faculties for such work. Purity, a requisite so important in the care of children; tenderness, patience, endurance in the face of seemingly trivial endeavors; sympathy, talkativeness, and other such character traits indispensable for the educating of children appear to be inherent in the female sex, and merely artificially acquired skills in the male. As nature is to art, so would a system of child rearing and education by women be to the present educational system. Even now the part they play is great; what would we be capable of without their assistance? O, what wonderful training for mothers of the middle class it is when a household of crying and screaming children tests their patience, and the questions of curious, bashful young girls and impudent boys confuse and embarrass them. It is incomprehensible to me how a good woman is able to handle so many heterogenous matters simultaneously—here she wrests knife, fork, and scissors out of the hand of little Field Marshall James; there she pulls harmful objects from the mouth of the omnivorous Bishop Peter; now she shoos the flies from little sleeping Henrietta; and how difficult it is to pacify the young madcap Karl, who jumps continuously from one pastime to another! How many vigils and how many daily cares are their share and inheri-

tance within the family duties which fall to their lot! And does not even
the lady of high station, who according to the custom and tradition of
the land possesses the harsh right to treat her little ones as foundlings
and is herself hardly busy at all—does she not still have much more to
occupy her time than her officious lazybones of a husband, who, overburdened as he is with affairs of enormous inconsequence and elegant
infirmities, nevertheless finds time to spin so many other such webs
outside the spinning rooms of his own council chambers, webs which
almost always wind up complicating simple matters and attempting to
impart an air of significance to things frivolous?

But what is that you say? Would women not, by virtue of their
timidity and an awareness of their own weakness, pamper and coddle
the children and make the human race even more feeble and delicate
than it already is? This is an objection which seems to have some basis
in truth; but in fact it is nothing more than an apparition which strikes
our imaginations with terror, and which must necessarily vanish the
closer women approach to their goal. Tenderness, or even actual weakness of the constitution, is frequently congenital and much less often a
consequence of delicate upbringing. In the latter case the skill of the
teacher can often restore in boyhood and early manhood whatever
well-intentioned, but poorly-understood delicacy of upbringing ruined
in the child. This fear will vanish only when the order of nature which
we have reversed is once again brought back to its previous state, and
we decide once and for all to give the opposite sex some guidance in this
matter. We have already partially given up turning children into dolls
and smothering them with soft feathers, and then, when they availed
themselves of their lungs, the only way out of their predicament,
anesthetizing them with soothing syrup[23] or a gentle box on the ears;
we will also surely cease to keep children away from water and fresh air
as soon as women begin to feel more comfortable dealing with the
influence of these two elements.[24] Attempts have already been made to
cast suspicion on the type of clothing children have worn up to now,
and to criticize it for that constraint and pressure which causes the effect
of oxygen on the entire body to be lost, the child's ability to exhale to be
impaired, his chest to constrict, his heart to be crushed, his strength and
vitality to slacken before its time and the whole machine, in effect, to
become overwrought. The tyranny of fashion! Even our painters and
sculptors are for their own part exposed to the unfortunate embarrassment of having to portray their subjects in some sort of idealized
costume simply because the altar of true good taste has no place for the
absurdities of fashion—an act of the most exquisite revenge by nature

on those who would disdain her! And while we are in the process of improving the status of women, nothing would be easier than to bring about some sort of clothing regulations based both on physical and moral considerations, then to produce such clothing cheaply, naturally, and simply, and thus to remove from the matter all the exaggeration and foppery now associated with it. Only from unpampered, stable, and solid *children* can we obtain unpampered, stable, and solid *adults*! Let women first feel strong themselves, then they will bear with their bodies children who are strong in both body and soul, and with the power of their spirit they will continually "re-bear" them their whole life long—that is, they will bring them into the world and educate them as well.

Why should the skin live in enmity with the sun?[25] Dashed hopes, oppression, and conflict are even less conducive to tractability of character and to the moral graces than the unyielding constriction imposed on us by our clothing. Courage, ingenuousness, and that all-embracing cheerfulness which can penetrate the deepest scowl and shine through the roughest exterior, these come only from an exalted feeling of liberty—and which is worth more to you, those equivocal Delphic utterances, or an unyielding honesty and uprightness? Honest and upright behavior paves the way for moral omnipotence, whereas the elegant life of manners brings about results utterly at odds with it. Whichever we choose will determine what the results will be. Does not timidity merely have its basis in the feeling of a lack of physical strength and in the constriction of the mind? A famous English general once noted that his troops never possessed more courage than when their bellies were filled with pudding and roast beef.[26] Hunger causes cowardice, want a dullness of the spirit, and oppression despair. The women of Sparta knew neither delicacy nor timidity. "I bore him for the Fatherland," was the reply of that heroic Spartan woman as the news was brought to her that her only son had fallen in battle.

If the difference between the sexes begins to appear at the time when children become young men and women, then the citizen must be grafted onto the individual—that is, one's status as a citizen must be tied to that given to him by nature, and his preparation begun for the various roles which he is to play within the state. Now, and only now, is it time for any visible sign of a differentiation between the sexes. From this point on, the separation of the sexes according to dress will eradicate forever all the worrisome consequences which the uniform of nature might perhaps cause among the weak, who will always be with us; it will transform boys and girls who knew each other as children into strangers (although not complete strangers—what would be the point in that?), and extinguish all but the vaguest reminiscences of their previous acquaintanceship. Would not this separation according to dress reaffirm once and for all that single difference between the sexes which was intended by nature, without thereby creating a distinction in the civil status of either sex and without exposing morality or the commonweal to the slightest danger? This is the single stroke which would bring child rearing and education in better relation to the respective sexual and civic responsibilities of the two sexes. Was not a similar arrangement worked out earlier among the Romans with regard to the male sex? And does not history tell us that the young man adorned himself with the love of his country and all the great character traits of the Roman the first time he wore the *toga virili* (the cloak of the man)? It is a shame to live one hour longer than one ought to live; but it is just as great a shame to begin living an hour later than one is capable of it. And just as the end is the crown of the work, and the Last Day is the judge of all those which preceded it, so we ought to set aside certain days and make memorial days of them. That day when the sexes are first separated, that day of one's initiation into citizenship, would be one of these days.

Yet the business of education must still not be taken out of the hands of the women entirely in this new epoch, and even less should we introduce a differentiation in the raising and education of the two sexes except with regard to those duties to which each is called by its very nature. During this period such duties would necessarily be taught by persons of the same sex, whereas all else, as far as the circumstances allowed or required, could be taught by persons of either sex without regard for this difference. Because men and women are in truth of but a single race, even after this separation of the sexes takes place a state of complete and utter alienation will not occur, for what God hath joined together let not man put asunder.[27] During this period, which for girls could last approximately until their sixteenth year, for boys, until the eighteenth, both sexes will need to be prepared for their role as citizens and given instruction in everything related to that role without regard for the difference between the sexes. It goes without saying that the goal of the full and complete development of the individual is not to be permanently disregarded. At most, it is to be set aside but temporarily. Would not then under such a stable arrangement both parts of humanity, regardless of sex, be placed immediately where they showed the best potential for being of use to the state? No longer accustomed to that greatest of all evils, boredom—which is to be feared more than death—young men and women would now need to receive tasks for which they are equipped by inclination and talent. Honor, privileges, and rewards would then not be a prerogative of sex, but the result of personal merit. Women, who previously were mere objects without name and rights, would in this way become persons as well as citizens of the state.

Plato wished to make the distribution of private capital and goods a matter for the law to decide.[28] As much justice as there seems to be to this idea, it would lead to many injustices if instituted. The capital and goods which women possess, on the other hand, even though they believe themselves to be managing them without our assistance, only *appear* to be under their control, for in fact they are the possession of the men, who never seem to miss the opportunity of bestowing blessings upon themselves with this cross which they keep so close at hand. How often cash-box frauds take place thereby is well known. Only when women decide that they can no longer afford to withdraw from the affairs of the state will they be restored to full possession of their wealth and have no need of anyone else in order to think and to act. And to this end women will have to assert themselves often, and willingly, before those principles which seek to give them honor because honor is due have become a matter of course.

The physiocrats,[29] in their system, consider the producing class of citizens to be the most useful; and since utility is the only criterion for the state in determining the hierarchy of its citizens, that is to say, since the principle of utility determines the fate of the citizen, can we then exclude an entire half of the human race from the honor of being citizens—and specifically, that part of the race which plays the most essential part in its own creation and reproduction? And having already unjustly and arbitrarily excluded them by virtue of our own hereditary authority, can we also deny them the return to the state of paradise? Will they not, if prepared properly beforehand, encourage, counsel, and assist with distinction wherever and whenever the state is in distress?

However, until the above hasty outline of a new order of things can be introduced in full form into bourgeois society—men, open your institutions of learning the sooner the better to the female youth of today, and allow them to take part in instruction and learning without letting yourselves be seduced by the fear of disadvantageous consequences! Examine that malicious and ubiquitous doubt which claims there will be much annoyance, resentment, scandal and many other unfortunate consequences—examine it and you yourselves will find it to be inconclusive. One can be afraid of fear, and one can also be afraid of help.

Should a reprehensible order of things, even if it has already lasted a thousand times a thousand years and we are overcome with a feeling of discomfort at the harm it has caused us, as well as at the prospects for a better future—should such a reprehensible order of things still be allowed to continue undisturbed merely because its modification *could* be associated with difficulties, perhaps even with serious consequences? Would anything great ever have been undertaken in the world if we had weighed the pros and cons as fearfully as this? Would man be what he is today, would he have made such remarkable progress if, after the manner of the elephant, he had fearfully inspected the ground for firmness each time before he moved a single foot forward?

Offense! It all depends on how one takes this word with its wide range of meanings. Our ancestors, who respected symbols, most certainly would have taken the most serious offense if in one of their educational institutions children with and without foreskins had come together to take part in the various courses of instruction. What disadvantages for Christianity would have been feared if a descendant of the house of Judah had learned his human and civic responsibilities together with the son of a Lutheran bishop from the works of the blind heathen Cicero! Yet who does not know of countries where this has been brought into effect without the slightest sound from the zealots, without anyone fearing that the foundations of Christianity would be shaken in the slightest?

"Morality would be endangered!"

How so? Do not boys and girls already receive their religious instruction simultaneously from one and the same clergyman in one and the same way? The institution is already there; it needs only to be extended. And what is to prevent us from granting those to whom we acknowledge equal rights within the church equal rights within the state as well? If girls and boys are trained together as *Christians*, why should they not be prepared together for their responsibilities within the state as *citizens*? Are we to deny the vocation of citizen of the state to those who, we admit, possess the necessary aptitude to be citizens of the heavenly kingdom? Why do morals not suffer in these coeducational schools, even though religious instruction is given during the very years when the sex drive is the most sensitive to stimulus? Are not the pupils there under supervision, just as they are otherwise? Would not a wise teacher or tutor know how to avoid at each juncture those conditions which awaken the sex drive and be able to direct his instruction toward the future duties and responsibilities of his pupils, so that the consequences would not be damaging, but beneficial?

"Will the opposite sex meet our expectations? Will it reward our efforts?"

So we wish to reap and yet spare ourselves the trouble of sowing? How will we assure ourselves of the fertility of the soil if we do not cultivate it? Has not every such soil repaid the toil which was expended upon it? And should we fear a different result here, if we could just overcome our inertia long enough to undertake a serious attempt? Nature places seeds in everything she produces, seeds which require only the proper conditions for their germination. Would not the women give honor to the status of citizen which we had opened up to them? And what affair of the state would suffer under their benevolent hand, providing they were not prevented from carrying it out by any special peculiarity of their sex? Would not everything stand to gain immensely by virtue of the competition which would arise between the sexes?

Not the nymph Egeria, whom Numa himself sought out for counsel; not the Pythia, by whom the heroes of old were advised when they made their laws or wished to conquer other lands; neither Aspasia nor Phryne, who schooled people like Pericles and Socrates in wisdom and the art of ruling—none of these shall serve as my example here.[30] For even if no one is willing to concede to the poetic virtues of these female heroes the glory and honor which they deserve, no matter! We have prosaic examples as well which will allay all doubt that the female sex, in spite of the fact that it was kept away from the stoa, the university, and the prytaneum (if not by formal legal means, nevertheless by tacit agreement, which is often even more inhuman and oppressive);[31] in spite of the fact that it has been excluded from the schools, where instruction and wisdom are to be found, still exhibits wise and learned women among its numbers, women who have made their names immortal by what they have done or written. It would not be difficult, in fact, to find names of women in many areas of the far-reaching realms of human knowledge and art who have a legitimate claim to respect and fame. I have already paid homage to a small number who have distinguished themselves by the greatness of their character.

So, then! Let history step forward and witness to the important part which the female sex played in the spread of Christianity and to the magnitude of its contribution in terms of morality and enlightenment! The Founder of this charitable religion, which is an ally of mankind and an advocate of the rights of humanity, gave instruction to the sister of his friend Lazarus, and also gave precedence to Mary over the merely domestic Martha: "Mary hath chosen that good part, which shall not be taken away from her."[32] The Book of the Acts makes mention of a pious woman named Tabitha, who not only distinguished herself by her work among the new converts, but also took active part in the spread of the gospel which she had come to believe.[33] Does not church history record the names of a great many women who confessed their faith with the courage of heroes, and whom neither the promise of torture nor reward could cause to waver in their belief? Women who, giving up all claim to honor and luxury, held to their conviction with unshakeable firmness amid contempt, ridicule, want, and persecution? The Founder of the Christian religion so often admires the devout faith of the female sex in his teachings, and rather than excluding them from taking part in the benefits of the wise and pure milk of his instruction, he seems to put great importance on the elevation and liberation of this sex. And when in fact this religion wishes to appear in its most charming, childlike form, does it not make itself manifest in little children and in the women who care for them? Women's hearts are, if I may say so, almost amalgamated with the teachings of this religion; for in truth the highest stage of human development is not speculative reason, not mere philosophy, but a certain something which, when it takes the name of the art of ruling, is an art form to which even nature subjugates herself without objection.

A long, cool draught can call back the spirit of life to the dwelling-place it had almost left forever; yet it can also be poison for the over-heated traveler. The sword which protects us can just as easily become our own murder weapon. A freedom which has been shaped and molded, a freedom quite different from mere eccentric behavior and farthest of all from its most blatant expression, utter licentiousness, such a freedom could be designated *Christian freedom*. And its school? The school of women. If men renounce their strength, which so easily degenerates into mere passion, and become true Christians by sacrificing revenge, bloodletting, and great shows of power, they begin to have the feeling that the possession of Christian virtues is a denial of their sex. But perhaps it would be the better part of valor not to dwell on this particular subject at present. . . .

Everywhere the genius and artistic spirit of man reaches into the world, we encounter the names of women who are contending for honors. These are not women who sought to satisfy their vanity in some other way because they experienced little success in the pursuits traditionally associated with the sex; rather, they are those who, driven by their intellectual faculties, merely applied the powers with which nature had so richly endowed them. What a position of honor is held by Anna Comnena among the Byzantine historians! The great daughter of Henry VIII, who chose not to rule England through Parliament, but whose every suggestion became a law for that body and to whom it paid daily homage; who, while not subduing proud Philip himself, yet conquered his invincible fleet, this queen found a woman not unworthy to record her deeds in the historian Kéralio. During the centuries of intellectual and spiritual darkness, when deepest night covered the peoples of Europe, when every longing of the human spirit lay torpid and utterly exhausted, it was the nun Roswitha[34] who sought to enkindle once more the holy fires of learning. Dacier and Reiske[35] distinguished themselves by their knowledge of languages, and how many women in England, France, and Germany have not made themselves famous by writing? Who does not know the names Macaulay, Genlis, Sévigné, or Laroche?[36]

"Women have never invented or discovered anything. They have never produced a Newton, a. . . ."[37]

And why? Was it not merely a matter of chance that from the beginning of time human beings have stumbled upon inventions? Does it not seem that nature, in the case of every human invention, has kept the best of her secrets to herself? Is it not she who reserves the best of her bread on the window sill?[38] Were not those discoveries and inventions simply placed into the hands of the inventors? Is it the fault of the women if they lag behind us in this regard, or is it simply that they have been denied all opportunity? Let us but make room for them in our pulpits and the chairs of our universities, and we will soon see whether (without prejudice to our dutiful respect for St. Paul, who did not wish women to have a voice in the affairs of the congregation[39]) they are capable of gaining our confidence here as well. There can be no doubt whatsoever that they will obtain for themselves even easier access to our hearts; in this regard the Quakers have already set an example for us.[40] The sermons of the women would often be to those of many of our clergymen as the sermons of Bourdaloue[41] to those of the bunglers of his own time: when they preached, they stole from the congregation; when he preached, he gave it back again. Just as our bodies can spread infection to others, so our moods and emotions are often contagious as well; and if it is on the whole not entirely incorrect that life and death lie in the eyes, and that certain people can, by means of this organ both kill and restore to life again, then it is the female sex especially which takes advantage of this ability. All their magic seems to come from their eyes. The eyes and the voice are the soul's vocabulary of love and hate; and who understands the language of the eyes better than women? It is by means of them that women are able to give continuity to their long speeches; and where is the man who is not able to testify to this eloquence? But do women speak only with their eyes? The whole life of a woman consists more in speaking than in doing; their words are generally their actions; and if we disdain a man whose life comes closer to being an encyclopedia than a history, this is certainly not true in the case of the fair sex, which speaks as one having authority.[42] The life of a woman could be described as a painting in conversation. What women *say* often comes from the heart far more than what men *do*; thus their discourse often has more of interest for the thinking and feeling being than the manifold deeds of men. One can, if I may express myself so, impart a certain coloring to his thought-paintings through his speech; and how many nuances are possible here, if one will but take his instruction from the heart which lies behind the words! One might suspect that women, accustomed to elaborate dress and cosmetics, would corrupt their thoughts and perceptions at the altar of adornment. Not so! They prefer to leave this adornment of the mind to our own sex. Even if many of them, because of their position and their sex, are required to be models of fashionable dress and the courtly vanities prevailing at the time, their manner of expression does not change its nature; their discourse remains all milk and honey.

Is genius wisdom? Are idle talk and sophistry reason? That which does not have its basis in common sense and moral religion is not true wisdom or reason. The imitation pearls and the gold foil with which the women adorn their bodies they leave to the men when it comes to speaking. The deepest truth can be clothed in the ideas of a simple man, and a truth which not even a Socrates can state in simple language is not much more than sophistry, with which we ought not to corrupt our mind and adulterate our hearts.

Women are born *Protestants*, and must worship a religion of freedom, the will of God manifested in the Spirit and in truth. They have little interest in the systematic structure of religious doctrine, and it is only with difficulty that one can entice them with doctor's degrees in theology. It is not important to them to prove the existence of God; rather they would be much more likely to sympathize with that new philosophical star which declares an undemonstrable God to be a postulate of practical reason, because He is necessary for our happiness and well-being.[43] "Whoever wishes to prove certain things," said Frau von ———, "either doubts himself, or desires to forestall politely the doubts of others." A very true statement, indeed! A minimum of belief, a mere mustard seed of belief,[44] along with the ability to imagine the possibility of the existence of God is sufficient to make everything out of us that can be made. The doubts of others, especially of intelligent men of good reputation, often entangle us in doubt without our even being aware of it. Women have God *in their hearts*; and since they well know that in view of the purposeful ordering of nature the First Cause must be an intelligent and reasonable one, they do not care how much or how little speculative reason can contribute to this belief. The basis of proof offered by morality (whether it is deserving of the honorary title of proof or not) produces a living faith in them. Many a man has given demonstrable proof of the existence of God, only to refute that proof by his own life.

To do His will remains the best proof that He exists. The greatest problem is to bring about such a *desire* in mankind—there is no lack of *insight* in the race. Benjamin Franklin, a man the likes of whom neither Greek nor Roman antiquity ever produced, once said: "Any man who fancied himself an atheist would be converted upon first seeing the beautiful and well-situated city of Philadelphia."[45] And the world, this great "city of Philadelphia," would it not also exert such a power over the atheist as soon as he stopped measuring everything by his own puny standards? In the end it is not so much a matter of what we believe, but of what our beliefs make of us.

The happiness of innocence, the dignity of nature, the craving for freedom, the joys of the quiet life, and the high value of the art of reconciling oneself to one's own destiny are the chief matters of importance for women, and as we may observe in our dealings with others, one's favorite preoccupations exert a definite influence on the mind and will. That variety of expression and restraint which we find in women is for them not hypocrisy, as it is for us; on absolutely no account will they utter certain things or become unfaithful to a certain purity of speech and fall into coarse innuendo or obscenity, even if such modesty and reserve were to prove less fascinating for their listeners. Purity of the body is closely related to purity of the soul and of speech.

Women know the rules of language as little as its limitations—they overstep the former and extend the latter. How many times have they not, directly or indirectly, enriched our language with new and felicitous expressions? Mediocrity could simply not prevail in this sex— whatever is distinctive in their speech is superior. Women even speak when they are silent, for no glance of theirs could ever be without its own language. Their unarticulated expressions of passion, by means of which human beings are able to penetrate so deeply into the hearts of other human beings, are unsurpassable. And when they really speak, who is more eloquent than they? Men often say nothing when they say too much, just as one proves nothing when one proves too much. In the words of women, even when they inundate us, are to be found purpose, gravity, and vigor; their eyes and their speech are on the best of terms, and women possess heaven and hell, life and death, weal and woe not only in their glance, in their eyes, and on their tongue; even their hearing is of the greatest importance. They hear differently from us, and who can deny the influence that one's hearing has on his speech? I know a very respectable man of high position who has the reputation of listening to everybody, and in fact he will grant an audience to anyone who wishes to be received in his anteroom. Yet the whole world complains that he does not listen—either he is preoccupied or incapable of understanding. And there also seems to be a kind of moral deafness even among those whose physical powers of hearing are excellent.

Women are masters of the art of listening. They are the original listeners, and I am not sure whether their greatest strength lies in listening or speaking. It is easier to deal with one's reading public than the circle of friends in which one moves, especially when this circle is composed of many witty women; and thus it is not because of the men but the women that I remain anonymous, no matter how much my treatise seems to be taking sides with the latter.

Women are too familiar with the human heart not to know how to reconnoiter even its most secluded recesses, to arouse its passions, or to anticipate their outbreak and meet them more than halfway. Who knows better than they how to soften their rage according to the dictates of their intentions, and certainly they are more successful at it than the most famous demagogue. Rome would perhaps have fallen back to its previous state of insignificance shortly after its founding if its newly acquired women had not espoused the cause of their abductors and assuaged the outraged Sabines.[46] What would have become of Coriolanus' native city if his mother had not been able to appease her son?[47] Without Roman pride and the noble challenge of a woman, Margarethe Herlobig, the Swiss Confederation would perhaps never have come into being.[48] A woman's powers of persuasion exceed everything that art has achieved up to the present. And their method of instruction? In truth, women are extremely instructive; they are as good at teaching as at child rearing. Whoever would reduce women to mere feeling and emotion knows nothing about feelings, emotions, or women. Does the heart instruct the head? Do our organs of perception and feeling deliver up unmistakable impressions to our powers of cognition to be compared with each other and judged upon? Or do our moral sentiments not rather stem from our powers of reason? Is it not the function of the mind to make certain basic principles of conduct, for example, so much a part of the heart that it views respect for the law as a habit, as a "feeling"? The heart can accomplish little without instruction from reason—it must be guided by the mind. The poet must first be consecrated in the temple of reason, and, if he longs for immortality, he must then combine the beautiful and tender feelings he wishes to express with such basic principles as these. Women understand that chemistry—one could even call it a more advanced state of the science—which is able to dissolve these basic principles into feelings, and thus without difficulty to make a habit out of what our theoretical and abstract sorcerer-philosophers can only express in the weightiest of words.

Women have morals; men, manners. The latter are acquired in childhood, learned by imitation, and imparted through social contact. The former depend on reason and the human heart. It is said that women are more miserly than men when it comes to charitable deeds—that they are by their very nature stingy. Not so! When they are inclined to charitable deeds it is as a function of the basic principles mentioned above, and not of some passing intoxication with pity, as is so often the case with us. Look how nicely they are able to modify the most venerable and traditional forms of etiquette and manners. Even in matters of love they fail to keep to the rules and the agenda. We have our Kubach,[49] and everything is set to a well-known melody. One could even say of women that "they love collectively, yet each of them loves differently."

They possess an extraordinary talent for hoping—expectation fills their entire being. To say that a woman is expecting is to say that she will soon become a mother. When *we* are happy, we desire that everyone around us be happy, and we urge this happiness on our own circle of friends to the point that, willy-nilly, they must join in with us. Women, when they are happy, make everyone around them happy. Their festivals are all celebrations of the harvest, Feasts of the Tabernacles[50] which have been hallowed by nature; at our own, we fire cannons. Women can manage without such dinner music (the eternal physical and intellectual death of all conversation). Thinking of God is for them the same as prayer; thinking of themselves tantamount to learning to die; to philosophize is for them a form of falling in love. Whoever thinks thus thinks well; whoever acts on these principles cannot be too far wrong.

Foreign languages are viewed, not without some justification, as the key to the repository of all learning and knowledge, and each language which we learn is in itself a little treasure chest of information we have found. A special talent is required to learn languages, a talent which is less often to be encountered among men than women. The methods we have traditionally used in our schools to teach languages were most certainly not invented by women, for they would hardly have chosen to begin such instruction with the grammar. Behold the schoolmaster, who must expend the energy of a beast of burden in making comprehensible to his pupils why the Roman placed his words in one particular order in his language and not in some other! Behold the pupil, who is to comprehend something which in the final analysis remains incomprehensible, as long as he does not know how the Romans spoke or wrote their language. Is not the art of teaching people foreign languages chiefly an art of women? And should we not give over the teaching of languages to them exclusively? A good memory, imagination, and a certain flair for detail seem to be the chief possessions of the women, at least in their present situation. Do we find many examples where a person has learned to speak French with any degree of fluency from a schoolmaster? Whoever learned to speak the language either spent some time in France or he learned it from his mother or governess. Hardly has the man begun to comprehend the rudiments of his subject when he immediately wishes to compose, generalize, and realize a profit from his work; slow and methodical gathering takes too long for him.

Who can deny that women possess a certain feeling for art? And does it not seem to be less a lack of ability than their present situation which is to blame for their having accomplished so little of note in the fine arts and the sciences? At times we can find more in the charming spectacle of powers grappling with adversity, even if often succumbing to it, than in momentous decisions and ostentatious victories; and does not even great Homer himself occasionally nod?[51] Are not even the most awake eyes finally overcome by sleep? Does not Brutus also sleep at times?[52] *Belles lettres* and the fine arts in general require a broad latitude, tolerate no oppressive constraint, and thrive only where the spirit, freed of its fetters, can traverse that realm of invisibility, the province of the imagination. Even with the greatest sensitivity to form and feeling, the most felicitous combination of talents, nothing great, nothing of perfection will be contributed by the women as long as the present oppression continues. The situation of the women can be compared to that of the present-day Greeks, who, with the same talents and under the same sky of their ancestors, will never produce anything resembling the unrivalled masterpieces of those ancestors as long as their necks continue to be forced under the iron yoke of the Turks.[53] How would it be possible for the female sex to soar into the higher regions as long as it is locked in a cage, its wings clipped by vile prejudice? If the body is weak, the soul tends to be so as well; and slavery does not allow those in its chains to fly even an inch above the ground. Yet a few have shown that they are children of the same spirit as the men, and am I mistaken, or is it a fact that they are less apt to snatch at every ray of a distant light than we are?[54] With better-exercised powers of reason, sharpened sensibilities, a richer fantasy, and a firmer character they will bear riper fruits; and in the realm of beauty, where they already have undeniable claims to greatness, they will perform deeds worthy of immortality.

And the poetic art—is not here to be found ample material for a new heaven and a new earth? And am I saying too much if I state that here as well a pathway is reserved for the opposite sex, along with palm branches which can be gathered here on earth, not far from any of us, even before we reach the third heaven, where we will be transported to unspeakable rapture?[55] Basic principles which are taught in a general way by human reason are made graphic by the poetic art through striking examples. The poetic art takes what reason knows to be intrinsically true and places it life-size before our moral organ of perception, bringing us thereby indescribable pleasure, the only pleasure which we may attain without sacrifice. And are we to say that this holy spirit was not poured out over the opposite sex as well? That they have not received these gifts? O, ye of little faith! As if Pegasus were created only for men!—this exceedingly good and gentle animal which had to submit to so much, this animal can tolerate no side-saddle?[56] And such a prejudice cannot be overcome?

It most certainly can. How magnificent are those feminine outbursts, the love songs of Sappho,[57] who even in Germany has had more than nine sisters. One of the most distinguished (Anna Luise Karschin)[58] not long ago returned home to her elder sisters after the poet Frederick the Great had made her a present of four gulden and Frederick William II, who is no poet, had had a house built for her. Do I need to do more than mention the name Elise in order to bestow on her mind and heart the rank which is due them, and which is further elevated by her exemplary modesty? Angelica Kauffmann,[59] the creator of beautiful forms, and others of equal stature have distinguished themselves as painters and continue to do so. The reproach that she makes masculine faces look too feminine is not without foundation; perhaps she is merely taking secret revenge on the members of our own sex thereby.

It is said that women will never master the art of portrait painting. If this were the rule, rather than the exception, I would attempt to explain it from the circumstance that they always paint into their portraits features from their own admirable souls, just as the men who painted Venus gave honor to the features of their own wives and daughters. Women painters tend to beautify or glorify the souls of the men in their portraits to the same extent as men painters add color to the cheeks of the women in their own.

Is it because men are more alienated from nature than women; or because nature really has more confidence in women and seems to display a preference for that sex; or is it simply that men so rarely enter the sanctuaries of nature that they are so uncomfortable in her presence? I do not know. Be that as it may, who among us men, whether poet or painter, can depict what he feels in the delightful sensations of nature or the fullness of his pleasure in them? Who of us does not succumb to the power of everything sublime and beautiful in the world continually streaming in toward him and either lulling him to sleep or so assailing him that he cannot comprehend its overwhelming impression?

Women can describe the pleasure they experience in their enjoyment of nature; intertwined closely with her, they are never at a loss for words in expressing her moods. They seem to be united in heart and soul with her, and because they are neither strung too tightly nor inclined to sink into sweet slumber, they do not lack the boldness to allow others, too, to have pleasure in their enjoyment through their descriptions. They can write in the first fires of their passion, while we have to let ourselves cool off first. Without a doubt we could have had many a female Ossian[60] if we had wished it; and what might our Karschin have become if we had not clipped her wings at a delicate age through instruction in mythology! Originality only flourishes in the cradle of liberty; and can nature ever be made truly perceptible to us through women until we men cease to dominate them, and until the spirit, heart, and tongue of the opposite sex are finally set free?

And what is the point of my saying all this? To stimulate men, if not out of a sense of duty, then out of artistic curiosity to stop withholding intellectual and spiritual freedom from these darlings of nature, to cease from stifling their powers any longer, and to stop retarding their reason by forcing them into premature imbecility.[61] The poets, the heroes, the wise men of prehistoric times saw a sun and viewed a nature no different from ours; that divine inspiration which the ancients possessed we can now receive with thanksgiving in the form of a new covenant with nature proceeding from the hands and hearts of our women.

Music? As unquestioned as women's talents in music are, the sex is nonetheless reproached for never having produced a true master composer. Without doubt they lack the courage here, as well, to strive for and attain this honor; they are satisfied to play the compositions of the masters of our own sex with sensitivity; they are content with being second-class. Yet on the other hand, the words can be exactly as the poet wrote them and the music played ever so precisely, and still often neither the poet nor the composer will recognize his work when a woman plays or sings it—she breathes a living soul into it. To create is good; to *preserve* is no less good. And women might always have remained second-class if a recent traveler had not made the observation that there has never been a great composer among the *castrati* either. If this statement is indeed valid for both *castrati* and women, the reason, it must be said, is an infinitely different one in each case; *castrati* create nothing; women, on the other hand, are fellow creators and the true preservers.

One should learn to write from men, and to speak from women. In the present state of oppression in which they find themselves, women find it more important to make everything that they themselves understand comprehensible to others as well, and to clarify that which we express in weighty terms. They smooth the way, know how to reflect and reproduce the mere glimmer of the most difficult idea and to depict the most abstract notion in clear and understandable terms, so that they would long since have brought great profit to all branches of learning if we had but granted them the freedom to ply a trade and the right to citizenship without requiring that they produce documents testifying to their male birth. If even now the women, although they are but tolerated and must work by means of concessions and favors, have already proven themselves valuable in this capacity, what will they be able to accomplish if they are no longer excluded so shamefully from truly dignified competition?

It is not the object of schoolroom instruction to make a master of every pupil. Moreover, the educational industry could hardly function with all masters and no apprentices. This industry produces vessels both as objects of beauty as well as for household and chamber use; it employs masters at the potter's wheel, even those who are masters only in one respect. Likewise, we are willing to call a master a capable teacher if he knows how to instruct an apprentice in the mechanical aspects of his craft. But have we not all had masters who never succeeded in training capable pupils in their art? Do not many lack the gift of clarity and the pure talent for teaching? And do not many as well doubtless lack patience, that most indispensable of virtues in a teacher, which the male sex laudably does not omit from its list of virtues, but one which is also only rarely characteristic of our sex? We like to show that in our wardrobe there are also unfashionable garments, but we keep them merely for the sake of having them, and not of using them. In the case of the female sex, however, patience is the most beautiful housedress they own, and it is the one which is most becoming to them as well. Is not a woman's patience capable of enticing sprouts from even the most unproductive soil? Can not the tenacious diligence of a woman give to even the most deformed human being if not a beautiful form, then at least a tolerable one; and if it is not able to make artists of all of us, do we not at least become patrons and lovers of art?

The criticism which is often made of women, to wit, that they love novelty and change, is not unjust; nevertheless, the cause lies not within the sex itself, but in our oppression of it. Perseverance and tenacity are certainly less characteristic of our sex than of theirs when the goal is a worthy one. Who of us at the present time can place a negative interpretation on their flightiness and fickleness; who find fault with their lives when it is said of them: "They live as if they were flying away"?[62] Who? Indeed, there would be far fewer such moral caricatures if we would decide to grant a greater role to the female sex in education and child rearing. And have women really only offered sacrifices to their friends the Graces, or have they not in fact penetrated into the holy of holies of human knowledge as well? In truth, here they have also known how to open doors, how to attain places of honor and maintain them with dignity—and this in spite of all the hindrances which prejudice, tradition, and base envy have placed in the path of their talents and enthusiasm. There will soon not be many branches of knowledge which cannot count among their initiates the names of a number of women who have worked actively therein, and I am not speaking of those who have merely scratched the surface in their dilettantism, but those who have penetrated to the very core of the matter with zeal and great effort, who have not merely tasted of this ambrosia, but who have satisfied their hunger to the fullest on this nourishment of the soul as well.

Women are without question capable of enjoying that inner freedom of the soul, and of applying their mind in the pursuit of that goal. But we have too often denied the existence of this latter faculty in the opposite sex, and affirmed the heart, reckoning only with that organ. As if the one were of any use without the other! And even if women would and could shut their eyes to the verdict of our criminal prosecution—is their self-ordained intellectual placidity ever going to be capable of yielding riper and more tasty fruits when we continually have the barbarity to profane its blossoms? Whatever women could not attain through intellectual freedom is strangled by the torrent of technical terms and regulations which we for our own part deliberately invent in order to confuse them and cause them to lose heart, so that they needlessly tire and give up. What a great pity!

And yet there are those who did not quit the field, who decided to persevere steadfastly to the end; and among those who took this final oath are to be found a few who let themselves be consecrated as administrators and teachers in the temple of the Muses. In the well-known Institute of Bologna Laura Bassi teaches physics, giving her lectures in Latin; and how long now has Signora Agnes of Milan[63] been teaching mathematics at this institution with approbation? And here, too, Lelli and his capable wife[64] reproduce the muscles and blood vessels of animal bodies with deceptive verisimilitude. Italy, this land which has alternately spread so much light and so much darkness over the peoples of the earth, this land has no scruples whatsoever about opening its professorial chairs to women. Of late Germany has created her first female Doctor of Philosophy, Dr. Schlözer;[65] and would we have received such a considerable amount of dependable information concerning the firmament if the immortal Herschel had not been supported so tirelessly in his work and observations by his sister,[66] who was in many ways very much like him in nature and spirit?

Doctors become just as ill as those who are not physicians, and the greatest philosophers are not only often unwise, but lose themselves to such an extent in speculation that they can no longer find their way. Women are very much for inner truth; and even if they do not possess the well-known impassiveness of our ministers and officials, they nevertheless know how to differentiate calmly and objectively between knowledge which is useful and that which is but dry pedantry. If spice and humor are lacking, the most richly set table is an abomination to them, and they will accept no invitation to partake of the show-dishes and table ornaments of the philosophers whatsoever. Must not the female sex then under such conditions have misgivings about appearing learned upon occasion? And yet, if it *is* capable of assimilating knowledge and imparting it to others with ease and visible profit, how can we argue that it lacks the talent to apply this knowledge in some other way to the best advantage of the state, as soon as the state deigns most graciously to remove the interdict with which a barbaric prejudice has burdened it for millenia! If those medieval knights, who among their various oaths and loyalties also bore the responsibility of protecting ladies, if they had but extended their limits farther, how much more estimable would their calling have become! It is unfortunate that these excellent men, who with certain exceptions were the most noble and intelligent of their age, did not, instead of protecting the women, seek to elevate them above such protection!

Although we can hardly fail to recognize the clandestine nature of much of the power of persuasion which the opposite sex has over our own, has not the greatest influence which women have exerted at all times on all civil and state affairs been quite visible and apparent? When it came to vast plans which needed to be carried out or canceled, it was the women who took over the chief role. They served as privy councillors for wise men and fools, regents and priests, monks and statesmen; they were always members of the closed committees of the council of state, for whose decrees the full assembly merely provided a secretarial function by adding the flourish of legal language. And who would not prefer to have a woman running things, even if she were a mistress, to our bellwethers of valets, court dwarfs and Heyducs,[67] who are but the parasites and darlings of the women at court anyway? Not merely by virtue of the tinkling playfulness and billowing banners of their wit; not merely through their discourse, strengthened by the rapid association of ideas, are women able to gain access for themselves; their powers of reason, flexible enough to make the most subtle distinctions and judgments, are capable of doing anything that should be required of them. How many a tyrant of a minister, who made light of the tears of his people and trafficked in their fortunes, has not learned from a woman how to steer back to a more favorable course? Women hold the strings by which cabinets are guided; they shuffle the cards with which Their Excellencies play; and just as new obstacles often give rise to new and unsuspected strengths, so they have often attained a high degree of strength by virtue of their weakness.

A soft and moderate character is peculiar to the opposite sex. Nature endowed it with great and undeniable talents for such moderation, and with only a little more philosophical reflection and more singleness of purpose, the fair sex would be able to teach us a certain noble insouciance in the face of so much that now annoys and vexes us—and such an insouciance is without doubt the crown of all life this side of the grave. Has not nature often far exceeded even Correggio[68] in the beauty and modesty which he bestows on his women? Where do painters find faces for the angels they paint? And what is impossible for such gentleness—even if it occasionally feels itself compelled to arrive at its goal by going backwards? What sharp contours and lively coloration women give to their fancies and the characters they weave into them! Their very first glance perceives the unusual in every matter, and since this ability has much of the miraculous about it, is it a wonder, then, that they often cast so much radiance even on everyday occurrences that these sooner resemble ceremonious events? Is it a wonder when they elevate a country supper to the dignity of a great feast? To unite increased clarity and intensity of light with greater magnification is the goal which, no matter how impossible and extravagant it may seem to us, they attain with very little effort.

The opposite sex as a rule is able to *captivate*, our sex only to *alienate*. Of us it is said: we are angry until our good side has been acknowledged without question. Women have a foretaste, we an aftertaste. Those wrinkles which old age has received from wisdom, or wisdom from old age, frighten off neither their wit nor their intellect—and nothing, neither intellect, nor wealth, nor beauty makes them shy. They are always on the lookout to be of service to their intellect, and soon find to their comfort something to criticize in the lives and the theories of our friends the philosophers, even where it is difficult to find anything to take exception to; and because they are born *naturalists* (in the true sense of the word) how easy it is for them to pluck a feather or two from our *artistes*! They have, to a far greater extent than we, a talent for freeing their intellect from prejudice and superstition, and are able to distinguish perfectly learned wheat from learned chaff and give meaning to Shakespeare's phrase: "[He] speaks an infinite deal of nothing." [69] Women are simply made for orienting the philosopher and bringing him back to reality when he loses himself in the cobwebs of his own systems (just as a well-known scholar once got lost in his own house—a house which had been in his family for years and he had inherited from his grandfather); like Ariadne,[70] they place a thread in his hand and call out to all who no longer can tell up from down, to all who have lost direction in their lives, "You are goldsmith, Mr. Josse!"[71]

The spirit of that philosophy which wishes ill to all demigods has long rested with the women. Who has known better than they that neither practical nor theoretical reason is capable of providing convincing proof of the existence of intelligible extrasensory beings, and that we stray into unavoidable contradictions when both types of human reason offer such objects up for sale. Women perceive clearly that our beloved generalizations are only half true, and positively insist that assertions of this sort be made more specific. They act according to obvious motives. Gamblers, sailors, and all those whose destinies are guided by Dame Fortune (speculators of all sorts not excluded) tend to be superstitious—is it then a wonder that women are less so than we? Handsomeness in a male counts nothing at all with them; and if we honor the rich man because he could help us if he wished to, they know full well that he will never wish to. Their unbiased soul will always find a way; and whoever does not possess a heart of stone—can he withstand their sincerity and the warmth of their feeling?

The wife of a lamp vendor had no misgivings about trying her luck with the poor soul of the philosopher David Hume. And he could find no other way to divert her missionary activity on his behalf from the inner light of his soul than to agree at least to purchase his external light from her.[72] Concerning the philosopher Terrasson, Madame de Lassay has said that only a witty man could be such a fool;[73] and if it were a historical fact that Charles XII wrote to his senate: "I am sending you one of my riding-boots; you are to obey its every command,"[74] then the wives of these esteemed men would have laughed loud and long. "All of us here are either princes or poets," said Voltaire, as he sat down to eat with a prince—and that is the true tenor of a woman's thought. They are not much for art galleries where for every connoisseur ten shoemakers put in an appearance and display their ignorance. They work quietly, to be sure, yet like their tutelary goddess, Nature, they prefer to work from the particular to the general. A certain indulgent magnanimity when it comes to historical judgment is, in general, a characteristic of the opposite sex; yet women know how to analyze and separate the extraneous matter from both a fact and a human being—no matter how complicated either of them are. Furthermore, they are able to communicate the total impression which facts and individuals make on them, something which is more difficult for us to do. Happiness, like truth and divinity, is a unity; to call forth this unity in all things is a sublime form of wisdom, and, to be perfectly honest, also more characteristic of women than men. With us it is often the case that a matter which is capable of more than one interpretation and which this or that odd fellow chooses to see differently becomes immediately the subject for a learned disputation. Here is where we then exhibit a highly developed dexterity in concealing quickly the grounds for doubt and then revealing them again; in adding to their importance and then subtracting from it; and in weighing the bases for decision in such a way that the balance must either rise or fall—even if, as is especially the case with facts, the probability that the truth could lie on either side of the question is more or less equal. The opposite sex has no love for such shadow boxing with a long list of carefully drawn-up arguments. But one thing is needful to this sex.[75] It will never poke fun at its public with sophistry; it is far less likely than we are to fall in love with an idea which is basically without substance; yet it also fears such specters less than we do.

It is said that strong truths are only for good minds (just as strong drink is only for truly able-bodied individuals), and that weak minds merely become giddy at such truths. Let us but test this out on the women, and we will see that there is no sort of truth which their minds cannot tolerate. We are too ready to believe that our own plans are organized with order and precision; women exhibit credulity only in regard to the fulfillment of their plans. They fear nothing high or low, nothing that ignorance or learning, wit or lack of it, reason or irrationality can do. If the power to carry out their plans were granted to them, they would accomplish more than we have accomplished. And if they began to sink, they would do as the dying Socrates, who, as he felt his feet becoming cold and stiff from the poison, stroked them and said, laughing in defiance: "Just so near does pain border on pleasure." [76]

Does this afford us proof of the happiness women experience at death? Do we even need proof? Watch men and women dying—if philosophy is but a preparation for one's own death, then women are great philosophers; and in truth, they are infinitely more practical about it than we are. Studying is but learning to die, it is said, and in the sense that one removes his spirit from his body and raises it above the latter, this is true; yet women have no need of such artifices in order to deceive death and ultimately defeat him. What is the good of such artifices anyway? To disdain death when he stands before us—that *is* wisdom; to attempt to deceive him through strategems only *appears to be* wisdom. None of us can draw another's lot; all of us alike are condemned to death—yet not as criminals, but as human beings. If it were up to the women, they would seldom trust the pronouncement of life or death to the doctors, or let the latter declare a case to be hopeless. Distrustful of the art of Galen, [77] women all prefer to put their trust in someone not of that fraternity when they feel more needs to be done. The tenet of a famous sect: "either reason or the rope"—either conform to life or leave it—suits women as if made for them. [78] Only he can be truly free, said a wise man of old, who has disdain for death. [79] What a great potential for freedom is exhibited by the women in their indifference to death! Can they thus continue to be so systematically deprived of their freedom in the face of such potential? Only he who considers himself to be more important than freedom possesses the soul of a slave and is unworthy of this freedom. Is such the case with the women? Life is a gift; let us view each day as something extra thrown into the bargain, something which we had no reason to expect. "Do not put off until tomorrow what you can do today," is the way women think, and there is no question that their bodily weakness, the limitations put on their freedom this side of the grave, and the status which not fate but the men have assigned to them, all contribute to their indifference to life. On the whole, these are the cause of the greater burden of suffering which has been laid upon their shoulders as human beings, while the men, it seems, have taken on a greater burden of civic responsibility as a certain compensation for this inequity.

The tears of women are seldom an indication of unwillingness and dissatisfaction, and often represent only a quiet, tender, and somewhat daring longing for more freedom within the state; thus one thing more than anything else helps prepare them for a joyful death: namely, their weariness with a life which hardly deserves the name. The belief that in the world beyond they certainly cannot be worse off is a naiveté which they hold to with great assurance at the time of their departure from this world (a true vale of tears for them). Death is their deliverer. They create for themselves another world where justice reigns, where they stroll upon rose petals under sunny skies—an Elysian idyll! A gentle, moving melancholy and quiet ecstasy help them to overcome themselves and the world, and to blend the bitterness of life with that of death. Watch women dying—how calm, how peaceful they are. As a rule, they die philosophically. If this were to become the case with our own sex, what a hue and cry would be raised over such resignation! Women die by Nature just as they have lived by her; she appears to offer them her hand in order to help them over the threshold. Women do not wish to die a little every day; they have no desire to witness the all-too-visible forfeiture of life which takes place the longer we live. If they reach a ripe old age, then they are even more fully aware of the travail of life, and death has no opportunity to overwhelm them suddenly, even if it should wish to. Socrates confronted those who brought him the news that he had been condemned to death with the reply that Nature had also passed such a verdict on the judges who had condemned him. Life gives us death, and death gives us life. Not only he who has passed his days in the sweat of his brow, but also he who has passed them in the full measure of his pleasure is glad to feel sleep coming on in the end. If sleep were not the elder brother of death,[80] it would not be so easy to die—in the end we but fall asleep for a longer time than usual. Why fear something which we all face, from which none of us will escape, even if he were to take the wings of the morning, and dwell in the uttermost parts of the sea![81]

If men learn the art of dying, then women learn the nature of death;

their heart knows no terror, it is not afraid. If one would derive comfort from becoming acquainted with death, he must watch women dying and not men. To be sure, men die more easily in war than under ordinary circumstances; nevertheless, death in battle is far less instructive than the death of a woman in childbirth on that field which nature intended for her. How beautiful is death here, a death for the fatherland! But I must stop now, otherwise I would betray all too clearly that I am only a man when it comes to death. Two women friends, whose lives nature chose to link with my own, died this mother's death . . .

This is how women die; and how do they *live*? Men base their actions more on temperament than principle; they are subject to external circumstances and let themselves be driven back and forth by them like a ship which has lost mast and rudder. They act out of indolence, desire, and need. In their hearts they are much more fearful than women—it only appears otherwise. They always unite themselves with other men, and often call *friendship* (O, the desecration of the word!) what should in fact be called *faintheartedness*. Friendship! Where is a pure and unsullied one? How seldom does the one gain from it without the other losing? Friendship is like a polished sword, which even a single moist breath will cause to rust. Yet friendship is life, for without it human existence would be utterly without value. Kings may offer it for sale—but friendship cannot be bought. And such true friendship—which, even if it cannot be counted among the seven wonders of the natural world, most certainly belongs to the great rarities of the moral one—such true friendship would occur more frequently if the women were permitted to say their vows before its altars as well. Any restriction in the sharing of personal confidences or in the mutual outpouring of the heart; any moderation in the disclosure of secret burdens invalidates all that friendship stands for and makes customary a certain pretense, which, while it may do yeoman's service in the fashionable world, nevertheless desecrates the altars of friendship. Our friendships at present are usually nothing more or less than cases of reciprocal favoritism from which both sides profit. And just as modesty is but the desire to be praised even more extravagantly, so friendship is an alliance dedicated to profiting even more completely. Our sex is too happy with things as they are to become true friends of the women; and as regards our friendships with each other, of which we are so proud, the women have not the slightest confidence in them. Can we (and how could women's logic reasonably interpret it otherwise?) flaunt our friendships and boast about our sacrifices when we do not once condescend to show justice to the women? If one thinks about it, our own life is but half a life because we do not authorize a life for the women. And how, then, do they live?

Although nowadays they succumb a little too often to sensuality—for which they themselves are less responsible than our own severity; although they are far from having become what they can and will become, nonetheless they exhibit on many an occasion a steadfastness and self-control which so often shames us. Their amorous escapades, which we exaggerate so terribly, arise more from an attempt to satisfy vanity than from concupiscence. They have no other pathway to Olympus than through their men; if another is opened to them, they will work miracles.

Women act out their little flirtatious pantomimes because it is the fashion, and because no intelligent man would dare to infer anything from them. But why do we so sharply condemn women for these pantomimes and yet regard vanity, coquetry, and voluptuousness as immaterial? We laugh over the woman who quickly responded to the praise bestowed in her presence on her neighbor's brown eyes: "But, my dear, these days brown eyes just aren't fashionable any more." Yet is it not we ourselves who induce the opposite sex to such replies? Do we not by means of our own vanity promote it in them as well? Let women but regain their strength, and you will perceive that amidst the deafening roar of the tempest and the terrible rolling of the angry sea, where we men are seldom able to make ourselves heard, they will appear and bid the wind and the sea to be calm.[82] For if one learns and ponders during periods of peaceful solitude those things which are to be applied when shipwreck is imminent, then it is not reprehensible to gather beforetimes, in order to have in time of need. And what if the women were able to make their own decisions even in the face of such storms and no longer had need to refer to a book of rules, which never seem to fit the individual case anyway?[83] What if . . . ? Yet let us consider not what this whale of the human race will become when we no longer throw it little barrels to play with,[84] but rather what in its present unfortunate condition it has been and is!

"Is the modesty which women exhibit in their actions really characteristic of them?"

The lesson of human experience spares me from answering that.

"Have women in fact ever really acted of their own accord?"

O, the insult this question implies! Without an Isabella America would perhaps not yet have been discovered, at least not by Columbus, or at a later time, and from a different direction. Ferdinand had neither the courage nor the decisiveness to lend his name to such a bold undertaking and to open up his coffers. Would Cicero have discovered the conspiracy of Catiline and received the title Preserver of the Roman State without Fulvia?[85] Charles V had only the beneficial influence of a woman to thank for the fact that his quixotisms achieved a better result than they deserved.[86] But why a long enumeration of such affairs of state in which women not only took part, but which were initiated, guided, and concluded by them; where they did not perform mere subordinate services, but were the spirit which moved upon the face of the waters,[87] the soul which determined and ordered the course of events!

For the last two hundred years France has been ruled by women—whether poorly or well is a matter which does not concern us here. That it has been ruled poorly is not the fault of women in general, but of those women cunning, audacious, and ambitious enough to wrest the reins of state from weak men who had either been entrusted with them by blind chance, or who, having been given their positions for extraneous reasons and then being faced with the difficult task of dispelling the tedium from an idle monarch, had hit upon the idea of taking over the much easier business of running the state themselves.

Since the time when Semiramis[88] swiftly and decisively seized the scepter and carried it with as much dignity as wisdom, many women, among them several whom birth had not destined for the diadem, have borne the title of regent. Are there not lands which list among their rulers just as many famous names from the one as from the other sex? If the French cabinet happens to have no feminine representative except for Chevalière d'Éon,[89] are we to accept this as proof of the incompetency of the female sex? In all that can be attained by reason, grasped by boldness, snatched by wit, and gained by good-naturedness, the fair sex will not be left far behind. Should venal souls sell their services to any or all in authority, the women will not forget what is decent.

If we knew what has happened in cabinets and councils on account of the influence of women, we would marvel at that most interesting of all performances, the deception of the imagination by which women attain their goals; we would admire the ingenuity with which a woman hatched the beginnings of a plot and carried it through all the secret passages of intrigue to a successful conclusion. Actually they seem to make use of those artifices on which the politics of today prides itself, only for the purpose of paying the men back in their own coin; basically they are less well equipped by nature with that political guile which, according to the rules of present-day practice, skulks about in the darkness. Doubtless we can expect from their powers of reason and from their hearts that they will purify politics and, for the good of mankind, bring it into a closer union with nature and truth. With their talent for ferreting out the innermost thoughts of others, they will outwit the slyest diplomat without His Excellency ever being able to wrest their secrets from them.

Yet even when faced with such artifice and deception, will women give up the magnanimity so typical of them? Will they yield up that willingness to deny themselves which stems from their genuine love of mankind? Will they, as a consequence of their art of understanding people and fathoming their innermost thoughts, stop being generous and subduing their own desires? Never! Weak men tend to place their confidence in evil men; women, on the other hand, to entrust it to noble men. Women hate treachery and the treacherous; we hate, if it is to our advantage, only the treacherous. We like it when such people bring us much, and only trouble ourselves to see that they take little or nothing in return. Women, far removed from political tirades, from political figures of speech, and from the sort of political *salto mortale*[90] which men like to perform, elect nature as their teacher and accomplish more than Their Excellencies do with their worn-out political tricks based on treachery and bribery, tricks which are far from even being worthy of the notorious designation "artifices."

Are women not capable of revealing and concealing things at their own discretion? Do they not possess an openness through which they accomplish more than through reserve and propriety? Do they not possess an incomparable suppleness in their thinking, a clarity of expression and a malleability in their judgments? The ever changing play of their features; their happiness and success at producing the greatest effects with the slightest means; their art of holding up a mirror before each of us in which *we* see what *they* want us to see; their facile tongue, through which they bestow on their ideas a power which overcomes all—these are characteristics which accomplish everything for them. One needs merely to perceive their effect on himself and to search in vain for its cause—a cause which the women are able to conceal very artfully. Even in everyday life they intertwine all the different personality types in society in such a pleasant way with their wit that one must simply stand back and admire the facility with which they do it. By seeming to lose their power of expression, or even to yield it up voluntarily, they achieve a language of rapture. They listen with the utmost care for every little idea the person they seek to win over lets fall. They know precisely his favorite dishes, his preferences, his strengths, his weaknesses, and possess a remarkable gift for making use of both good fortune and bad. How admirable! Our own sex seldom understands how to profit from good fortune, and almost never how to find happiness in adversity.

The lack of discretion with which we so often charge the women is only a bad habit of the common sort of female, and the males of this type are hardly an exception—in fact, they almost seem more loquacious. Because women talk much, we have accused them of indiscretion; yet our own sex deserves this reproach infinitely more—almost always when we are full of sweet wine or in love, but oftentimes when we are intoxicated neither with wine nor with love. Many cannot even be prevented from revealing their own shame. No soldier can describe his conquests with such enthusiasm as a dandy his own. Has not the reproach been made concerning Mirabeau, the most recent of the golden-tongued orators of history, that he could not keep silent about anything? The willingness of even good people to listen to everything, including secrets, proves how few truly respect such confidences. Many of our sex have so many secrets of their own that they can hardly concern themselves with others' secrets conveniently, and some are low enough to demand shamelessly other confidences in exchange for confidences so entrusted.

Whoever is not true to himself and does not consider it ill-advised to make his misdeeds known, will think it justifiable, if not in fact excusable, to betray his master or his friend. Men easily convince themselves that they may betray the confidence of a lesser man for the good of another who stands higher in their eyes. Many a judge has no scruples about eliciting confessions under the pretext that he will not make use of them. "Do I not have a greater duty to the state," he asks, "than to obligations such as these?" Thou art mistaken, traitor!—it is to virtue that we have the greater duty. Our duties to our country hardly nullify our other duties, and a citizen must never cease to be a human being. Even in war we must not give up the prerogative of being a friend to our friends! Men can also maintain a certain traitorous silence, a way of shrugging their shoulders or of uttering but half a word—or even the first syllables of that word. This Judas betrayal by means of a kiss, this loquacious silence, certainly removes the burden of guilt from the opposite sex. Let us not speak of the indiscretion of women!

Even less should women be forbidden to take part in the inner workings of the state, since at present they are entrusted with the management of their entire household, and their performance at these duties, even in the judgment of us men, is commendable. Most certainly we would then have fewer tyrants who watch with pleasure from solid ground as others suffer shipwreck, or who, by means of the charitable institutions under their jurisdiction, cast straws amidst the blaring of trumpets and rolling of drums to those surrounded by rising flood waters. We would have fewer leeches who on the one hand see to it that every object of financial value is identified and properly accounted for, and on the other squander the sweat and blood of their subjects without measure or purpose; who try to lure the chicken right out of the pot of the common man; who begin their administrations with pillage, just as miserable field commanders begin their occupation of a city; and who, in order to avoid the rumors of new oppression, give *redoutes* and balls, dinners and suppers, doing precisely what Alcibiades did when he cut off the ears and tail of his best dog![91]

If anyone denies that the female sex possesses the ability to perceive matters in a larger context; to set up regulations for whole kingdoms and then carry them out on a large scale; to comprehend far-reaching plans and, in short, to raise its ideas to the level of the universal, he betrays very little familiarity with the way of the world and is drawing his conclusions only from its ability to undertake minor matters and perform detail work, the single function which is presently entrusted to this sex.

The talent for figuring is remarkable even in the most common of women, although they seem to pay little attention to our methods and often retain their own arithmetic after they have been exposed to the mysteries of the numbers according to the usual method of instruction. Their methods of figuring and writing are dear to me regardless of their irregularities and the fact that our present legislators of morality cannot yet decide among themselves whether the ability to write, at least, is useful or harmful to the female sex. Do we not have enough men who know no better way to keep watch over their daughters than to forbid them pen and ink? According to his observations on France, Storch, a recent traveler in that country, found in the school of the famous tachygrapher Coulon de Thèvenot in Paris girls among whom several had very quickly attained an astonishing facility in the art of writing—and is the art of writing not more than mere orthography and calligraphy?[92]

Up to the present time, we have regarded many things which pertain to the field of agriculture and the management of the state as insignificant. Many domestic animals have not been utilized according to their inherent potential, and as a whole it could be said that it is no small field which waits for women's hands and heads to make it bear fruit. In fact, one could almost say that our entire agricultural economy is already in feminine hands, especially that part which is conducted on a large scale. How we men have been able to subvert—or should I say *invert*—everything in such a masterful way!

And thou, O hallowed Justice! An insurmountable object to those who, like pilgrims crossing the Alps, wish to assail thee without boots, alpenstock, or guide! Thou mystical aristocrat who hast so often placed thyself between a prince and his people—ostensibly to serve as a mediator to both, yet in reality only to be master over them—may I have the audacity to address thee? So often has it been thy misfortune that even the foremost of thy officiants have not known what to do with thee, and I myself do not quite know the reason why none of them knows what is right and proper. Their opinions and judgments, which are designed to solve matters (and even claim to do so), are but new riddles themselves. Thou hast ever been a paltry crutch on which the state has limped through its existence, and more than this, thou hast been of such a malicious and evil nature that thou hast bored through the hands of even those who leaned upon thee in trust! How often have thy judgments been but contaminated Host, which men have received with all the pomp and ceremony surrounding High Mass. Even in thy golden age thou wert but a peep show wherein exquisite rarities and beautiful figures run by clockwork could be seen.

Lawyers have always counted in their profession a certain number of *élégants*, and who has not heard people talk of *elegant* jurisprudence? Even the most sagacious lawyer is frequently at a loss to know what to do in his personal legal affairs, and thus it often seems that the all-too-great art of administering justice is for man, although he was created by God as an upright and forthright being, an utterly unsuitable concept.

Should improvement in the status of women ever be extended to the administration of justice, and the law cease to be a monopoly of an especially paid male class, then, and only then, will we begin to see that this administration is not merely a matter of uttering incomprehensible formulas which owe their effect to nothing more than the presence of a sword next to the scales of justice.[93] Rather, such administration must make the effort to inform and convince both parties concerning what is legal and what is not, if it is to deserve even a part of the honor which it has now so boundlessly and dictatorially assumed for itself. It is said that Necker is virtuous so that he can boast about it; Lafayette[94] so that he may truly be virtuous and not merely appear so. Would this not also be the case with judges from both the male and female sexes?

Already the idea is beginning to make itself felt that only equals can pass judgment on equals if the law is to be a living entity instead of a lifeless one. Would it not meanwhile be a monstrous injustice to exclude women from judge's benches and the jury room before that glowing ember bursts into flame? How would it be if the opposite sex were to take part in the administration of justice; if quarrels and lawsuits could be handled by good women as well as by good men (*arbitri*)?[95] Would not the administration of justice be rendered more perfect thereby?

Individuals whose behavior is characterized by nothing more than its legality have no personal standards of behavior. They are, in fact, useless servants who do what is bid them, it is true, but who nevertheless bring about nothing of value thereby. Human laws and passions are often so closely related that whoever follows neither reason nor his conscience (i.e., practical reason), often turns out to be corrupt in spite of his law-abiding ways. And who is able to accept the truth of this better than the opposite sex? Who can sense better than they that those forces by means of which others are now becoming free can also be a true test of liberty for them? Unadorned objective truth has always, historically and in every other way, counted for more than falsehood, no matter how dazzling the latter may appear.

Moral reason is a dowry granted by nature to all men in equal measure. The most basic principle of universal law, with whose application the element of force can be indissolubly associated, is the principle:

"Resist every retrogressive step in the perfection of mankind," and is itself an integral part of the highest material law of morality:

"Perfect all mankind."

Is perfection not the highest stage of the development of all one's powers into a unified whole? Without wishing at this point to incur the displeasure of any particular philosophical school, may I be permitted, in the interest of convincing justice just how much she is at odds with herself, to note that the perfection of all men appears to me the ultimate purpose of moral law? And what does mankind desire more than this highest development? Should not for this very reason the law be extended to all men? Can a rational being be considered merely as a means to higher goals?

Good legislation is certainly the masterpiece of the human race, and whoever knows from his experience with our nature that the customs of nations are attributable for the most part to the effect of their laws will not take it amiss if I lead our lawyers back farther than the ordinary members of this profession are accustomed to going. In special cases where women already sit on the judge's bench, that is, in certain *privilegia causae*,[96] they exhibit a mastery of their own sort, shaming their husbands, who usually ruin everything as soon as they take it upon themselves to represent their wives.

It is said that "women would be too harsh"; yet what does justice have to do with emotions? "They would be too meticulous in their research and inquiry," it is said. But can one afford to be less than meticulous when it is a matter of the guilt or innocence of a human being? Women certainly do not lack a memory capable of retaining a legion of laws; nor do they lack the patience to hear out the eternal accusations and defenses of the parties involved with a good and pure heart; nor the eloquence to calm the storm of passion and hurl the flood of rhetoric back to its overflowed banks. How skillful would be their attempts at reconciliation!

Up to the present women have had no more serious business to attend to than affairs of the heart. To be sure, if all at once they throw themselves into the affairs of the state—just as if they were to fall from the sky, without any preparation, without having been granted the additional legal rights or helped onto their political feet—would it be a wonder if, according to eye-witness reports from France, occurrences of hysteria disappeared and were replaced by maladies of an even more severe nature?[97] Serious matters are too precious and sublime in women's eyes for them not to be willing to sacrifice everything for this one pearl of great price.[98] Let us therefore introduce the opposite sex to new situations in moderation, and bring them gradually into contact with ever more serious matters, and such cases of hysteria, as well as other even worse maladies of the body and soul, will vanish. The pipers and fiddlers were dispatched from the scene as the daughter of Jairus was to be raised from the dead.[99] Even our population would experience an increase: "Now life is worth living," the women would think. How has it been possible that the entire world up to now has failed so utterly to recognize what is advantageous for humanity? That it has kept women locked up like dead souls in a psychodocheum,[100] never authorizing them a real life, but only the appearance of one—an existence as a kind of knight of melancholy countenance? Many of our traits would be exalted and ennobled, others more gently blended; we would not so often be heroes merely out of anxiety or fear; we would not find so many legal fortune hunters and puppeteers in the courts; not so many shallow and coarsely drawn judges, lawyers, and whatever else they are called, if women had some voice in the administration of justice.

Speaking in terms of the state as a whole, the Romans were not especially gifted in financial matters; and quite often the sinful thought has crossed my mind that this could be the reason for the bitter hatred which has existed between lawyers and financiers even to the present day. And if women were allowed to take part in the administration of both justice and finances, I would wager that this hatred between Herod and Pilate would soon come to an end, with both parties being converted to a way of thinking more in keeping with the rest of humanity, since now the financiers often dabble in law, and those in the legal profession rarely think twice before entering the realm of high finance. As a matter of fact, could not the lawyers often enough be said to serve as officers' orderlies in our state Department of Finance? O Themis![101] O goddess, thou hast but to open thy sanctuaries to thy race, and thou wilt experience miracles without having to lift so much as a finger!

When we men, not satisfied with being masters over the souls of the women like a sultan,[102] seek to be defenders and protectors of their bodies as well; when we begin to extend our grasp greedily in every direction and toward everything, we force the opposite sex to renounce all claim to the *healing arts*, a business for which they have an undeniable propensity. And why are the healing arts in the larger sense not the free province of both men and women? Do women not in fact have the feeling that they have been especially called by nature to such a business? And do they not, in spite of all the regulations, the surveillance, and the punishments, still carry on with this so strictly forbidden handiwork? And what is even more remarkable, have they not also availed themselves of the opportunity to make something of themselves thereby? Frau ———— in ————, for example, cures the maladies of all the members of her household without paying the slightest heed to the invective and threats of experienced professors of medicine, and cannot bring herself to accept the strict orthodoxy of these gentlemen, even though they have gone to great lengths to prove to other equally insignificant women "physicians" this orthodoxy in a manner worthy of the Inquisition. Be on your guard, Madame, that you do not fall head over heels into similar controversies and become answerable for your unsophisticated and unprofessional treatments!

In several of the provinces of Spain the women do the barbering, and in this regard the Marquis de Langle[103] is of the opinion that this ought to be the case universally, since the soft, smooth, and plump hands of women are better suited than ours for lathering the chin and handling a razor. While I cannot exactly concur with the reasons which led this patron saint of women to his conclusion, I heartily accept his conclusion. The fear of assassination, not always totally unjustified in some, would certainly diminish, if not completely vanish, if the opposite sex were to take over this dangerous skill entirely. The talent which the opposite sex possesses for healing and surgery proves beyond the shadow of a doubt the excellence of their powers of observation. They quickly notice the slightest passing change of color in our faces, the slightest alteration in our expression or in the look in our eyes. Their glance is capable of perceiving every—even the most insignificant— sign of tension in our muscles. Their sense of touch is more delicate and is able to feel a pulse beat long after the coarser hand of the doctor has ceased to observe it. Not even the slightest whisper eludes them; they understand those words which trembled on our lips and died there, and often they can read our very thoughts. Moreover, they never fail to make practical use of their carefully collected observations. Even now, in spite of the meager store of their knowledge, and without the help of professional training, they undertake cures which force from even the most experienced physicians if not an overt, then at least a covert expression of approval. How much farther they would be if admittance to this profession were granted to them—an admittance which a fraternal spirit fraught with jealousy has refused them up to now. If only the temple at Epidaurus[104] and the immeasurable treasures of nature were opened to them and they were initiated into the secrets of this art as its priestesses—how much would be gained for humanity!

At present a matter of great concern to us all, the health of mankind, still finds itself in a deplorable state because many of our physicians are not content to act as servants of nature, but seek to dominate her by dint of force. Is there no domain over which we do not wish to extend our rule? The healing powers of those who stand close to nature are so simple and effective that they can heal any malady with but modest means, just as that simplest of foods, bread, is the daily fare on every man's table, rich or poor. Nature is so beneficent that she desires to make us healthy by means of our illnesses. Illness is a warning bell summoning us to repentance. Nature makes us aware of ourselves, and with that she attempts to entice us into believing that she is our good and rightful mother. And is she not just that? The pain we experience—how much could be said in its defense. In fact, nature seems to be using our pain to poke fun at us. There are cases in which pain and the danger to our health have little to do with each other—the pain of a toothache, for example, in which the suffering is significantly greater than the danger—and in other cases where the opposite holds true. Nevertheless, in all such cases more—indeed, infinitely more—can be expected from the opposite sex than from our own. A special kind of charitableness toward the ill and defiance toward the illness is characteristic of them. We need but to watch them suffer pain and express compassion, to see them offer condolences, comfort, and courage to be aware of their gifts for healing.

We are all convinced of the great extent to which a rational, well-ordered life contributes to the maintenance of our health. We are just as convinced of the importance of the proper preparation of food and drink; and yet this largest and most important aspect of the science of healing is left entirely to the female sex without their being provided with the slightest knowledge of what should be prepared, or how to prepare it if the machine that is our body is to be maintained and not destroyed. Perhaps through the intercession of women it could come to pass that our food and drink would become our medicine, and that we would no longer be permitted to make use of medicine of any other sort. Would we not then be able to forfeit fully half the loathing which accompanies the taking of medicine? In short, the countless legions of trials and illnesses would be reduced substantially if women were judges and physicians. Is it not much easier to *prevent* illness than to *cure* it? Is it not more beneficial for the state if fewer of its citizens are stricken by disease in the first place than if they do contract diseases and then have to be restored to good health again through the physician's art? And is it really health which these gentlemen are peddling to the sick? In point of fact, it resembles health even less than that which we pay such an exorbitant price for in our courts of law resembles justice.

Fathers of the state, instead of erecting clinics and medical institutes, build schools for women—schools in which our foods and beverages could be studied and tested more closely; where women would be taught to prepare meals in such a way that they are both good-tasting and free from harmful ingredients of any kind; in short, where they could learn to safeguard the lives and health of the citizens of the state. And even in a moral and ethical sense, it would be advantageous for both the state as well as for public morality—the latter being, of course, one of the chief concerns of the state—if women were permitted to practice medicine.

Women doctors would necessarily gain the confidence of patients of their own sex much sooner than our own physicians do. The patients would perceive their own frailties much sooner and with less constraint; and the doctors, experienced in the ways of nature and the disposition of the female body with its periodic emptyings, would be able to trace the source of the malady, as well as to give advice and assistance with more assurance. With that the treatment of female illnesses would cease to be the disgrace of our physicians; rather a certain perfection in the art of healing would be attained thereby, at least insofar as perfection is possible in this world.

Modesty, that virtue which so magnificently adorns the opposite sex and without which all grace and charm lose their efficacy, that virtue which can be supplanted by no other—is it not often the reason why women conceal their infirmities so long that they are beyond all hope of treatment? Or that they prefer to reject all medical assistance even at the risk of their lives? How many have been brought to the grave by a mere infection, when, had they been but a little less modest, they could have been saved in a moment? How many have forfeited their lives in cases of difficult childbirth, who could have been saved and borne the state more citizens if obstetrics were a woman's art—if we did not leave merely the more mechanical aspects to the midwives and preserve the theoretical side of this art for ourselves? Under such circumstances, is it then a wonder that among women in the cities of London and Dublin one out of seventy of those who are treated by midwives dies in childbirth, whereas only one in 140 of those who avail themselves of the assistance of male obstetricians dies upon giving birth?

Truly, it still remains immoral for a married woman to expose her body to any man except her husband! Does not such a breach of modesty cast out everything that we are wont to call respectability? How many cases like the one at Villacerf[105] may already have occurred—even if they continue to go unrecorded—in which a doctor in the throes of passion no longer knew what he was doing, and in order to seduce a young woman, or even to win her, guided her onto forbidden paths, or often in fact brought about a gruesome death without ever having had the slightest intention of doing so. If one has any idea what jealousy can do to a person, does he not tremble at this thought and at the circumstance which requires us to entrust everything to the physician, with only the miserable consolation of knowing that should anything happen we would lose our case in any law court of the land!

In like manner, we continue to allow male instructors to teach women music and dance, and seem either not to realize or to ignore wilfully what dangerous ground this is for the female sex, and how many have already fallen victim to the temptations inherent in such relationships.

We permit men to dress women's hair and never suspect what manner of thoughts are excited and desires aroused thereby. We forget that running our hands through someone's hair causes a certain physical stimulation—if not in both parties, then in at least one of the persons involved—and we overlook certain postures and attitudes which can reveal a great deal to an attentive observer. To be sure, we have slowly begun to transfer these matters to the hands of the women; yet this is still a rare occurrence dictated by economic necessity—a consideration which, in the face of so many others more important, is hardly a consideration at all.

Women's clothing, too, should be fitted and fashioned only by women. The manipulations performed by a male tailor or shoemaker are unseemly and inappropriate as they have to do with the female sex. In short, if the state were serious about employing this great and noble half of its population in a useful way; if it felt the important obligation to treat those equally and according to their rights whom nature herself had created equal, and to restore their rights along with personal freedom and independence, as well as with the merit and honor of citizenship, the weal and welfare of the state will everywhere begin to increase. If the state were to open to women its council chambers, its courts, lecture halls, commercial establishments, and its places of employment; if it were to grant to the presumably stronger male the monopoly of the sword only when it cannot, or does not, wish to keep from butchering people in the attainment of its ends; and if, moreover, the state does not draw a distinction between the sexes and chooses rather to follow the wishes of nature and what ought to be the desires of bourgeois society as well—that is, if society is not to be ashamed of its origins in nature—then not only will the weal and welfare of the state everywhere begin to increase, but people will multiply like willows at the side of a brook, and humanity will approach its true destiny with great and rapid strides.

Still, I had only intended to provide a few suggestions, and now it might be said of me that I had earned that title which was once applied to Edmund Burke by his fellows in Parliament when they dubbed him "the dinnerbell," because most of them got up and left when he began one of his perorations. Truth needs no cosmetic, and whoever writes for beauty's sake alone subjects himself to the fate of a good many women of our present corrupt age who would much sooner half freeze to death than give up the slightest claim to the privileges of fashion.

How is that? I seem now to be hearing objections from all sides to every one of my previous chapters! Nonetheless, I shall let nothing daunt me, even if the objections should become but repetitions of repetitions, for in the end it is not I, your humble servant, who is at fault, but rather (without mentioning any names) my honored opponents whom I have requested to dispute a few points with me. And who are these my opponents? Are they not the authors of those *chroniques scandaleuses* written and uttered against the fair sex, an assembly of misogynists and much-married men, eunuchs as well as the most virile, masculine types (who believe they are also the best of men, for they assume that physical need forms the closest bond between the sexes), fools and wise men, saints and rakes, sultans and self-appointed guardians of female purity? And yet, in the final analysis, can any of them ever truly change mankind or do violence to nature by anything he does or says?

"The woman only exists for the sake of the man!"

I agree, and the man for the woman! Friend, have you never known a woman, who, her charming simplicity notwithstanding, exhibited a noble grandeur?[106] A strict and chaste propriety in spite of her free and open manner? A woman who was capable of a searching inquiry into your ways, even though you trusted each other implicitly? To win hearts is never a woman's object, and yet she wins them all. That noble lack of specific intention and design to which poetry aspires is so characteristic of her—and how much she accomplishes thereby! Her glance, which forces its way through the bolted church doors of our hearts and discovers our innermost desires and doubts; her power to exalt or to cast down anything she wishes; her freedom from joy and sorrow, and the constraints of fear and hope; her ability to live for the day without giving thought to the cares of the morrow; the rapid and overwhelming effect of such a woman, born to be the autocratic ruler of our hearts—these things not only raise her to the level of her male friends, the magnitude of her dignity is even capable of making them her subjects in the end!

All mere coquetry, you say? Well, then cosmopolitanism is stoicism,[107] and the noblest human virtues in life and death are coquetry as well! By nature women ought not to love every Caius, Titus, and Sempronius,[108] but the sex as a whole. In marriage, it is true, the woman becomes the wife of one man; yet, having become accustomed to this state of affairs, her manner of thinking begins to become more general and to extend itself. If a man of some stature were to take over the role of a woman of equal rank—tell me honestly, would he be able to play the role with the same spirit and animation as she plays it? You are annoyed, friend? Wherefore think thou evil in thy heart?[109]

"All the evils of bourgeois society are the work of women!"

Of women, who are but ciphers in political society, and who would have no influence whatsoever except through the men who represent them? And just why are the evils the work of the women? Because the women led the men to them? The foster children led their own guardians? Because of that influence which even we cannot deny the women, that influence which even slaves exert on their masters?

Behold, then, the vengeance which Nature cannot deny herself when we give offense to her great majesty! If you cease to withdraw from the women those portions to which they have an undeniable right, you will automatically put an end to the insidious intrigues which women presently conduct to the disadvantage of their husbands and the state as well. Reason is but the image of the divine, and when we are confronted with it we are duty-bound to acknowledge its superiority. Or does the value of the opposite sex for us have its basis not in reason, but in sensuality? Ah, my good friend, can we ever, as long as we wear these garments of our mortality, can we ever truly vanquish our sensuality? Do we not through our sense organs and their perceptions meet reason more than halfway? Is not human reason grounded in sense perception? Are the senses not the final arbiter of our reason? Do they not raise reason to its true value? Is reason not of the feminine gender? Must not reason, too, as a function of its office, make itself perceptible to the senses, in order to be able to conquer the heart? Would we not cease to be human and become supernatural beings if we renounced the true nature of man? And is the supernatural also not unnatural? The highest refinement of anything is always closely related to the simplicity of its form. It is our lot in this life to play the role of the human being—is it so insignificant as it seems, and does he who is faithless in lesser tasks deserve to be given greater ones?

In marriage the woman finally attains completion through the man—to the same degree that he is completed through her. Man and woman together constitute a complete human being. The distribution of human characteristics between the two sexes leaves no doubt as to the veracity of this conclusion. And do I need to repeat that the physical size and strength which the man possesses over against the woman in no way implies any kind of moral superiority in our sex? Neither sex has the slightest value without the other; together they comprise humanity. We are all playing with the same deck of cards, and Nature has joined man and woman in such a way that no mortal can put them asunder.[110] Thus intertwined, their hearts and their wills become one. Jealousy of one's authority is a lever by which only the weak can be stimulated to action. And what manner of group can be formed without the women? If you were to associate with a woman merely for the sake of relieving boredom, although she meant nothing to you at all, before you even became aware of it your souls would engage and you would not be able to part from one another—and this without love or even mutual inclination exerting the slightest influence. This harmony is a result of the sex drive, that secret inner feeling which confirms the divine words: "It is not good that the man should be alone." [111] Without Eve, Adam is but an animal, and Eve without Adam but a cloistered nun. Who has not had occasion to observe that all social groups consisting entirely of men have their beginning in Paradise and end with the Last Judgment! One is astounded at the sudden turns which men's conversation can take when they are alone; women tie everything together and bring it into context, even though everyday social conversation with good reason follows the example of the English garden in avoiding precisely laid-out pathways.

If greater spiritual strength were a direct consequence of greater physical strength, then this treatise would have been much abbreviated, and to consider improving the status of women would not have been worth the trouble required. But if it is man's spirit which constitutes his true essence and being, then the supposed unfitness of women for the affairs of state, the arts, and the sciences is merely a pretext and no reason. In fact, women are not always more weakly built than men.

"Not in certain cases? Not in the lower classes, for example?"

No, not even as a general rule. In the province of Champagne in France, where the inhabitants are a fine, healthy race of people, the women, at least according to those who have traveled there, are stronger than the men. And how many young rakes and profligates are there who have had themselves inoculated with the serum of old age while they were still in their youth, in order to have as little chance of dying of old age as they would of smallpox!

I shall now endeavor to offer my opponent reasons for the above assertions, trusting that he will do likewise in his own good time. Granted that the female in general—that is, among all peoples, as well as within the whole animal kingdom—is of a weaker, more delicate, and fragile constitution than the male; that the nerves of the female are more pliant, irritable, and sensitive than our own—what do we conclude from this? Do we conclude, for example, that the female body is not fit for extended mental exertion? That because of their lively imagination they are incapable of remaining with anything for a long period of time? That mental exertion and concentration is not their strong point?

But are there not scientific pursuits which require a mind characterized by pliancy and delicacy? Can we draw inferences concerning mental capacity purely from physical strength alone? And if so, does not the most powerfully built day-laborer have the best qualifications to be a Lutheran bishop? The most superior men have often had the weakest bodies. Great souls have seldom chosen powerful bodies as their companions; friend Hume and a few others excepted, the great minds have, as a rule, been small and sickly types. "Fat paunches," runs the wise old proverb, "have lean pates." Even Alexander and Frederick the Great were small in stature, just as heroes in general usually have not been able to lay claim to great physical size.

Or again, have physiologists been able to prove that their naturally smaller stature has made subordinate beings of the women, blocking their path to all that is noble and great—so that even if boys and girls receive the same instruction and are prompted by the same motives to intellectual fulfillment, the former always outstrip the latter? If such observations had ever been verified, then we would be compelled to believe them—even if our own eyes told us otherwise. But my dear fellow! Where shall we find such a storehouse of experience? It certainly has not been collected. Where have experiments been made? And should this not be the first step, before we begin to deny certain talents and faculties in such a way? Never has there been a lack of mind and heart among those women who have outstripped the men in some particular field. I refer the reader to the beginning of this wee bit of a chapter, where my words are so richly adorned with their names. And why should we quarrel with each other at all, when a single glance out of the window of one's study—providing the view is not distorted by colored glass—can and will refute the prejudice resulting from the scorn which has been heaped upon the women.

(My opponent is proceeding in the same manner as many others of his ilk: he is not debating the ideas themselves, but the incorrect assumptions which he has made from them; not me, but himself.)

"Admittedly" (a not unexpected beginning for such an opponent), *"admittedly, the Queen of Sheba made the pilgrimage to Professor Solomon in order to hear his lectures on philosophy; and I suppose we can hope that he did not dismiss her without some tangible blessings of his school."* [112]

You are referring to his school of wisdom, of course? If not, I shall find myself compelled to give you back that "admittedly" of yours with interest. Does not this royal pilgrimage (the "admittedly" notwithstanding) prove clearly how desirous the fair sex is of knowledge and wisdom? And to be perfectly frank, what do we truly know anyway? Are not women at times of the opinion that they really have no use for a philosophy in which we rack our brains in the most laudable fashion in order to be able to say with absolute conviction that we know nothing?

Can we then deny that they possess sufficient mental energy and the faculty for deep thought and penetrating observation? If my opponent will agree that we cannot, then this battle, too, will have been decided in favor of the women. Children of the wealthy are often just as run-down as the hovels of the poor, and a long period of disuse can weaken one's powers considerably—but can it not heighten them as well?

"Those characteristics which are peculiar to the female sex have nothing distinct and positive to offer bourgeois society."

Who could maintain that proposition? Women possess self-esteem and the self-discipline which derives from it. Is bourgeois society really much more than a household on a larger scale? Or do you not even feel that the household is the proper place for women? Where are those private social groups which can exist for any length of time without the company of women? The greatest part of their attraction they owe to the women, whose cheerful and airy manner puts everything aright and is able to render the weightiest topics tasteful, pleasant, and understand-able. The women find the most appropriate expressions for the thoughts of the men, and I have often had the opportunity to observe the opposite reaction as well: that men seek to enliven the thoughts of the other sex by means of their own well-chosen words. For every rule the women have ten examples at their fingertips which either confirm or refute it; their powers of imagination, nurtured by true good taste, are able to breathe a living soul into the most abstract of concepts. We seek to know much, women to understand much; we prefer to think about an idea, women to talk about it and to bring it into circulation. As a rule they tend to become patrons of learning, rather than of the learned. Less vain in this regard than we are, they consider it less important to be learned than wise; they respect wit, and make use of it as one of those weapons which nature has given them for attaining respect and then maintaining it. They enliven their social circle through this faculty, and ward off every impertinence and act of rudeness; their agreeable dispo-sition tinges everything with good will. They grind the rusty edges off the pedant so that he becomes tolerable, and if Newton should avail himself of a female hand to have his pipe refilled for him, they know how to turn this inexcusable distraction to his advantage; when he writes on the Revelation of St. John, it is the protection which they bestow upon him which prevents him from doing himself any real harm.[113] What a great advantage for him! Nothing is so difficult to forgive as personal merit, and yet women seek to bring nothing under their protection so eagerly as this. A certain irritability and sensitivity is closely bound up with genius; the germ of our misfortune often lies hidden in our good fortune; and how diligently women must work here to guide our efforts along the best path and restore our equilibrium! Fame and solitude are seldom the best of friends; women seek their reconciliation and possess means for settling their differences. By adding a breath of fresh air, they drive off the smoke and haze which collects in the works of our writers—a haze which in time would come to becloud everything. They arrange tournaments of wit at their dinners, and then delight in leading the foray. They do not contradict the way my opponent does, but often only so that we might realize that it takes two people to make a conversation. When learned men skip over thoughts the way we sometimes skip over pages while reading, women fill in the gaps, they bring everything into context. Their encouragement supports the deserving writer when little boys ridicule his balding pate; their aegis covers him from the fiery darts of jealous mockery, so that the best authors rise with their assistance to the level of respect they truly deserve, and which they most certainly would not have attained without these guardian angels. Without the encouragement of women they would have begun to wither before their fullest flowering—their physical powers would have fallen prey to the rigors of the writer's life long before their time. All the honors which our academies have to bestow cannot hold in check the inflamed wit of a mocker within our own social circle—and do we wish to say that women, who shield us so magnificently from such people in smaller circles, would be unable to be as effective in larger ones, or even within the state as a whole?

An English traveler once made the observation that French women were most brilliant at times of festivity and enjoyment, English women in the shadow of domestic tranquility and the secluded life. Let us permit women entrance into the business of the state and we shall find that not only the English breakfast table and the French Assembly will be the recipient of that gentility and goodness which they so readily disseminate wherever they are, but the affairs of the state will benefit as well. They are the salt of the earth which gives flavor to everything;[114] they are the light of the earth which illuminates our way—whether as the moon of our domestic life or as the sun of our state. Not only the inborn morality of their beautiful souls;[115] not only the ability of their heart to search into the innermost regions of human feeling and sensitivity; not only their penetrating glance which, like the stone of David, kills Goliaths;[116] not only these, but such character traits, too, as we find lovable in children: their noble simplicity, the goodness of their heart, a soul beyond all human fears, their carefree trust in the Father in Heaven as well as in a just and amenable ordering of the world; these traits would transform the business of the state, and we would behold a new world wherein justice and mercy resided.

It would be an unforgivable piece of mockery if we were to attempt an answer to the question as to why the administrations of female rulers are better than those of men by saying that it is because the men really have hold of the tiller; for by using the same method of reasoning, must it not be the women who have the tiller firmly in hand when men are the rulers? Even this bit of mockery, as little as it is substantiated by historical evidence, only goes to prove that women know how to appreciate good advice—and is this not only rarely the case with men? Yet I have been called merely to reply to the objections raised against the fair sex—how is it that I have now begun to apologize for them?

"One of the main duties of the woman is to raise her children. But in order to be more certain of shining in society she neglects this duty, which then must be taken over by wet nurses and governesses. And if a mother with divided loyalties actually does undertake to bring up her daughter, is it a wonder if she at first displays her with pride, yet shortly thereafter begins to look upon her as a rival?"

My good fellow! Is the raising of children only the duty of the mother, or does this responsibility not also fall to the father? Do not the children belong to both of them? And if the father, ignoring this responsibility, does not curtail his social activities, why, then, should the mother? For what are children raised in the first place, if not to play a role in society—from its smallest to its largest circles? And is the mother to deny herself the privilege of becoming acquainted with each of these circles? Is she to raise her children for society without ever learning herself what society really is?

"The great weakness and effeminacy of our century is to be attributed to the women, and to the tone which they set for society."

One of the most unjust reproaches I can imagine is contained in that statement. Are we as weak and effeminate, I might ask, as those "cultivated" peoples which lock up their women? As a matter of fact, the opposite sex actually provides an opportunity for the youth of our own to practice gymnastics: if it were not for the women, the art of dancing— for which our young men even now hardly possess the strength— would have disappeared entirely. Weakness and effeminacy began to appear in our sex a long time ago, and doubtless it is for the most part the women we have to thank that these traits have not caused greater damage up to now. That vanity which at present cleaves to the female sex will disappear when we render accessible to them those things wherein they can show themselves to better advantage. Until now their complete concern has been the art of pleasing men, and a young girl has considered her quest to be ended when she has had the good fortune to enlist the services of a young man whom she deems worthy of her. Give women other things to occupy their time and they will abandon these trifles, these girlish playthings, and begin to consider external appearance far less important than a great many of our own Narcissuses, for example, who are able to see in the mirror which women hold up to them merely the reflection of their own dainty selves.

Are we not in fact satisfying our own vanity more than the demands of nature or the wishes of intelligent women by what we have granted to the opposite sex? It is not to be denied that even a virtuous woman finds it difficult to consider a certain kind of coquettishness a fault, and that, while remaining completely faithful to her husband, she can be so loving and ingratiating in her encounters with men of distinction that they cannot help showing her their heartfelt gratitude. In spite of this, it is never her intention that desires of any sort be awakened thereby, and if they should be, the thought of satisfying them is farthest from her mind. And any man who would think of capitalizing on these feelings is either naive, or a great boaster, or both. Within the current state of affairs this coquetry in everyday life serves to render social intercourse more pleasant—one courts, if I may express myself so, the soul and not the body, and there exist in fact what one could call "cicisbeos of the soul,"[117] the most innocent and harmless beings under the sun. A certain equality among men, reminiscent of the innocence of the primal world, hereby comes into being; and so long as women have no part in the affairs of state and we discuss no serious business with them or even in their presence, just so long will this coquetry continue to be a necessary evil—without which our social organizations would be the most insipid, unstimulating, and boring affairs on the face of the earth.

The reproach of my opponent that "women spend too much time in the adornment of their bodies" brings the war home to him, for is it not we who dispute the existence of a soul in women and who limit them to a body alone?[118] Is the human body really to be considered as mere ballast which the soul has taken on simply to facilitate its passage through the world? Or is it not rather a respectable part of the human being? Whoever once called the soul the guardian spirit of mankind— was he so far wrong? Let us refine women in the fire of service to the state the way we refine gold to give it a more brilliant color, and they will by no means neglect the soul for the body.

"Women have an uncontrollable propensity for splendor which causes them to lead their husbands to prodigality and eventual bankruptcy."

Are you really serious, my dear fellow, when you maintain that or are you merely joking? Ah, I see you are serious! Well, then, what was it that led them onto the pathway toward splendor? Was it not the rank and position of the man? Must they not often sacrifice some of their fondest wishes to this rank and position? Is not their natural inclination toward solitude and country life?

"Country life?"

Absolutely! At the hand of the woman Nature seems to be willing to let us become more intimate with her, even seeking out opportunities to have us taste of her milk and her honey and to behold the entire spectrum of her delights. Those noble effusions of tenderness who inhabit our cities and courts seek out the countryside only when they desire a stimulating change of pace, and how often must our land continue to be misused for the purpose of brightening the spirits of the city dweller and the courtier, spurring them on not to greater heights of virtue and propriety, but to further excesses of wantonness! They desire the cleaner air of the country merely to gain strength for some new manner of debauchery. Women also seek out the countryside, but do not wait to be banished or driven to it. They create, in fact, their own countryside, which they sow and cultivate by means of their salutary powers of imagination—and how effortlessly they become rich thereby. Have you never seen the unalloyed joy of a woman in her own world, her cheeks reddened by the glow of an inner peace and her whole being radiant with the salutary power of her imagination? But in the real world—how insignificant is her role! The women have drawn all the blanks in the lottery of life, we, all the winning numbers.

And if there do exist women who do not fit my description—were they not already seduced as fiancées to untimely expenditure through numerous presents from their betrothed, the cost of which far exceeded the latters' meager fortunes? Once such women have taken command, to relinquish their authority becomes both difficult and intolerable for them. And if we do succeed in bringing them down a peg or two afterwards, is it excusable for us to commit such deception with impunity? Is it even decent for us to play the *Pastor Fido* as the fiancé, just so we can become the *Orlando Furioso* as the husband?[119] Just so we can cast our wives from heaven into hell, from Eldorado into the public house, where we expect to compensate them with a bit of shadow-play on the walls?[120] This is the way traveling comedians were once adulated in Paris—yet in the end they were even denied the honor of a decent burial.

"Women become easily excited to anger; but anger accomplishes nothing, particularly in matters of state."

And whence this anger? Is it on account of their impotence; is it because we allow them no legitimate power of any sort? What is the good of entering into consultation when one lacks the power to carry out the decisions which one reaches, no matter how wise they may be? I would be the last to deny that when a person breaks into a rage he is incapable of perceiving the still, small voice of his own soul,[121] just as we are hardly able to hear each other's words during the raging of a tempest. But the other side of the coin—for how many people has the repression of their anger caused permanent injury to life and health? And if I grant, for the sake of argument, that women have not mastered the art of taming their anger externally and conjuring up a certain appearance of repose—are not those faults which we do not conceal our least significant ones, and generally but manifestations of a human weakness from which the saints themselves were not entirely free? Those faults are and will remain the most dangerous which come to us in sheep's clothing, but inwardly they are ravening wolves; ye shall know them by their fruits.[122] "Be ye angry, and sin not," are Paul's words to the Ephesians.[123] Is not anger a kind of weapon with which we can often render good without doing harm? How would women be able to accomplish the rearing of children without the help of this home remedy? Are there not individuals, uncircumcized in heart and ears,[124] to whom it must be pointed out forcefully and energetically just what is in the best interest of preserving peace and harmony? Does not anger often give all matters a certain verve and animation?

"Women are not called to the business of the state because they have neither the understanding nor the desire to cultivate friendships among themselves." (Let it not be overlooked that it is my opponent who is so friendly as to think of friendship, and not I.)

This is the most unjust criticism of all. I do not deny that without a certain bond of so-called friendship, actually better termed *openness*, and of good-natured acquaintanceship, matters of state would be considerably hindered in their fulfillment. The machinery of the state, unfortunately now all too artificial in its structure, would continue to resist simplification, for without such a bond no unity can be established within the state, and everything remains a jumble lacking order and purpose. But who of us is in a position to deny that women possess the powers of concentration, the ability to assess a matter coldly and rationally, the delicacy of feeling, the charming good will, and the willingness to sacrifice necessary for the task? Even now one finds friendships among them which are the equal of ours. It is only the prejudice of the men which has denied them the capacity for friendship. Are they not more tender, more faithful, more indomitable and incorruptible than many men, in whom envy and rivalries of every sort adulterate the true feelings of the heart and turn friendship into a grant of favors for favors returned, into an exchange of objects, rather than of hearts?[125] Damon and Pythias friendships[126] are rare, and all the less to be expected in the monotony of the woman's everyday life, in view of the trials and tribulations which are absolutely indispensable to secure forever the bond of such an attachment. And how different these Damon and Pythias friendships are from the equilibrium required for conducting matters of state, which necessarily has its basis in mutual agreement and understanding! Because of their sex, women now must at least seek to win hearts, if not to be utterly fascinating; and if they are not adored, they must at least be loved. But if we free them from this sensuality, their vanity, their curiosity, and their present inclination toward pleasure will be refined and ennobled. They will not cease to be women—how miserable we would be if that should ever happen!—they will merely cease to be the women they are now. The first step is up to us, and it depends solely on our contrite resolution to bring the revolution about. We must become different men, and everything, especially the women, will change with us. They will then measure us by the new standard which we have applied to them.

The moral status of women is very naturally based on their legal status. Since a young girl is not permitted to give loud and clear expression to her selection of a lifetime companion, she sees herself thus compelled to leave this business to her eyes, which, once accustomed to this method of invitation, can never give it up entirely. Moreover, society seems to have granted this fashion a certain degree of respectability, in that this game of glances is now played by all, and loses thereby the impropriety which would otherwise accompany it. Such glances, by means of which the women exert a kind of control which one might call "ophthalocracy," or "rule by the eyes," and which express a most pleasing sort of friendship, these glances have their own social contract,[127] as well as laws which are so precise and specific that one knows exactly when the allowed limit has been "overglanced." "Unto the pure all things are pure." [128] Who has not found in the delightful sport of secret love a most certain pathway to happiness? The pleasures of secrecy are heightened to the level of spiritual dignity, to an enchanting delicacy. Yet this happiness which the young women have caught sight of through their glances, this power of attraction through which they exert their effect on our young men by no means puts an end to their dilemma if they later have the honor to come under the domination of these men. They must then continually scheme to set limits to this domination through their many artifices, and are forced at times— and who can blame them?—to use their eyes to enter into alliances with trusted acquaintances for the purposes of concealment. And no matter how innocently such friendships begin, such relationships based on protection often carry within themselves the seeds of guilt and shame. From individuals of their own sex they can expect no help, and the friendships they form among themselves are of a unique and altogether different type. But are there not just as many true friends among women as there are friends among men? The enlargement and enhancement of women's capacity for friendship depends entirely on improving their status. How unfair it is of us to demand from women—whom we even deny the dignity of supposing them to be persons—more than it is possible for them to accomplish! One could almost say that the laws we have adopted to care for their possessions—in the same way that we care for the possessions of minors—completely neglect their person in favor of these objects. Women who are capable of becoming mothers are no longer children! The bitter, and not undeserved reproach leveled at our sex that "there are no longer any children nowadays"—is it not more closely tied to our cruelty in treating women as overgrown children than we realize?

"Fickleness is such a characteristic trait of the female mentality that women are incapable of serious reflection and the protracted and steadfast application of their powers of investigation to any object, regardless of what it might be."

The largest segment of the opposite sex—that comprised of the women in the middle class—has but a single means for keeping itself occupied, never deviates from this task, and only knows from hearsay what boredom is. This latter phenomenon arises from a kind of over-abundance of preoccupations, and belongs as a rule to the characteristics of the men, although women of the higher regions also take part in this vice, becoming weakened and even ill when the pleasure endures longer than they are accustomed to bearing it. Her Ladyship the Countess was bored at the theater today because of the fancy dress ball this evening, but that will become tiresome, too, if she can enlist no accomplices in her search for diversion—and even if she could, time, in its petty pace, would not be urged on thereby, for her *cicisbeo* and constant admirer, bored to tears himself, will be supping as a guest at the table of the Prince, and cannot just then play love games with her. There is but a single game in which the fair sex finds too little to do to keep it busy. Does this sex ever really and truly live? I think not—it merely plays at the game of life.

I find, in general, that fickleness is not more or less typical of their sex than it is of ours; in fact, it is rather a certain surmounting of the affairs of this world which characterizes them. They know how to cast themselves into the darkness of obscurity, and yet shine all the more brightly for it. Silent service is their contribution—and where is even a trace of fickleness here? In their choice of a life partner they act less precipitously and with a greater realization of the permanence of the union than we do—the twenty exemplary old maids for every old bachelor attest to this fact.

"The liveliness of feminine emotions and of the feminine imagination, as well as the women's all-too-sensitive nervous system is the cause of their fickleness and the merely transitory enthusiasm they show for intellectual matters; moreover, they seldom exhibit true interest in the great questions of human knowledge and understanding."

But in how many of our own sex is such perseverance to be found? Who can maintain an enthusiasm for a scholarly or scientific subject equal to our very first burst of zeal, and then remain faithful to that subject until death? Do not almost all of us have, in addition to our own vocation, an avocation which we call our recreation, but which really is more important to us than the former? Our true devotion is reserved for this avocation, and through the blessing of God we are often able to rise farther and faster in it than in our chosen profession. Have not kings milked cows, mended fishing nets, turned buttons, painted, and the like? Leibniz was as little a professor of philosophy as Wieland a professor of poetry;[129] and just what *are* these "great questions of human knowledge and understanding" for which nobody from the opposite sex has exhibited true interest? The patience and perseverance of women is in fact greatly to be admired, and do they not give daily testimony to this by not shattering those molds into which force and chicanery have poured them? By raising children and guiding them onto the paths of righteousness, often only to see them spoiled by the blind love, or just as often the blind harshness of their fathers? By dealing with their husbands (all-too-frequently only overgrown children themselves) as gently as they would deal with any evil which could not be avoided, and by lifting them up, carrying, and guiding them in order to support them at least passably? And is it really necessary for everything to be forged in the heat of the fire? For every fantasy to be painted in flames? For everything we say and think to shoot like an everlasting firework across the sky? The world knows of other beneficial elements besides fire. Unbridled imagery, sparkling aphorisms, sentences of exquisite form drawn from the depths of human wisdom— may they never cease to be of infinite value to us. Yet there are also thoughts whose value lies in their gentleness and quietness, thoughts whose justification is their incitement to human activity.

And if the intellectual endeavors of women are attended by a certain timorousness—is it any wonder, when their only access to the republic of letters is by stealth? By their very nature they are more impertinent than we; the feeling of powerlessness to act toward and address others in conformity with their rank and privilege is a feeling which is alien to them. Their gift of light and unconstrained conversation will never allow their utterances to be disfigured with hackneyed phrases and parenthetical insertions, which are hardly more pleasing aesthetically than flies which have fallen into one of our favorite dishes. To bestrew their conversation with such idle phrases is but a waste of time for them; to attempt to charm by elegant and affected speech is tantamount to regarding pleasure as the basis for man's existence.

Observe rulers and princes—how nervous and fainthearted they are! Court ceremony seems to have been invented solely to help them out of their timidity. Yet on the other hand, there also exists a noble and exalted freedom which is the result of a clear conscience—just as all our emotions are affected by this latter faculty—and this freedom is peculiar to the opposite sex. Why, then, should women authors act so timorous and embarrassed, when language open to the spontaneous bursting forth of emotion possesses a strength and power against which nothing can prevail—except perhaps the arrogance of our criticism, which seeks to prevent the women from rising in every way possible? Women know how to elevate perceptions to the level of observations; and if we men are capable of raising propositions to the level of principles and slaying our thousands with them, then women would slay their ten thousands[130] with their wit if the men did not continually seek to cripple it with their profundity—a quality which, in the final analysis, is of little or no importance. Women are endowed with the knack for bringing all their mental faculties into play in their witticisms—and do they not succeed remarkably in catching the idea of the matter thereby? Are they not able to vary, in an exquisitely beautiful way, the eternal monotony to which they have been condemned, and to reveal a high degree of attentiveness and sagacity? But how can they withstand the deluge of technical terms with which we assail them? How withstand the ponderous erudition with which we chide them and drive them out of the temple of learning, whose inner sanctuary is really so very simple and unpretentious? Why do we say they lack intensity and depth in their thought, or creativity and great enthusiasm for learning, when they give us countless unsought and unpretentious demonstrations of these every day? Subtle and original qualities drawn from nature are more frequently encountered in this sex; what their descriptions and characterizations lack in sharpness of outline (although these are rarely inaccurate), they replace by their lively coloring and shading. Just as they know how to adorn their bodies, so they also adorn their thoughts. The suitability of their choice of words and the magnificent simplicity of their application endow their style with unexcelled clarity.

An author creates the greatest memorial to his own work when his characters remind us of ourselves; when his writing goes straight to our hearts; when we feel that little or nothing would be lacking if we were to have written the work ourselves; when we imagine that we his readers would have been fully capable of dictating the work through the pen of the author, or that he had seen it in our hearts and made it known to us—such a reflection of ourselves is both profitable and enlightening! But we men let ourselves be tormented by ideas, as Socrates was by his daemon;[131] like Plato, we consign ourselves to a republic governed by ideas. And just as he who continually casts an unsympathetic eye upon a single point finally sees only what he wants to see, so with the eye of our soul we begin to take windmills for giants, village inns for castles, ponds for great oceans, and an Abderite farce for a well-thought-out financial operation.[132] As if that were not enough, we all too often allow our very words to play the master over us as well. We misappropriate their meanings or set arbitrary limits to them, and then fall victim to our own self-imposed limits when we wish our words to accompany us in our flights of speculation, or when, in striving for the epigrammatic and pithy, we demand that they say more than they do. We deliver our manuscripts to the publisher with the express intention of reaching an educated audience, or of having our work read aloud before privileged or unprivileged circles.[133] But in spite of the fact that it may make a better impression if the content is, or at least appears to be, more instructive than some hastily sketched piece by a woman, the latter's work will doubtless show more individuality and reveal a kind of intuition which we, in spite of, and perhaps even because of, our stupendous learning are unable to lend any of our works to the same degree. The work of women is lighter and more superficial, but therefore often all the more to the point, penetrating, and accurate. Women do not love long words, for in them a main syllable subordinates the others to itself and gains dominance over these. They do not prefer long sentences and clauses, for they are not well enough acquainted with the ancients, whom they find difficult to read and comprehend. Women seldom permit an expression of truly luxuriant growth to spring up, and if one should happen to do so, then it is always a wildflower which does not exceed the bounds of modesty. With us it is reflection, with women sentiment which has the upper hand. I use the term *upper hand* because reflection, too, gives a helping hand to feminine sentiment; and if in their essays and treatises the irregularities are not always all smoothed out, yet these retain more that is characteristic, more that is original than our own.

Let us but raise their sights beyond the kitchen and the knitting needle; let us give them training and guidance and they will soon surpass us in acumen and depth of thought, while their common sense will prevent them from losing themselves in the clouds. Alas, who of us, when reference is made to the privileges claimed by our sex, can keep from calling out with the prophet Daniel, "Behold, these are your idols!" [134]

"Women cannot stand to be left alone."

Not alone? My dear fellow, if one were ever to paint a portrait of loneliness, a woman would have to sit for it; otherwise we would never capture a true likeness.

"Or at least they cannot ponder the solution to a problem all by themselves."

And yet at every opportunity men request their counsel—and how good it is for them, the government, and the state itself, when men do this! O, how gladly men cast the burdens from their hearts onto their women by entrusting them with their secrets! And how much, how very much women must bear! Yet for their own part there is hardly a one of them who does not die possessing something known only to her and to God, something which no father confessor will ever hear, and with which she approaches time and eternity unafraid. Our own secrets often vanish like ghosts in the night; theirs are etched into heart and soul. If our own thoughts often get away from us, and then resist every—often repugnant—effort to call them back again, women, on the other hand, do not allow their thoughts such exuberance. "What I meant to say . . . " is something one will seldom, if ever, hear from women. Their memory is more trustworthy than ours, and it would be hard for one of them to be as absentminded as Terrasson, losing their memory to the extent that he once did. Women consider absentmindedness to be an affectation, and cannot keep from laughing when it is told of Terrasson that shortly before his departure from the marketplace of ideas he assigned everything he possessed, including his mental faculties, to his administrator Luquet, so that when his father confessor inquired at his last confession concerning any sins which might still remain on his conscience, he was forced to reply: "You had better ask Luquet."

"Women are not independent and cannot stand on their own two feet," you say?

This is a criticism which, no matter how well-glued it might appear, simply will not hold up under the strain. When we men are hovering between fear and hope[135] they immediately come to a decision and show themselves to be resolute in body and soul. It is the birth of their children which makes them so bold; in matters less important than this they do not consider it worthwhile to lay so great a claim to decisiveness, and are content to let matters take their course. Whatever we accomplish redounds to the credit of our teachers; what they do reflects credit on them alone.

In political matters they will not, however, side with any particular party, but cast their vote for what they think is best—while we spend our time filling rooms with hot air. The sheer complexity of our political machinery prevents us from accomplishing anything, the unending flow of words prevents us from doing anything, and the everlasting tallying of votes prevents us from ever deciding anything. Who of us has not at some time become annoyed by the incessant tuning of the instruments before the symphony ever began?[136]

"Why should we awaken the Jesuit order from the dead by giving privileges to secret Jesuits, to Jesuits 'en tapinois' (the fair sex)?"

Why? Because the secret ones do more damage than the public ones (that is, if they keep nothing secret themselves); because the public ones then cease to be Jesuits; and because hidden diseases are the most dangerous. How else is the fair sex ever going to attain the status of an order?

"Mistresses of good breeding have been the cause of far less evil than those of humble origins—for example, than a Pompadour or a du Barry." [137]

Correct! Thus we should take women as wives, not as mistresses.

"No, thus we should let women remain in their obscurity!"

Absolutely right, if they are to become mistresses. But if they are to follow their divine calling and be wives, then we should not seek to elevate them by means of baubles and trinkets, but with legitimacy. Are the Turkish pashas and viziers, the beys of Egypt the more humane for having learned to know the poverty of the people at first hand during their early years?

"What kind of refutations are those?"

Are your criticisms any better?

"Anything can be defended."

And anything criticized.

"Well, I would not want to be a woman for anything in the world."

Nor would I.

"Which of us, then, is right?"

Whoever was speaking the truth.

"And who was speaking the truth? Was it not the one who was right?"

Whoever espoused the cause of the oppressed and carried the banner of humanity.

"Of humanity?"

Are not women human beings as well?

"Of the oppressed?"

Are we not their tyrants?

"Well, then, long live the knights errant!"

May they have long lives and happy countenances, if their errantry is directed toward the good of mankind.

"And if they have no Dulcineas . . ."[138]

They have none other than sincerity of intention, the Dulcinea of our philosophers.

"This book was not written on account of a woman, by any chance?"

Not on account of a woman, but of women. None of them knows I have written it, and, if God so wills it, none of them will ever know.

"And why did you not seek out the strait and narrow path where excesses and deficiencies are avoided, and which wends its way carefully between both?"

Because there are few who tread this path.

"But that is better than many!"

Not always, when we are talking about the virtues and vices of society as a whole.

"And what about the middle road between skepticism and naiveté?"

A wretched half-breed of a thing. Either this way or that, is my motto, and not: this way and perhaps that, or: both this way and that. Yes or No—whatever lies astride these two is rooted in evil.

"And the laws—will this book take them on as well?"

The least of my concerns! Let the laws take each other on! Let the dead bury their dead.[139] And indeed, the laws themselves sometimes act as if there existed forces within humanity which were not a part of it.

"What is that supposed to mean?"

There exist laws which suppress the power of the individual in order that the total power of humanity will be the greater. And yet it is obvious that the total power will be greater only if the sum of the powers of the individuals is greater. Our state political economists are making a grave miscalculation when they fail to include the women in their tabulations.

"But when they take into consideration the purpose of bourgeois society . . ."

Ah, then the good gentlemen are even farther off in their calculations. Is there any other purpose than that of protecting individual liberty and preventing the encroachment by any person on the freedom of another?

"And that applies to the two sexes as well?"

Are the women not moral beings, just as we are?

"And justice?"

It is all on my side. That which has value in one's own country is lawful and proper. Whatever holds good in the world at large is truly just. That is just which the greatest number of people take to be lawful and proper.

"And whoever acts in a way which the greatest number of people take to be lawful and proper, is just. A just author, for example, is one who writes in a way which . . ."

Correct!

"What if we were to tally our votes now?"

I would win, providing only those voted who were themselves above the reproach: "Understandest thou what thou sayest? Knowest thou what thou doest?" [140]

"I grant you your argument for improving the status of women—but why start with the state?"

Because we do not need to grasp at twigs and even leaves when the trunk is so close at hand.

"And the tone of this book . . . ?"

It has been determined by the material with which I have had to work, by the slivers and shavings which have fallen from my bench.

At this point my readers of both sexes who have grown weary of the above rather lengthy series of arguments and counter-arguments may choose to catch their breath and refresh themselves by contemplating the simplicity and straightforwardness of such a literary technique—or perhaps they may not. Whatever suits their fancy . . .

VI / The Application of the Ideas Proposed

$\int$F IT IS INDEED TRUE that the entire operation of a successful financial system or a wise governmental administration depends upon the theory and application of pressure,[1] then we men, at least, have not yet chosen the proper method of applying such pressure, for in truth, through the manner in which we treat the opposite sex we lose even more than it does. It is said that the same holds true if rulers attempt to extract the virtues of industriousness and obedience from their subjects by the application of the seven plagues multiplied seven-fold.[2] Pressure and friction do bring about supernatural effects in the case of magnetism,[3] it is true, nevertheless, the pressures exerted in a political system have not yet been able to excite that talent for divination which can quench thirst without water and stay hunger without food. It is a wretched state of affairs when we have no other law than the will of our sovereign; and whenever the ever changing moods of the despot, his attacks of indigestion, choler, and flatulence take the place of Numa and Solon[4] in his reign—who would care to be a subject to such government as this? It is already insufferable to be subject even to the best of all men if he wishes to rule paternally over a people which has long since ceased to speak, understand, and think like children. But behold! This is precisely the wretched state of affairs in which the opposite sex finds itself entangled. The times have passed in which continual feuding kept everything in a state of fear and unrest; where robbery was thought heroic and ruffians were seated at places of honor. Yet, which is worse—to be certain of one's fate, or to suffer injustice under the protection of the law? How can we rob an entire sex of its rights and privileges under the sanctimonious pretext of serving the best interests of all? How can we often act as if we were at the beck and call of our own female slaves, and even more often actually pay heed to their hints and suggestions, all the while continuing to tyrannize them in every other way? Does not love almost cease to exist altogether and turn into the mere lust for power, revealing this abominable desecration of a holy institution, through jealousy, at a very early stage, even at the first blushes of an incipient inclination? The bashful youth fondly embraces his beloved when they are together, and pines for her when they are apart, only to lay down the law callously and haughtily when, shortly thereafter, he has become her husband. Vanity and fear of shame are generally the basis for any mettle which the men possess; women have theirs by virtue of their temperament. If the true state of the world is ever to become apparent, it will have to happen in the theater, for in the real world we only have time for farces. Where can one find Abderite trials to equal those offered up daily by the present relationship between men and women?[5] If an intelligent being from some other planet had the desire and the time to undertake a tour of this great ball of clay of ours, and if he were thereby to ponder in his heart the relationship which exists between the sexes, would not the travel journal of this intelligent being upon his return to his home planet constitute one of the severest condemnations of our civilization possible?

A mere code of laws is inferior to universal reason. Further, a code of laws does not provide a procedural technique in the determination of universal reason, for the former can neither serve as its own proof, nor can one derive from it any standard by which it may itself be evaluated. And how long will we men continue to resist reason? Human beings are fond of laying the blame on others, and when they find none who willingly offer their backs for such burdens, then it is nature herself who must submit to the denunciation.

Thus it follows that our own most worthy sex has not been lacking in excuses which serve to place the blame for things entirely on the fair sex. It is disgraceful enough that we are unjust, but to remove the guilt of our unjustness from ourselves and assign it to the opposite sex is worse yet! "The woman whom thou gavest to be with me," said Adam of old, "beguiled me"[6] —and such faithful Adamites have we remained even until today that we never fail to disavow in the best legal fashion the guilt implied in the second-class citizenship which we assign to the opposite sex! The poor creatures! If they wished to enter into formal negotiations with us they would not even be granted a hearing; how then can they ever hope to prompt us to take more serious steps on their behalf? They have no Leonidas,[7] no Franklin, no Washington; they are not Spartans, not Swiss, not American colonists. But can they not have all this, be all this? Marie Antoinette and Lafayette are two equally great figures who will both shine in the history of the French Revolution.[8] For centuries before this the character of Europe had not changed—despotism and slavery, superstition and barbarism ruled supreme. And why should we not now be able to raise women, too, to that rank which is due them as human beings after an equally long period of oppression? A great many of them seem to have grown weary of the chains which the law depicts to them in such glowing terms, and to be harboring an irresistible urge to smash them, rather than to continue playing with them as a child plays with its rattle.

Furthermore, it shows what little confidence we place in them when we sugarcoat everything that is to be taught to women and give it to them in easily handled knitting-basket size, as if they were too weak and frail to hold anything larger than a duodecimo volume! The question: "Understandest thou what thou readest?"[9] would apply sooner, I should think, to all our dandified fops in duodecimo format than to a refined and high-minded woman. . . .

And even if the intellectual labors of women, as soon as they begin to exceed the bounds of everyday living, are for the present no more than bas-reliefs, they will yet one day be capable of more than this—for it is we who keep their intellect on a leash, so that we may prevent them from walking alone. An eminent pedagogue in ——— once had gingerbread baked in the shapes of the letters of the alphabet so that his pupils might more easily get their ABC's into their heads. Alas, the little dears got the gingerbread letters no farther than their stomachs before they all became quite ill. This gingerbread method is the usual error which we make in the education of the opposite sex. We wish neither its intellect nor its will to come to maturity. Women are as yet like biscuit ware;[10] but then are we completely baked ourselves? And if so, what does it mean to be compared to porcelain anyway? Böttcher[11] tried to make gold and succeeded only in inventing porcelain. What is man?[12] "Midway from nothing to the deity," says Young; and our pious Haller, wishing to refrain from taking the name of God in vain, calls him a "wretched intermediate stage between the angels and the beasts of the field"—may God have mercy on our souls![13] Friederika Baldinger's autobiography, prefaced by Sophie von Laroche, assures us that "as a woman I was passable; how small I would have been as a man!"[14] Begging the lady's pardon, but must not also each and every man say just the opposite of himself in return—as long as *to be a man* does not mean more than *to be a human being*? And by the same token, does not the modesty of Friederika Baldinger imply a criticism of our own sex in reference to our tendency toward self-exaltation?

Our own Herschel, who because of his sister Caroline, as well as in connection with astronomy, has earned mention more than once before in this treatise, maintains that the central forces[15] function not only to sustain the universe, but that they exert a formative and restorative influence as well. Moreover, he is of the opinion that other types of attractive and repellent forces could also be at work in the structure of the universe. Could not then results be achieved beyond our wildest dreams if there existed in the human realm as well such central forces which attracted and repelled in the same manner?[16] If Herschel is able with his telescope to reduce to single stars what the naked eye sees as shapeless nebulae, how easily the Flamsteeds and Mayers[17] would be able to expand their catalogue of stars on the female, or better yet, the human horizon if both sexes were of one heart and one soul!

Do I go too far in asserting that the oppression of women is the cause of all the rest of the oppression in the world? Truly, personal valor and gallantry do not always play a role in fate's selection of our rulers. It is through magnanimity, and not cunning, that one must seek to overcome one's foes; and it is now, and always has been, unfair to exploit others' lack of experience. The preservation of the rights of even a single citizen—is it not more important than the defeat of a hundred enemies? What is right in the opinion of a majority of mankind is, translated into plain language, as it must be—right in a higher sense of the word. This higher, or *true*, right has its basis in the very nature of things and has been purified of the dross of capriciousness and Turkish despotism. Do we then want to believe (and in a certain sense one must *want* to believe in order to believe) that, in accordance with the above-mentioned principle of the majority the millennia-old slavery of women has its basis in such a true right or in justice? I, personally, do not want to believe this. Not everything which we suffer in silence redounds to the credit of our inward man.[18] Look around you, and you will find that most of the injustice in the world has its basis in the attempt to act in a manner that mere popular opinion considers to be right.

Who, without doing violence to the principles of logic, could possibly maintain that even after women have attained a higher level of culture and moral integrity, they must nevertheless be maintained at a certain fixed level in society, and that between now and the Day of Judgment because of their inborn destiny, they could come only so far and no farther as members of society and as women? Our own prospects for development are to know no limits, while their path is blocked by barriers? Great Goodness! I am certainly not questioning here the particular roles assigned to women by society on the basis of their sex alone—these are as immutable as those of the men. But that the woman's intellect and will should stagnate while the man's press ever onward—such a misfortune would make a mockery of the Enlightenment!

Perhaps it might be possible to liken men to food and women to drink—for only food and drink in conjunction hold body and soul together. The awareness of life's necessities is what brings about progress in the human race, and the Creator seems to have granted us the power to invent such necessities in order that we might learn to satisfy them by the sweat of our brow.[19] Self-esteem, an inclination to a state of well-being, an aversion to pain are also motivating forces which bring man farther and farther along in his development; and the opposite sex is just as aware of these forces as we, if not more so. Was it perhaps the arrangement between the sexes which necessity and these motivating forces brought about in an attempt to urge humanity more rapidly to its goal by means of collective effort—was it this arrangement permitting woman's entry into society which was ultimately responsible for her present status? Not in the least! It was Eve herself who was responsible for drawing up the first contract regarding woman's place in society; could she possibly ever have imagined that also here the first were soon to become the last?[20] Did we ascribe to the opposite sex with their full knowledge and consent the motto which stands written on the gates of hell, namely: "Abandon all hope, ye who enter here";[21] or is it not sooner the case that the woman's place in society is used to give sanction to her position in nature? Should not in the former, as well as in the latter, all men be equal? Nations and peoples are as equal to each other as individual men, and the sexes as equal as peoples. Was it not through the oppression of the weak that the internal decay of every fallen state first began, a decay which then gradually had as its result oppression and destruction from without? What really matters to us in our dealings with others—a playful wit, waggish utterances, and reckless flights of fancy, or truth and right? How can we make any claim to justice in society, when we show none? Can we men, who so ignobly have set ourselves up as masters of the female sex, deny that from the beginning we have never fully understood this authority? And from the looks of things today, that we have made no advances in this particular science at all since then? Can we conceal it from our consciences that we are the author and cause of every female fault, and that most of the good which we have in us we owe to the opposite sex?

Fainthearted men will, to be sure, condemn me severely for supposedly stimulating the vanity of women and providing further nourishment to the overblown ideas which they already possess concerning their own worth. Nonetheless, good people, by means of your alarmist fears that I might have advanced too far in my determination of a woman's destiny you prove that you yourselves are weak instead of strong, and that through this weakness you have completely reversed what you suppose to be the natural order of things. And furthermore, you show that you lack the intellectual strength and capacity which you would deny to the opposite sex because of your envy. In fact, you should actually thank nature for using women to encourage and inspire you to continue your development, rather than to seek fig leaves to cover your proud indolence. As soon as women are considered to be human beings and given credit for possessing the power of reason, one can no longer place limitations on their intellectual faculties. Least of all are *we* in a position to pass judgment on their psyche, since we are hardly impartial in the matter, and since we have learned to look out for our own interests and to be shield bearers of authority so much better than the opposite sex, which has remained much more faithful to nature. Where inner strength is not lacking, opportunity alone is needed to give it expression, and only when mankind prohibits the use of reason will it ever come to a disavowal of that state of affairs in which not all persons possessing human reason are equal as human beings. Only when excessive pride overly refines and subtilizes the calling of the human race do we turn away from the true development of our natural talents, and only then do they turn away from us as well. How unfortunate this can be!

We have learned from experience what influence education, climate, and other external circumstances have on people (men not excluded). The wine-grower remains, even in fertile lands, the symbol of indolence and the dissipated moral character which is its result. Women only know how to use the weapons which nature has given them; we season our legal treaties with learned arguments, strike temporary bargains, and know how to disguise our weaknesses so that they are no longer evident. And yet it is precisely this which makes us maintain rashly that mere curiosity, not a thirst for knowledge; mere encouragement by others, not their own free will; mere vanity caused them to dabble here and there in intellectual pursuits—and at that with rather little success and without distinguishing themselves particularly thereby.

But aside from the fact that the purity of the man's intellect or his intentions scarcely deserves to be praised and that selfishness, along with its entire brood of vanity, pride, avarice, and adulation continue to plague the male sex severely; aside from the fact that even the most learned man, if he were ever to be brief about it, would need but a scant three weeks to confess all that he actually *knows*, or even what he truly *believes*, showing that his knowledge and prophecy are still imperfect at best; aside from the fact that there is a difference between the gingerbread of theory and the bitter wine of experience, in the final analysis all intellectual pursuit and all scholarly activity (if it is not merely intended to serve as space filler or to enable us to pass time more pleasantly) has for its goal the moral improvement of mankind. And has it accomplished this? If so, then I withdraw shamefaced, retract everything in my treatise that smacks of vindication, and rest my case with the humble request to grant the opposite sex time and space for moral repentance through an improvement in its status, and to permit it obligations and responsibilities under the laws of the state—those full and clearly defined obligations and responsibilities which ought to be the right of every citizen or member of a state.

And now the conclusion of my treatise? Machiavelli wrote *The Prince* in order to bring the subject of a republic of despots up for consideration—and I wanted no more than this. If I have juxtaposed ideas which are usually thought to be unrelated, then grant me this, if you would, and let each follow his own path—for if every book sang the same tune, what would happen to all the readers? Not to mention doers of the word![22] A mere treatise can never ignite a mighty, all-consuming fire, and if it is said that Rousseau, Voltaire, and Montesquieu brought about the French Revolution, then we are forgetting all about North America. It is one of the signs of the present age when rulers prove to be better acquainted with their books than their subjects, and when people are too fond of the external form of a system to exchange it for what is basic and consistent in their philosophy of life.

Sympathetic regard for those who are weaker bears the stamp of the divine; and if committees for the supervision of state officials have proved to be an excellent arrangement for a ruler and his people, and one that rewards their patience,[23] then why do we not wish to entrust the supervision of the entire human race to the female sex—to those who have never been accustomed to basing their actions on what is imaginary, rather than what is real, even if we do try most despicably to accustom them to reading nothing but novels, in order that they may be kept from ever coming to know the real world thereby. Women have more intellect than they have learning; men more learning than a coherent philosophy of life, and our own sex forgets all too easily that it must first seek virtue and integrity if all else is to come its way.

It was not my intention to write a grammar in which a whole list of exceptions follows the rule. Training in drawing should precede practice in penmanship, and if the theory of a number of experienced pedagogues has any merit, history should be taught backwards. I shall consider myself sufficiently rewarded if people applaud my endeavors as a whole, even though further elaboration may rightly prove necessary. A book which stimulates thought is often better than one which exhausts the subject and, in doing so, treats its readers as children. Hints and suggestions often bear more fruit than long sermons; and when a writer is unfaithful to that great office which nature has entrusted to him, namely, the protection of man from public injustices, then he deserves to be the object of those injustices himself.

In times gone by the German woman has always counted for more than the women of other countries, and I am certainly not outside the bounds of truth if I assert that at the present time as well, German women, just as they are now, would be more receptive to, and fit for, an improvement in their status than all others, whatever their land and tongue, and whatever advantages they justly or unjustly proclaim over the women of Germany. We awaken sleepwalkers by calling them by name; and should not our honorable German gentlemen sober up from the cooling draught which this treatise serves up to them?

There are writers who, when they do not trust themselves to succeed with their own sex, preface their writings with the white lie that they composed them for the welfare and edification of the opposite sex. Many a literary pirate, as well, believes himself to be acting honorably when he breaks the freshly baked bread of another without even adding butter and milk to it to give it a different appearance, and does this at the expense of the opposite sex—as if the gentleman earned his bread in the service of that sex, or the latter were no longer capable of eating it except when broken into crumbs!

"But why all these proposals for consideration and plans for improvement? For even if it is true that they make no claim to the preemption of others, and although they are content to serve more as modest hints than as warning markers or danger signs, they are nonetheless not able to promise concrete results, since we still do not know whether, and to what extent, they will be able to pass the crucial test of practical application."

Absolutely right! But then why all the pulpits and rostrums? Has not mankind been filled with liars, ingrates, robbers, misers, and jealous people from time immemorial? Birds of prey, it is true, have always eaten the more modest of their fellow birds as soon as they were able to gain mastery over them; human beings are capable of understanding that to be better *is* better, and that they in fact can become better—are they ever and always to remain birds of prey? I am comforted by the belief in what I consider to be the intention of God the Father for the human race, as well as in the restless driving spirit of the race itself, once it has been awakened and set into motion. The beneficial air of the mountains is without doubt the cause of the homesickness of the Swiss in far-off lands; but what is there that could persuade the opposite sex to remain in its present place? It will desire to leave as soon as we decide that we want it to.

It is with reluctance that I must now address myself to a group of people to whom I never would have given a second thought, had not the sight of some quite fresh tracks just startled me a bit. That I am not referring here to literary critics should be quite obvious. There exist among this group many stouthearted fellows who mean no harm, even though they have lately begun to adopt a peremptory tone of voice which was hitherto rather unusual. Let them go right on being dogmatic and dictatorial—everyone seems to be that way these days! I really have nothing against these good gentlemen, who hang on our books like beneficent leeches in order to suck the bad blood from them; rather it is my heartfelt wish that this bloodthirstiness will redound to each according to his rank and merit. But when mere mosquitoes pursue me just for the sake of a few drops of blood in an effort to make me divulge my name (truly but a few drops of blood), then I would ask these anecdote-suckers to consider that a book does not become a hair's breadth or length better just because we know that this person or the other wrote it. In the world of writers there is no hereditary nobility; and why do we wish to turn the republic of letters into a monarchical, if not indeed a despotic, state? Why not allow each individual as much freedom as is humanly and politically possible? Otherwise we will have "geniuses" without genius—men without the talent and power of expression characteristic of genius who, painfully aware of their intellectual shortcomings, snatch at anecdotes in order among truly learned people to play the scholar they are not, and, barring another Miracle of Pentecost,[24] never will be!

Who would deny that those who are scholars by profession, for example Kant or Heyne,[25] have brought about great progress in the various branches of knowledge? Surely that master of philosophical knowledge Kant would not be delivering such powerful works at his patriarchal age if he had not become thoroughly familiar with his material when his life was in its prime, and if he had not been accustomed to thinking out his ideas first in his teaching. His lectures were the touchstone for his philosophical principles. But a businessman could hardly give his book such care and attention. If the *Critique of Pure Reason* comes into the world under the name of Immanuel Kant, who can complain? But if a businessman is its author, what difficulties face him! The city president envies him if he is also a counselor; and if he is himself president, his ministers are green with envy. Called to the common life, he must adjust himself to its demands and move with the times—and for the businessman they are only too often hard times. Criticism does little harm to the professional scholar; an imprecise intellect, on the other hand, can be the ruin of the businessman who writes, in that witless antagonists will take up every trite and hackneyed idea with pleasure and sport with them purely with the intention of provoking the good man. The scholar by profession passes on the ball thrown to him by the unfriendly critic; the businessman-turned-author can only throw it back. His writing is held accountable for every misfortune in his business career; the complaints of every deceitful party are certain of a hearing, simply because this Decernent, Instruent, Referent, or whatever else these "enten" [26] call themselves, is an author and did not take the time to please everybody.

And the reverse side of the coin? Would not many a writer use his reputation in the scholarly world as a scarecrow in order to elevate himself to the status of a touch-me-not? [27] Would not his supervisors bestow on his literary endeavors what amounted to a pension at the cost of his official position, and burden others with those affairs which should be his responsibility? A vocation is a many-faceted thing. A man who among authors is still a president, and among presidents is merely an author deserves the chastisement of a Johnson, [28] whereas an author who reveals as little of his political associations to the scholarly world as he does of his scholarly associations to the political sphere deserves, it seems, to be doubly honored, in that he neither has need of a foil nor tries to coax his way from the one realm into the other by flattery, but is everywhere and always his own man. The autobiography of a man of this sort can, after he has retired from political or even natural life, truly serve as an excellent textbook for our own life here on earth.

Frederick the Great, himself so sorely plagued by poesy that this daemon would not desist from courting him even in the heat of battle, once said to one of his civil servants, whose memory I celebrate today on the anniversary of his death: "I will make you a ———; but you simply must stop this writing—such things are distracting, and you must let nothing distract you in the performance of your duty, do you hear?"

Yes, indeed, and he that hath ears to hear, let him hear.[29] If such are the sentiments of a royal author (in the manner of the royal prophet David), how much is to be feared from princes to whom, aside from the aptitude for ruling, no others have been granted! And how much more even from ministerial authors who, too dull to possess the slightest critical insight themselves, jealously seek to win their spurs by attacking writers far superior to them in intellect and talent? Whether one or none of the preceding cases applies to me is not the issue; no one would deny that they are drawn from life. And may I just add that literary critics, like all other judges, ought not to be respecters of persons, and that it is contrary to a critic's duty to attempt to make the name of the author the object of his examination?

How much would I give to have been spared this conclusion to my treatise! The fact is, I really do not know how best to make it conform with the spirit of the work, except to note that this epilogue was not directed at those dear and noble souls who would very much like to know my name for the simple purpose of binding themselves closer to a writer with whom they feel themselves so much in accord. May God in His inscrutable wisdom publicly forgive these dear and noble souls even for whatever they might have done to me in secret! May the cares and passions of life be made easier for them at the hands of well-meaning women! May everything on earth be easy for them, in life as well as in death!

Notes to the
Translation

CHAPTER I

1. This is a modification of the expression "Knight of the woeful countenance" ("El cabellero de la triste figura") applied by Sancho Panza to Don Quixote in Cervantes' novel of that name.

2. According to legend, Socrates, although his body was handsome and powerfully built, possessed a homely face.

3. The widow of the French burlesque poet and dramatist Paul Scarron (1610–1660) later became Madame de Maintenon, the second wife of Louis XIV, hence the comic allusion.

4. Hippel here refers to the ancient Greek fable concerning Democritus, who was perpetually laughing over the state of mankind, and Heraclitus, who continually cried over the same condition.

5. Hippel apparently alludes to Cervantes' Don Quixote, and the propensity of the hero to see an "enchanted castle" in every inn he encounters along the way.

6. According to Herodotus, Xerxes, upon surveying the magnitude of his army at Abydos, first congratulated himself on his good fortune, then wept out of pity when he thought of the shortness of man's life and considered that of all his army not one would be alive when a hundred years had gone by.

7. Cf. Exod. III:8 and XVI:3.

8. The Fates or Parcae.

9. In Book V of The Republic, Plato had considered the position of women and children in the ideal state, concluding that "no practice or calling in the life of the [state] belongs to woman as woman, or to man as man, but the various natures are dispersed among both sexes alike; by nature the woman has a share in all practices, and so has man, but in all, woman is rather weaker than man" (trans. W. H. D. Rouse). Hippel here pays humble tribute to an early expression of his own thesis, although he will later question its final conclusion.

10. Hippel alludes ironically to the German proverb: "Ein gutes Gewissen ist ein sanftes Ruhekissen" ("A clear conscience is a soft pillow").

11. René Nicolas Charles Augustin de Maupou (1714–1792) was Chancellor of France from 1768 to 1774. He upheld the King in his plan to override the parliament of Paris, and sided with Madame du Barry against the Duke of Choiseul. After the exile of the Duke he,

196

the Duke of Aiguillon, and the Comptroller General Abbé Terray formed in 1770 a triumvirate known as the "Maupou Parliament," which in time became unpopular because of its excesses.

12. Hippel refers to the lamppost as a symbol for intellectual enlightenment and, ironically, for "equality" among men as well, in the sense that the phrase "les aristocrates à la lanterne!" became one of the rallying cries of the French Revolution, and many a nobleman met his end hanging from just such an object of "illumination."

13. As will become apparent later in the chapter, the author here addresses himself to an imaginary lady of the fashionable world with whom he wishes to dispute several questions. The reference to the number of admirers is censorious, for while it was in the wealthier classes that reforms could most easily be introduced, Hippel clearly feels—along with Rousseau—that the women of these classes had strayed farthest from nature, and thus from a "natural" equality which had existed at an earlier time. The statements in italics which follow in the dialogue are those of his imaginary female opponent.

14. Undoubtedly Catherine the Great (reigned 1762–1796) is meant.

15. Hippel refers here specifically to the *Messias* of Friedrich Gottlieb Klopstock (1724–1803), which was the first work of German literature to introduce unrhymed "free rhythms." Because of the nature of the topic treated (the passion of Christ), little attention is devoted to the female characters of the work.

16. Cf. Matt. XII:31–32.

17. *Statesman* 266c.

18. In Aesop's fable "The Frogs Asking for a King," the frogs, grieving at having no established ruler, send ambassadors to Jupiter to beg for a king. Perceiving their simplicity, Jupiter casts a huge log down into the lake. The frogs, terrified at first by the splash and the size of the log, soon dismiss their fears and, after finding that they can climb up and squat on it, come to despise so inert a ruler. After some time they begin to think themselves ill-treated, and send a deputation to Jupiter to request another sovereign. He then gives them an eel, which proves no better than the log. When they request a third ruler, Jupiter, displeased at their complaints, sends a heron, which devours them all.

19. Hippel makes a sly derogatory reference here to the French revolutionary Assemblée Nationale.

20. Chimborazo was long believed to be the highest peak in the Andes (el. 20,498 ft.). Tornio is a town in western Finland on the Swedish border.

21. Charles Marie de La Condamine (1701–1774), a French scientist, was sent in 1735 to Peru to measure an arc of the meridian. The French mathematician and astronomer Pierre Louis Moreau de Maupertuis (1698–1759) acted as chief of the expedition sent by Louis XV in 1736 to Lapland to measure the length of a degree of the meridian.

22. Hippel here clearly refers not only to the general idea of toleration of the Jews, which arose as a consequence of the advocacy of religious tolerance *vis-à-vis* all confessions and sects during the period of the Enlightenment, but more specifically to a treatise entitled *Über die bürgerliche Verbesserung der Juden* [On improving the status of the Jews], written by Christian Wilhelm Dohm and published in Berlin by Friedrich Nicolai in two parts, dated 1781 and 1783. Hippel most certainly derived the title of the present work from Dohm's book, although apparently little more, and it would do an injustice to Hippel's originality of form and content to assume that because of the similarity in the titles his work is merely a copy of Dohm's, with the essential arguments reworked to apply to the situation of women rather than that of the Jews. Parallels between the two works exist, in fact, only with regard to the use of reason in overcoming prejudice and the argument that the state would benefit greatly from the increase in population which would be brought about by the addition of these two groups to the ranks of its citizens. The population argument also became a favorite of other later advocates of female equality, and can be found not only in the work of Hippel, but, for example, in Wollstonecraft's *Vindication* and Tallyrand's *Rapport sur l'instruction publique* of 1791 as well.

23. Matt. XII:34.

CHAPTER II

1. Throughout the eighteenth century until the discovery of the Rosetta Stone in 1799, the word "hieroglyph" was frequently used to denote a figure, character, or mark which was thought to have a mysterious or enigmatic significance.

2. See St. Augustine *The City of God* XIX. 25.

3. A reference to the Judgment of Paris in Greek mythology. According to the legend, at the time when Peleus and Thetis were to solemnize their nuptials, all the gods were invited to the ceremony except the goddess Eris, or Discord. Furious at her exclusion, she threw a golden apple among the guests which bore the inscription: "To the fairest." Thereupon Hera, Aphrodite, and Athena each claimed the apple for herself. Zeus ordered Hermes to entrust the decision to the shepherd Paris. Paris decided in Aphrodite's favor, giving her the golden apple. This won for Paris the eternal hatred of Hera and Athena, who helped the Greeks in the Trojan War—a war caused by Paris's abduction of Helen, "the most beautiful woman in the world." However, Hippel here ironically combines this legend of the fall of Troy through an apple with the account of the Fall of Man in Genesis brought about by the same fruit. In this case, if Paris (man) bestows praise on Eve (woman) through his gift, it is not her beauty which he honors, but rather the fact that it was she who brought him to his fall—that is, who freed him from his unconscious, instinctual state and thereby prepared him for the breakthrough of "reason" (in psychological terms, the conscious mind). In this sense Eve is given greater credit for the founding of human civilization, the ultimate creation of man's conscious mind.

4. Orphans and other juvenile wards of the state were under the guardianship of the Children's Bureau until they reached their majority at the age of twenty-five. In Hippel's version, Eve, as the more mature of the two orphans(!), takes over responsibility for her spouse in the absence of such a bureau.

5. The wording is that of the monarchist Hippel and represents not so much an intentional distortion as a sneering paraphrase of Paine's statement in Part II of *Common Sense* (1776), which reads as follows in the original: "In short, monarchy and succession have laid (not this or that kingdom only,) but, the world in blood and ashes. 'Tis a form of government which the word of God bears testimony against, and blood will attend it."

6. Gen. I:26–27 and III:16.

7. In older Germanic law, a plaintiff, if accompanied by six witnesses, could bring a man to trial, in which case the latter's right to an "oath of purgation" (permitting him to clear himself of the charge) was then denied.

8. In this difficult passage, Hippel apparently equates iron with the male sex and the magnet with the female—ostensibly because of the magnet's power of attraction over iron. It seems to be his intention to show the equality (of respect) in such a relationship, but the "woman-hater" (probably Scheffner) in the paragraph below rejects this comparison, wishing instead for the women to be steel. The emphasis seems to be on the highly refined and noble qualities of the metal, rather than its hardness. This comparison is in turn rejected by Hippel, because steel, by virtue of its process of manufacture, is also subject to being interpreted as mere "adulterated iron," and "pure and unadulterated right stands on the side of the women."

9. Hippel here refers to the theory of "preformation" popular from the seventeenth to the early nineteenth century. According to this early notion of heredity, the new organism was already present in complete form in either the egg or the sperm at the time of conception, gradually becoming visible as the parts grew in size. Hippel here sides with the "ovists" against the "spermists," who sought to minimize the contribution by the female to the heredity of her progeny.

10. This is to be understood as a thinly veiled criticism of the philosophy of Gottfried Wilhelm Leibniz (1646–1716), who taught that the existing world, as the work of God, must be the best of all possible worlds, for if a better world were possible, then God's

wisdom would have recognized it, His goodness would have desired it, and His omnipotence would have had to create it. In Hippel's time the belief was no longer widely held.

11. See Romans VIII:22.

12. Acts XVII:28.

13. Cf. Gen. III:8–9.

14. This phenomenon is called "couvade" or "men's childbed." "Among the theories that have been suggested to account for the couvade is that during this period the father has to take care of himself to avoid an injury that could be transmitted to the child by sympathetic magic. Another is that the father asserts his paternity by appearing to take part in the delivery. A third explanation is that the father simulates the wife's activities in order to get evil spirits to focus on him rather than her" (Charles Winick, *Dictionary of Anthropology* [New York: The Philosophical Library, 1956], p. 137).

15. The famous chess-player of Wolfgang von Kempelen (1734–1804) for many years astonished and bewildered Europe. Kempelen's automaton was later revealed to be a fraud utilizing a complex system of mechanical devices to carry out the movements of a concealed player.

16. The first successful flight in an air balloon was made by the brothers Mongolfier in 1782.

17. "With the degree of doctor of both branches of medicine," a play on the phrase "in gradum doctoris utriusque legis," "with the degree of doctor of both laws," i.e., canon and civil.

18. Cf. Matt. VIII:5–10.

19. Cf. Gen. XLI.

20. The parasang is a unit of length (about 3½ miles). Hippel means here that any army—even a very large one—can easily be defeated by a solidly massed one if it is weakened by being extended over too great a territory. But in a larger sense, the entire passage is a satire on the women of the upper class for whom the rigors of both motherhood and an active social life proved so great that they were not able to fill their roles in either sphere successfully. In the next paragraph Hippel repents of this momentary descent to mockery, however.

21. Cf. Exod. III:2–6.

22. Carolus Linnaeus (Karl von Linné, 1707–1778), a Swedish naturalist and founder of the "Linnean system" of nomenclature in botany and zoology. He was the first to develop the criteria for defining genera and species, and insisted on a uniform usage of specific (Latin) names for all plants and animals.

23. The Italian ecclesiastic writer Girolamo Rorario (1485–1556) wrote a curious treatise entitled *Quod Animalia bruta saepe Ratione utantur melius Homine* [That brutes often reason better than man], first published in Paris in 1648, and translated into German in 1728. In his work *De l'esprit* (1758), the philosopher Claude Adrien Helvétius (1715–1771) proposed the idea that all man's faculties may be reduced to physical sensation, the only difference between man and the animals being one of external organization. In the philosophy of René Descartes (1596–1650), chemistry and biology are both subsumed under the one science of physics and reduced to a problem of mechanism. Such a reduction, he believed, would afford an explanation of every phenomenon of which we have knowledge, and the most daring and remarkable application of this theory was to account for the phenomena of organic life, especially in animals and man. All organisms are in this way regarded as machines which by virtue of the laws of motion have arranged themselves (always under the governing power of God) in the particular animal shapes in which we see them.

24. In the year 1493 Pope Alexander VI (Rodrigo Borgia) set up a line of demarcation from pole to pole one hundred leagues west of the Cape Verde Islands in order to settle the conflicts arising from Columbus' first voyage. Spain was given exclusive rights to the region west of the line in return for converting the heathen; Portuguese expeditions were to keep the rest. By means of this arbitrary line, and the Treaty of Tordesillas at which it

was ratified in 1494, Portugal was able to claim Brazil after its discovery in 1500, thus altering irrevocably the history and culture of the entire South American continent.

25. Cf. I Kings XVIII:21.

26. According to tradition, Manco Capac was the first father of the Incas of Peru and founder of the Inca monarchy. The legend represents him as the child of the sun, sent with his sister and wife to civilize the Indians. One story describes his northward advance toward Lake Titicaca, where, with a golden wand which he sank into the ground at a spot depicted to him in a prophecy, he founded the city of Cuzco. Manco Capac may have been a real person, most probably the chief of a small tribe who by force or policy reached Cuzco (already an established city), and after attaining leadership there, laid the foundations of the Inca empire.

27. Japheth, the youngest of Noah's three sons, was thought to be the ancestor of various nations in northern Asia and in Europe which comprise the so-called Indo-European race.

28. The preadamites were followers of the doctrine set forth by Isaac La Peyrère (1594–1676) in 1665 which held that only the Jews were descendants of Adam. The Gentiles, being descended from men who lived before Adam, were thus considered to be free from Original Sin. La Peyrère later recanted, but a sect arose from his teaching.

29. Cf. Gen. XXVIII:10–15.

30. The "Pharisee" of this and possibly the following line is St. Ignatius of Loyola (1491–1556), the founder of the Jesuit order. Hippel's hostility toward the Jesuits most likely stems not only from the fact the the Society of Jesus did much to roll back the tide of Protestantism in Europe during the Counterreformation, but also from the natural antipathy of a staunch rationalist and son of the "enlightened" eighteenth century, which in general regarded the Jesuits as the symbol of dogmatism, intolerance, and treachery. Paul Kluckhohn (*Die Auffassung der Liebe in der Literatur des 18. Jahrhunderts*, 3d ed. [Tübingen: Niemeyer, 1966], p. 310) and Arthur Warda ("Hippel and Rousseau," *Altpreussische Monatsschrift*, XVI [1879], 298) take this "Pharisee of more recent times" to be Rousseau, in which case the Theresa of the next sentence would be Thérèse Levasseur, Rousseau's wife. See the notes to Chapter III for Hippel's opinion of this relationship.

31. St. Theresa of Avila (1515–1582) was a Spanish mystic writer and the originator of the Carmelite Reform. Although her accomplishments in active life were of great importance, she is now regarded more for the beauty of her inner life as it is revealed in her religious writings. In her efforts to bring about reform in her order she was aided by the Jesuits, for which she always remained grateful, even though in later years she learned to mistrust many of their methods. The reference to the casting of the first stone is from John VIII:7.

32. Zenobia, Queen of Palmyra, was a joint ruler with her husband, Odenathus, and succeeded him when he died (A. D. 267). Known for her wise and prudent rule, she is said to have marched on foot at the head of her army and to have shared in its toils. Under the cloak of an alliance with Rome, she stationed her armies throughout Asia Minor, and, on Aurelius' succession, openly defied Roman power. Her armies were defeated by Aurelius in 271, and the beautiful queen was brought back to Rome to grace the emperor's triumph. She was later pensioned and given an estate by the Roman government.

33. Anna Comnena (1083–1148), the daughter of Alexis I, Emperor of Constantinople, was a Byzantine princess of distinguished beauty, learning, and talent. At her father's death in 1118 she conspired unsuccessfully to place the crown on the head of her husband, Nicephorus Bryennius. She then devoted her life to writing, completing a chronicle of her father's reign, the *Alexiad*, which contains a description, as seen from the Byzantine viewpoint, of the events of the First Crusade.

34. Taganrog is a southern seaport in Russia situated on the Gulf of Taganrog, the northeast arm of the Sea of Azov.

35. "I was in anguish when he painted me."

36. Hippel refers to Frederick the Great, at whose court Voltaire resided from the year

1749 until 1753. Frederick disdained the German language, preferring to write his verses in French, a diversion he continued to the end of his life.

37. In 1769 Turkey (whose reigning dynasty was known as the Osmanlis, or Ottomans) opened war against Russia to prevent the spread of Russian hegemony in Poland, and suffered thereafter long years of disastrous reverses at the hands of Catherine's armies. At the Peace of Kuchuk Kainarji (in Rumania) in 1774, Turkey was compelled to recognize the independence of the Crimea, to cede a number of important cities to Russia, open the Black Sea, the Bosporus, and the Dardanelles to Russian shipping, and to pay a war indemnity of 4,500,000 rubles, as well as to grant amnesty to Christians involved in uprisings against their Turkish governors, and to acknowledge the right of Russia to protect Christians in Turkey. This treaty was one of the most advantageous ever concluded by Russia.

38. In choosing this incident to illustrate the brilliance of Catherine's reign, Hippel perhaps gives more credit than is due. The "depredations" of Emelyan Pugachev (1726–1775) must in fact be considered as unsuccessful attempts to lead the serfs in revolt after their efforts to complain to Catherine of the misrule of their feudal landlords had failed. Athough she had expressed sympathy for the lot of the serfs and had taken some steps toward bringing about their emancipation, her unwillingness to act contrary to the interests of the nobility later caused her to accede to its wishes and prohibit complaints of misrule. The peasants, in desperation, then resorted to flight, assassination, or rebellion.

39. The reference is to Prince Henry II of Prussia, the brother of Frederick the Great. Henry served the Prussian cause faithfully in both diplomacy and war, and in the autumn of 1770 he let himself be persuaded by Frederick to accept the invitation of Catherine to visit Petersburg, that he might both strengthen relations between the two powers and assess the situation at Catherine's court at first hand.

40. Margaret, Queen of Denmark, Norway, and Sweden (1353–1412). In order to weld the three kingdoms over which she ruled closer together, she summoned a congress of the three councils of state and other dignitaries to Kalmar in 1397, and on Trinity Sunday of that year the joint coronation of her infant cousin Eric brought about the unification of the kingdoms. She then continued to rule, although not as regent, beyond the period of Eric's minority until her death.

41. Christina, Queen of Sweden from 1644 to 1654, became queen-elect at the age of six (1632). She was a major force in bringing about the Peace of Westphalia, which ended the Thirty Years' War. Highly cultured and devoted to learning, she was known as the Minerva of the North. Her beneficent rule saw the founding of the first Swedish newspaper and the first country-wide school ordinance. New privieges were granted to the towns; and manufacturing, trades, and mining also made great strides during her reign. Having secured the election of her cousin Charles Gustavus as her successor, she abdicated the throne in 1654. Later she embraced the Roman Catholic faith and eventually settled in Rome, where she became a patroness of the arts and the friend of four popes. A militant protector of personal freedom as well, she espoused the cause of the Jews in Rome until her death in that city in 1689.

42. Sophia Charlotta, Queen of Prussia, born 1668, died 1705, was the grandmother of Frederick the Great and sister of George I of England. One of the more remarkable and cultured women of her day, she is described as being articulate and full of mirth, with a very swift and sharp intellect which often confounded the court philosopher Leibniz, whom she consulted on theological problems. She was the author of a religious pamphlet as well as several musical compositions, and noted for her literary and philosophical tastes, which did much to brighten the austere Prussian court during this period.

43. Cornelia was the mother of Sempronia, who married Scipio Aemilianus, and also of the two famous tribunes Tiberius and Gaius Gracchus. After the death of her husband (Tiberius Sempronius Gracchus) she devoted herself to the management of her estate and her children. She was much admired in her time (second century b. c.) as a cultured woman of great virtue and accomplishment.

44. According to Pliny, when the husband of Arria, Caecina Paetus, was condemned to death in A. D. 42 for being privy to a conspiracy against Claudius and hesitated to kill himself at the emperor's command, she stabbed herself and handed him the dagger with the words: "Paete, non dolet" ("Paete, it does not pain me").

45. In general, the Stoics held that if life ceased to be pleasurable it was permissible for the free man to end it; and Seneca, in his *Letters to Lucilius*, even argued eloquently in defense of suicide as an escape from suffering and the infirmities of old age. Peregrinus Proteus, a Cynic philosopher, seeking the best possible method to make himself conspicuous and to obliterate the memory of his earlier crimes, committed suicide by burning himself alive at the Olympic Games in A. D. 165.

46. In Chapter IV, Hippel discusses at some length the influence of Roman law and the Justinian Code on Germanic law as it concerned the status of women.

47. Cf. Isa. LXVI:24.

48. Cf. Mark XII:17.

49. Cf. Rev. XII:8.

CHAPTER III

1. By answering the riddle put by the Sphinx to the inhabitants of Thebes, Oedipus freed the city from the depredations of that monster and received as payment the hand of his mother, Jocasta, thus unknowingly fulfilling the second part of the Delphic prophecy that he would slay his father and share his mother's bed. In the eighteenth century it was customary for learned societies to offer a reward for the best answer—in treatise form—to specific questions previously insoluble and whose solution, it was hoped, would reveal new horizons for scholarly investigation.

The reference to the thirty pieces of silver (cf. Matt. XXVII:3–8) is perhaps meant to imply that the answer to this question, as well, might bring down upon the head of the riddle-solver—if he were to become aware of the specific details concerning the beginning of such subjection—greater grief than if he had left the question unanswered and never received the reward.

2. Since the third century the desert in Egypt around ancient Thebes has attracted colonies of anchorites who desired to pursue the ascetic life. This manner of monastic existence (*koinobion*) quickly spread throughout the Christian church; and this desert, for the eighteenth century as well as for later periods, served as a virtual synonym for the ascetic religious life.

3. "Ici repose l'homme de la nature et de la vérité." Hans Jakob = Jean Jacques (Rousseau); Hippel often uses the more pedestrian German form of Rousseau's name in his writings, ostensibly to poke fun at the latter's social aspirations.

4. Cf. Gen. XVI. The quotation at the end of the paragraph is from Gen. XXI:10.

5. See the Parable of the Cave in Book VII of the *Republic*.

6. Cf. Matt. VIII:10.

7. *World-patriotism* is a term commonly used during this period to express a belief in the idea of commonality and fraternity among all the peoples of the world (cosmopolitanism). The notion that all men were full and equal fellow-citizens of a supranational human community with its basis in universal human reason originated with the philosophy of the Stoics and Cynics, and found its full expression in the Enlightenment's humanitarian ideals of freedom, equality, and tolerance.

8. Cf. Gen. XIX:17–26.

9. Charles de Marguetel de Saint-Denis de Saint-Évremond (1613?–1703), a French soldier, poet, and essayist, was a royalist and one of the many victims involved in the fall of Nicolas Fouquet. He fled to Holland and finally England, where he was kindly received by Charles II and given a pension of £300 a year. He also found favor with Charles's successors, James II and William II, one of whom presumably granted him the honorary post of keeper of the royal flock of ducks.

10. The "rhinoceros at court" is Rousseau, who was born in Geneva and spent much of his later life in France. In 1766, seeking a new refuge, he had gone to England, and upon the assistance of Hume had entered into negotiations with the King of England on the subject of a pension. In April of that year Voltaire published his open letter to Rousseau which contained, along with criticism of Rousseau's philosophy, the statement that in England, "the country of beautiful women and good philosophers," Rousseau would no doubt attract the same attention "as the king's elephant and the queen's zebra." The letter was widely circulated in London at the time. Hippel's version probably reflects the accumulation of twenty-six years' alteration in retelling the anecdote, and its inclusion here is no doubt intended to poke fun once again at Rousseau's social aspirations in the face of his renowned ignorance of the social graces and profound distaste for polite society.

The "atheist-in-residence" is Voltaire, a thoroughgoing Deist, who had resided at the court of Frederick the Great from 1750 to 1758. His attacks on esablished religion and the historical veracity of the Bible, particularly in the *Dictionnaire Philosophique*, doubtless form the basis of Hippel's rejection of his thought. In a larger context, however, the passage may be seen as an attempt to discredit both the fowler and the fisherman, both Rousseau and Voltaire, as extremists who attempt to snare men's minds with the baited traps and hooks of their thought.

11. The quotations in this paragraph are from Christ's Sermon on the Mount and his parable of the rich fool; see Matt. VI:34 and Luke XII:20.

12. According to Ovid's account (*Metamorphoses* VII, Fables 5 and 6), Aeacus, the son of Zeus and Aegina and a man renowned for his piety, besought his father to help him repopulate the island over which he ruled after a plague had destroyed its inhabitants. Zeus thereupon turned a swarm of ants into men, who still possessed the traits of industriousness and frugality characteristic of their former existence.

13. Membership in the ascetic religious society founded by Pythagoras entailed a strict discipline of purity based on silence, self-examination, and abstention from certain foods, particularly fish, the flesh of oxen and rams, and beans.

14. In the seventeenth and eighteenth centuries "natural" gardens designed to create idyllic effects were called "English" gardens, in contrast to the geometric formal gardens favored by the French, which represented for the Enlightenment the triumph of human reason over the chaos of nature.

15. Cf. Matt. XXII:30.

16. Ironically, the prototype of the secret society in the eighteenth century was the Masonic Order, of which Hippel was an active and enthusiastic member all his life. Cf., however, the Introduction to the present work, note 50.

17. Hippel makes here a double thrust at Rousseau, for whom the "social contract"—an agreement between individuals to subordinate their own rights and powers to the needs of their community as a whole—was the most important bond in human existence, and who consented to marry Thérèse Levasseur only after 22 years of cohabitation and four children, all of whom were sent to the foundling home shortly after birth.

18. In the Roman Catholic church, a bishop *in partibus infidelium* is a titular prelate who bears the title of an extinct see.

19. This statement is probably not directed so much at the German people in general as at its princes, who carried on an export trade in soldiers for most of the eighteenth century to maintain the magnificence of their courts. Thus, for example, over thirty thousand German troops were "lent" by their princes to England for the American Revolution for a subsidy of more than half a million pounds sterling.

20. Gen. XXV:29–34.

21. The original text refers at this point to the institute of the *venia aetatis*, which was a declaration of majority and the granting of its privileges to certain individuals who had attained the age of eighteen, instead of twenty-five, as required by common law. This declaration could only be made by the territorial prince or the court of wards, however, and not by the individual himself.

22. Cf. John X:16.

CHAPTER IV

1. The first encounter by the Roman army with elephants in the battle at Heraclea against Pyrrhus, King of Epirus, in 280 B. C., certainly produced the effect Hippel describes here, but the only "Indians" at the battle were the trainers of the elephants and the beasts themselves, which were almost certainly Indian elephants.

2. Cf., for example, Lev. XII and XXVII; Numbers XXVII, XXX and XXXVI; Deut. XXIV.

3. Hippel's text quotes Justinian *Digest* XXXII: "servi pro nullis habentur."

4. The reference is to courtesans and mistresses.

5. In early Germanic law property could only be passed down to blood relatives of the deceased. Those who had no heirs could create them by means of a herital contract tantamount to legal adoption, providing such a contract had the approval of the popular assembly, or of the king who took its place.

6. Hippel traces the beginning of the reception of Roman law into Germany back to the discovery of a single manuscript during the Middle Ages at Amalfi, but it is now known that the Roman influence on the legal system began earlier than this. For a discussion of such influence, see the Introduction to the present work.

7. Cf. Tacitus *Annals* XII.3, and Suetonius *Vespasian* XI.

8. In his *Germania* of A. D. 98. Hippel's relation of the folkways of the ancient Germans according to Tacitus differs from the latter's only in the respect that he wishes to assign the defect of indolence to the pleasure-loving Romans alone, when in fact it is for Tacitus a chief character trait of the Germans as well: "During the intervals of war, [the Germans] pass their time less in hunting than in a sluggish repose, divided between sleep and the table. All the bravest of the warriors, committing the care of the house, the family affairs, and the lands, to the women, old men, and weaker part of the domestics, stupefy themselves in inaction: so wonderful is the contrast presented by nature, that the same persons love indolence and hate tranquillity!" (Oxford translation, chap. 15).

9. Vellede was the most important of the prophetesses among the ancient Germans. Little is known of her other than that she flourished around A.D. 70, and later was captured and taken to Rome in triumphal procession, after which she disappears from written history. It was customary for a prophetess to remain a lifelong virgin and to dedicate her life to her task; some, like Vellede, also withdrew to a tower in a deep wood in order to enhance the effect of their prophecies. From this tower utterances were disseminated among the people by the relatives of the prophetess, all others being forbidden to approach the holy shrine.

10. Cf. Diogenes Laertius *Aristotle* V. 20.

11. This right, while existing in ancient times among such groups as the Hebrews (cf. Deut. XXIV:1–4), seems not to have come into Germanic law from Roman law, but to have been customary among the Germans from the beginning. The ancient Germans acknowledged three kinds of divorce: 1) "statutory divorce," resulting from the outlawry of one of the spouses; 2) "divorce by mutual consent," the normal form of divorce; and 3) "divorce at the will of one party," originally existing in favor of the husband only. This implied unlimited power in the husband to free himself from his wife by repudiating her on grounds of adultery, a secret attempt on his life, or her sterility. The introduction of Roman law, in fact, finally empowered the woman, in a few cases at least, to declare herself free of her husband by her own act—for example, in cases of extreme mistreatment.

12. In all primitive societies, the virgin is endowed with a special magical power enabling her to work miracles, serve as a sacrificial offering pleasing to the gods, or, in the medieval Christian church, to walk unscathed before the devil under the protection of a special grace from heaven. Vestiges of this belief remained in Hippel's time and can still be found in modern attitudes and practices concerning marriage.

13. The original text introduces the Latin term *consuetudines*. In Roman law, *consuetudines* were long-standing customs observed by the ancestors of a people, and defined by classical jurists as the silent consent of that people. These were often of great influence,

and the emperors sometimes found it difficult to oppose such customs, even though they were not legally binding. Hippel here assigns greater "natural right" to these laws formulated by the people and arising out of the day-to-day interaction between the sexes than to those laws which derive from the male sex guided solely by the dictates of its own powers of reason.

14. Matt. XVI:26.

15. II Cor. XII:10.

16. The reference is to a decree of the Roman senate which prevented women from acting as bondsman or surety in a contract (*Digest* XVI. 1. 1–2).

17. *Digest* I. 5.

18. Justinian *Novels* CXXXIV. 9.

19. Mark I:3.

20. Matt. XXIII:24.

21. Along with black, the state colors of Prussia.

22. The petition is "But deliver us from evil," and the explanation in Luther's *Small Catechism*, to which Hippel refers, reads as follows: "We pray in this petition, as the sum of all, that our Father in heaven would deliver us from every evil of body and soul, property and honor, and finally, when our last hour has come, grant us a blessed end, and graciously take us from this vale of tears to Himself in heaven."

23. Cf. Gen. VI:5.

24. See, for example, Thomas Carlyle's *The French Revolution*, Book VII, "The Insurrection of Women," and Michelet's *Les femmes de la revolution*.

25. I.e., as a result of having been sold into bondage. See Gen. XXXVII–L.

26. Montesquieu, *The Spirit of Laws*, Book VII, sec. 17.

27. Hippel attributes the following rhyme to Luther, but others consider it merely proverbial, although contemporaneous with him:

> Ein jeder lerne seine Lektion,
> So wird es wohl im Hause stohn [stehen].

28. That is, the husband of a married woman is considered by law to be the father of all children born to her during the time of their marriage, and the question of his biological paternity cannot be subjected to an investigation.

29. Matt. VI:33.

30. The reference is probably to a popular interpretation of the ideas of Julien de La Mettrie (1709–1751), the father of modern materialistic philosophy. In works such as the *Histoire naturelle de l'âme* [Natural history of the soul] and *L'Homme machine* [Man a machine], La Mettrie advocated the notion that the soul can be identified with the human brain, and that various faculties of the soul such as judgment and imagination can be explained in terms of their related organic causes. The implication is that since women have smaller bodies and hence smaller brains, they also have smaller souls. La Mettrie met with great criticism during his life because of the antireligious nature of his materialistic philosophy, and finally found his way to exile in the Prussia of Frederick the Great, at which place Hippel doubtless became acquainted with his thought.

31. Alcibiades (ca. 450–404 B. C.) became the leader of the radical party in Athens about 421. He was later accused of profanation and sentenced to death, whereupon he fled to Sparta and became an open enemy of Athens. In 412, having aroused suspicion in Sparta as well, he took refuge with a certain Tissaphernes, who had deserted the Spartans and professed his willingness to help the Athenians. The Athenians then recalled Alcibiades from banishment in 411. After having achieved a number of military successes for the Athenian army, he returned in triumphal procession to that city in 407 and was immediately given command of all land and sea forces. He later fell out of favor once again and was treacherously assassinated in Phrygia in 404.

32. See Chapter III, note 13.

33. The monster surnamed Panoptes, "the all-seeing," was appointed by Hera to be the guardian of the cow into which she had transformed Io in a fit of jealousy at Zeus's love for

her. Zeus, however, sent Hermes to slay Argus and deliver Io, whereupon Hera transplanted the eyes of Argus into the tail of the peacock, her favorite bird.

34. Cf. Acts XXIV:25.

35. The original text makes reference to the *restitutio in integrum*, a term derived from Roman law designating reinstatement into a former legal position.

36. Cf. Luke II:19.

37. "Malbrough s'en va-t-en guerre" was a popular French song composed after the battle of Malplaquet (1709) to ridicule the victorious Duke of Marlborough. Its theme was the "death" and "burial" of the English commander. Hippel implies of course that war is one of the "utterly masculine" affairs in which women have no desire to take part.

CHAPTER V

1. In the eighteenth century, both names had pejorative connotations; *vandalism* remains today the generic term for malicious destruction, while the word *gothic*, for the enlightened European of that period, smacked of all the superstition, religious fanaticism, and barbarism of the Middle Ages from which he now felt himself delivered at long last by the power of his reason.

2. Matt. XVIII:2–3.

3. See also Chapter I, note 16. Since it is the effect of the Holy Spirit on the human heart which makes men desire forgiveness for their sins and to do the work of God, the sin of blasphemy against, and rejection of, the Holy Spirit is the only unforgivable sin, because it prevents the agent of forgiveness from doing its work. By analogy, the "sin against the Holy Spirit" of women is a rejection of the sex to the point where one no longer allows it to have an effect on his heart. According to Hippel, at this point reconciliation is no longer possible.

4. On August 27, 1791, Frederick William II of Prussia and Leopold of Austria met at Pillnitz to discuss the French situation. This resulted in the Declaration of Pillnitz, which stated that the two powers would intervene in French affairs only with the unanimous consent of both the powers and England. The French, however, interpreted this as an outright threat of interference, and declared war against Austria on April 20, 1792, and Prussia in July ("War of the First Coalition").

5. Matt. X:27.

6. The right to freedom from persecution because of religion was again granted during the French Revolution after over one hundred years of religious persecution. The edict of November 19, 1787, also reinstated Protestants in their civil rights. The Constitution of 1791 (to which Hippel is referring) distinguished between "active" and "passive" citizenship by means of a system based on property, and extended one of the two forms of citizenship to all adult males. Thus although the women were still excluded from citizenship, those Protestants who qualified were now eligible for "active" citizenship, which alone carried with it the right to vote.

7. Louise-Félicité Guinement de Kéralio (1758–1821) was a minor novelist, whose best-known work, the *Histoire d'Elisabeth, reine d'Angleterre* [History of Elizabeth of England] in five volumes (1786–1789) was highly regarded in her own time, although it is considered to be somewhat prolix and overblown today. During the Revolution she edited, with others, the *Journal de l'Etat et du citoyen*, which appeared in eighty-seven numbers from December 31, 1789, to March 29, 1791. After August 30, 1790, its title was changed to *Mercure national ou Revolutions de l'Europe, journal démocratique*. This paper was one of the first to embrace republicanism in 1790. Hippel is apparently not aware that the journal had ceased publication a full year previously.

8. An exhaustive search has not revealed the text of this letter. More than likely, however, she refers to the fact that the paternal power of Customary law had been transferred to both the father and mother together after the Revolution. This action corresponded to other legal restrictions on the power of the father in France, and had its

basis in the view that the state constituted the true head of the family. Thus it could be argued that mothers, who had already attained legal equality within the family, deserved equal standing within the state itself.

9. Cf., for example, Matt. XIII:23.

10. The German text quotes Hobbes, *Leviathan*, Chapter XVIII, *bellum omnia contra omnes* ("a general melee; anarchy").

11. Hippel's explanation for this statement is to be found at the beginning of the paragraph immediately following.

12. The Augsburg Confession of 1530 and the Formula of Concord of 1577 are fundamental declarations of doctrine within the Lutheran church.

13. Hippel here modifies the phrase *clam, vi, aut precario*, the Roman legal expression meaning "by stealth, force, or importunity."

14. The legal subjection of the woman by her husband had its roots in two distinct historical traditions: Indo-Germanic custom and canon law. In the prehistoric Indo-Germanic period, the husband enjoyed a position in marriage so superior to his wife that the language had no word for the conceptions "marriage" or "spouse." Legally, she occupied the same position in relation to him as any child in the family; and as a consequence of this, forms of adoption were common in the marriage ceremony. In the Middle Ages, the church, otherwise the energetic champion of equality between the sexes, strove to strengthen the husband's position in the matter of marriage. Starting with the presupposition that the woman was a being of inferior worth and that marriage was created basically in order for man to avoid the sins of the flesh, it based its authority on the words of the Apostle Paul (for example, I Tim. II:9–15) and taught that the wife should be at all times subject to her husband. The result of this was that the husband was recognized as the "mundum-holder" of his wife, or as it was expressed in the medieval period, her "guardian" or "steward," the "master" of the marriage relationship. Such a marital stewardship (*Ehevogtei*) everywhere rendered the wife incapable of independent action or independent control of her own property without her husband's consent, and everywhere the administration of the collective marital property was a matter solely of concern to the husband.

15. Cf. Gen. I:26–27 and Gen. II:23.

16. The women's quarters of a Greek house.

17. Cf. Matt. XVI:26 and XIX:14.

18. Cf. Plato *Theaetetus* 149a–151d (esp. 150b).

19. The philosophical ideas of Jean-Baptiste Robinet (1735–1820) concerning nature are contained chiefly in two works, his *De la Nature* [On nature] of 1761–1768, and the *Considérations philosophiques de la gradation naturelle des formes de l'être* [Philosophical considerations regarding the natural gradation in forms of being] of 1768. He argued that behind the apparently random distribution of suffering and pleasure in the world there lies a fixed order. The universe is animate, and all forms of being, including planets and stars, possess the power of reproduction, the individual being only a means for propagating the species. He held that in all of nature there is a gradation of beings, each degree of development representing a higher step in the fulfillment of nature's original plan.

20. André Ernest Modeste Grétry (1742–1813) was a French composer whose works were important for the development of the comic opera. After about 1790 he devoted himself chiefly to literary and philosophical studies, at first in Paris, and later at Rousseau's hermitage in Montmorency. Hippel intends with the quotation to let Rousseau, who refused to allow the women the same privilege as he requests here for himself, to reveal the extent of his hypocrisy through his own utterance.

21. A highly florid aria in bold, marked style was characteristic of Italian opera.

22. Cf. Eccles. I:7.

23. Hippel refers specifically to theriac (*theriaca Andromachi*), or Venice treacle, a compound of sixty or seventy drugs, pulverized and blended with honey, used as late as the eighteenth century as a universal remedy.

24. That is, as soon as women themselves are permitted to roam freely in nature and

become acquainted with the potentially beneficial effects of judicious exposure to her elements.

25. This passage probably contains more than a mere censorious allusion to the fashion of the day which required women, in order to preserve that pallor of complexion then considered beautiful, to avoid at all costs the rays of the summer sun. If one views the passage in a larger context, Hippel seems to imply that greater harm will result if women in their oppression continue to live in enmity with the "sun" of human liberty.

26. A well-known remark in Hippel's time and before, not directly attributable to any one individual. The most notable expression of it is to be found in Shakespeare's *King Henry V*, III, vii, 149–54.

27. Matt. XIX:6; Mark X:9.

28. Cf., for example, *Laws* XI. 923.

29. A group of French philosophers and political scientists, followers of François Quesney (1694–1774), the physiocrats opposed governmental restraints on the economic order out of a belief in the natural acquisitiveness and competitiveness of man. If nature were left to rule ("physiocrat," from *physis*, "nature," and *kratein*, "rule"), they maintained, man would be enabled to produce products in greater quantity and variety, as well as of better quality. The physiocrats regarded land and raw materials as the sole source of wealth, and divided society into three classes: a *classe productive*, of farmers, miners, and fishermen; a *classe disponible*, those holding military or administrative positions; and a *classe stérile*, consisting of artisans who prepare the products and tradesmen who bring them to the consumer.

30. According to Livy (I. 19. 5), Numa Pompilius, legendary second king of Rome (traditionally 715–673 B.C.), feigned nocturnal consultations with the water goddess Egeria in order to restore reverence for the ancient gods and legitimize his religious reforms.

Pythia was the name given to the priestess who served the oracle at Delphi. The words which she spoke after inhaling the sacred vapor were believed to contain the revelations of Apollo.

Aspasia was the mistress of Pericles from the time of his divorce (445 B.C.) until his death. She was a woman of considerable intellect who conversed with Socrates and was herself a teacher of rhetoric. She was later accused of both immorality and using undue influence with Pericles to bring about the Samian and Peloponnesian Wars, although Pericles himself, the real object of these attacks, defended her eloquently and successfully.

Phryne was one of the most beautiful and talented of the *hetairai* (courtesans) who became influential mistresses of men of political, philosophical, or artistic distinction in the Greek Golden Age.

31. The Greek stoa was a public hall set aside for general purposes, one of which was to provide an opportunity for walking or conversing under shelter. The word *prytaneum*, commonly used to designate the meeting-place of the rulers (*prytanes*) of the Greek city-state, is here used figuratively to represent all political institutions from which women were excluded in Hippel's day.

32. Luke X:42.

33. Cf. Acts IX:36–42.

34. Roswitha, the first "German" woman poet (ca. 935–after 1000), wrote exclusively in Latin. A nun in the Benedictine cloister at Gandersheim, she was the author of poetical chronicles of the Emperor Otto I, as well as six comedies after the manner of Terence.

35. Both Anne Tanneguy-Lefèvre Dacier (1654–1720) and Ernestine Christine Reiske (1735–1798) were married to famous classical scholars, and both also became well known for their own work in the classics, Dacier as a translator of the *Iliad* and *Odyssey* into French, and Reiske as her husband's collaborator and, after his death, his successor. She is chiefly known for her translations of classical works into German.

36. Catherine Sawbridge Macaulay (1731–1791) was a historian and thinker whose eight-volume *History of England* was highly regarded in the eighteenth century. She was

greatly admired by Mary Wollstonecraft, and the latter's *A Vindication of the Rights of Woman* owes much to her *Letters on Education.*

The works of Stéphanie Félicité Ducrest de Saint-Aubin, Comtesse de Genlis (1746–1830), a noted French pedagogical writer, were widely read at the time.

Marie de Rabutin-Chantal, Marquise de Sévigné (1626–1696), was a French epistolary writer best known for her correspondence with her daughter, thought by many to rank with the finest literary monuments in the French language.

Sophie von Laroche (1731–1807) was the first woman author in Germany to write popular novels. Her most famous work, the *Geschichte des Fräuleins von Sternheim* [Memoirs of Miss Sophy Sternheim], is a sentimental novel after the manner of Goldsmith and Richardson. A second novel, *Rosaliens Briefe* [Letters of Rosalie], deals with the position and duties of women.

37. Although Newton's scientific writings were understood by very few of their own sex either, it appears that one of the most common arguments offered by the men during this period against the participation of women in intellectual pursuits in general, and scientific ones in particular, was that their sex had never produced a thinker of the towering stature of Isaac Newton. Thus, in his popularized biography of Benjamin Franklin, published in 1815, "Parson" Weems inserts into the well-known debate between the youthful Franklin and his friend Collins concerning the intellectual abilities of the female sex the question by Collins as to whether Franklin knew of any young woman of his acquaintance "that would make a Newton?" Franklin's reply (in Weems' words), which may serve as an interesting contrast to Hippel's argument, is here reproduced in part:

> And pray, sir, answered Ben, do you know any young man of your acquaintance that would? But these are no arguments, sir,—because it is not every young man or woman that can carry the science of astronomy so high as Newton, it does not follow that they are incapable of the science altogether. God sees fit in every age to appoint certain persons to kindle new lights among men.—And Newton was appointed greatly to enlarge our views of celestial objects. But we are not thence to infer that he was in all aspects superior to other men, for we are told that in some instances he was far inferior to other men. [M. L. Weems, *The Life of Benjamin Franklin, etc.* (Philadelphia: Uriah Hunt, 1845), p. 26]

Thereupon follow several anecdotes designed to illustrate the fallibility of Newton in everyday human affairs. Others, however, sought to bridge the alleged disparity between the female intellect and that of Newton not by lowering Newton, but by attempting to raise the intellectual aspirations of the women, the best example of which is perhaps provided by Francesco Algarotti's *Sir Isaac Newton's Philosophy Explain'd for the Use of the Ladies*, trans. Elizabeth Carter, 2 vols. (London: E. Cave, 1739). The original Italian version had appeared in 1737.

38. Hippel refers to the practice in Germany of setting aside on baking day the best of the bread for future consumption.

39. Cf. I Cor. XIV:34–35 and I Tim. II:11–13.

40. Virtually from the time of its founding in the seventeenth century, the Society of Friends has regarded it as a limitation on the work of the Holy Spirit to place the responsibility for teaching and preaching in the hands of a single individual, to the exclusion of all others. In this way the teaching of St. Paul mentioned above was circumvented, and it became permissible for any man or woman during the worship service to read the Scriptures, offer prayer, or utter any teaching as seemed appropriate for the occasion. The sect, moreover, does not believe that there exists Biblical evidence that the gifts of teaching and prophecy are confined to the male sex alone.

41. Louis Bourdaloue (1632–1704), noted French Jesuit theologian and court preacher (1670), was one of the most accomplished pulpit orators of his day. The published edition of his sermons (1707–34) encompasses sixteen volumes.

42. Cf. Matt. VII:29 and Luke IV:32.

43. The "new philosophical star" is Kant, and the argument is found in the *Critique of Practical Reason*, Book II, Chapter 5.

44. Cf. Luke XVII:6.

45. The quotation given here is a translation of Hippel's German version. Diligent search has failed to locate the original version in any of Franklin's writings, and it thus most probably represents an offhand remark uttered during the course of one of his sojourns in Europe, and then transmitted orally across the continent by his many foreign admirers.

46. Livy (I. 9–13) writes that Romulus, finding difficulty in obtaining wives for the men who had gathered around him in the new city founded by him and his twin brother Remus, invited the neighboring tribes to a celebration of games and used the occasion to carry off a number of Sabine virgins. After the Sabine fathers attacked in revenge, their daughters strode *en masse* into the heat of battle and pleaded successfully with both sides to cease fighting.

47. According to Roman legend, Gnaeus Marcius received his surname from the Volscian town of Corioli, which he captured after being impeached and condemned to exile by the Romans for his opposition to the distribution of corn to the starving plebians. After capturing many other towns, he then turned his Volscian army on Rome itself, advancing to a point close to the city in 489 B.C. Here he encamped, and would listen to none of the entreaties of the distinguished citizens of the state until finally a delegation of the noblest matrons of Rome, headed by his mother and wife, swayed him from his resolve to attack and destroy the city.

48. Margarethe Herlobig, the wife of Werner Stauffacher, persuaded her husband to form a league of like-minded Swiss against the depredations of their Austrian governors early in the fourteenth century. Closely tied to the events following the formation of this league are those surrounding the legend of William Tell, and both the actions of Tell, as well as those of Margarethe Herlobig (under the name Gertrud Stauffacher), were later immortalized by Schiller in his *Wilhelm Tell* of 1804.

49. The writings of Quirinus Kubach (1589–1624) on Germanic public law and the Justinian Code were still regarded as authoritative in Hippel's time.

50. The Feast of the Tabernacles was the last of the appointed Hebrew festivals under the old covenant and to be celebrated, according to Exodus XXIII:16, "in the end of the year, when thou hast gathered in thy labours out of the field."

51. Cf. Horace *Ars Poetica* 358–60: "and yet I also feel aggrieved, whenever good Homer 'nods,' but when a work is long, a drowsy mood may well creep over it" (trans. Fairclough).

52. Cf. Plutarch *Caesar* 62 and *Brutus* 9; Shakespeare, *Julius Caesar*, I, ii.

53. Greece was subject to Turkish domination from 1456 until 1821.

54. Hippel probably alludes to the tendency of many thinkers in Germany to persist in regarding France as the source of the newest intellectual trends of the day.

55. The reference to a "new heaven and a new earth" is from Rev. XXI:1. In Hebrew tradition, palm branches were considered symbols of joy or triumph. Paul's "third heaven" is found in II Cor. XII:2.

56. A saddle, from the Middle Ages even to Hippel's time, like a chair, which enabled women to ride with both feet on the same side of the horse. Pegasus, the winged horse of Greek mythology, became the symbol for poetic inspiration.

57. Sappho was a Greek poet of great lyrical gifts (ca. 612 B.C.?), who appears to have been the center of a female literary society at Mytilene in Lesbos.

58. Hippel refers to Anna Luise Karschin (1722–1791), a German poet celebrated during her lifetime—although in excess of her poetic gifts—as the "German Sappho." It is difficult to know whether Hippel intends what follows to be understood ironically or not, for he surely must have known that Karschin rejected the paltry gift of four gulden in a well-known poem of the time as degrading to both her and a "great king." On the other hand, irony would seem inappropriate at this point, and it is out of character for Hippel to criticize the official actions of his late sovereign. The statement that she "returned home to

her elder sisters" refers to her death the previous October. "Elise" is a variant of "Luise."

59. A Swiss portrait painter (1741–1807), Kauffmann worked for many years in Italy and England. She was highly regarded during her lifetime for the grace and charm of her portraits and historical paintings, many of which are still represented in the principal galleries of Europe.

60. The Scot James Macpherson created a literary sensation in all of Europe when he published what he claimed to be poems by the Gaelic bard and warrior Ossian in 1760. The poems were received by an overly refined and hypersensitive continent as a new return to *Volkspoesie*, the unrefined, powerful, and heroic poetry of the people, and were influential in developing the thought of the "Storm and Stress" and Romantic movements in German literature. A controversy arose at once concerning the genuineness of the poems, and they are now considered to be, for the most part at least, the work of Macpherson himself.

61. This expression is probably derived from Diderot's reference to women as "enfans imbéciles" in his short essay "Sur les femmes" (1772).

62. Cf. Psalm XC:10.

63. Laura Maria Catherine Bassi (1711–1798), one of the great prodigies of the eighteenth century, was as renowned for the excellence of her Latin style as for her experiments and discoveries in the field of air compression. She was awarded the doctorate at the age of twenty-one, and shortly thereafter given a pension by the senate of Bologna out of gratitude for the honor which her presence at the Institute reflected on that city.

Maria Gaetana Agnesi (1718–1799), attained such skill in mathematics that she was permitted by the Pope to succeed her father as professor at Bologna. Her great work, *Analytical Institutions*, was translated into English by the Cambridge mathematician John Colson, who thought so highly of the work that he studied Italian in order to undertake the translation.

64. Ercole Lelli (1702–1766), a well-known Bolognese sculptor, had been commissioned by the Pope in 1747 to construct life-size models in wax for the enhancement of anatomical studies at the Institute. He later worked with a certain Signora Anna Manzolini (no relation) to perfect similar models of the uterus and fetus in order to improve the instruction then given to midwives. Their work was later extended to include models of all parts of the body, and was subsequently instrumental in the establishment of a chair of anatomy at the Institute.

65. Widely celebrated in her day for her precocity, Dorothea von Schlözer, later Baroness von Rodde (1770–1825) received a remarkable education during her childhood through the efforts of her father, a distinguished professor who wished to prove that women were capable of great intellectual accomplishment. She began at the age of three with the study of foreign languages, and by the age of eleven she had mastered virtually every modern European language as well as Greek, Hebrew, and Latin. She also had made great progress in the study of natural sciences. In 1787, at the age of seventeen, she was granted the degree Doctor of Philosophy after a rigorous, although at that time necessarily private, period of testing by a professor on the faculty at the University of Göttingen.

66. Caroline Lucretia Herschel (1750–1848) served as the assistant to her brother, the Anglo-German astronomer Sir Frederick William Herschel (1738–1822), in his observations as court astronomer to George III. She is credited with the detection of three nebulae and eight comets. In the year 1797 she presented to the Royal Society an Index to the observations of Flamsteed (see note 17, Chapter VI) as well as a full list of the errata in the *British Catalogue* of stars. She was later honored by the Astronomical Society and the King of Prussia for her work.

67. "Heyducs" refers to footmen in Hungarian uniforms.

68. Antonio Allegri (1494–1534) is known by the name of his native city. Hippel doubtless refers to the treatment of light and shadow which enabled Correggio to endow the figures in his religious paintings with the look of supernal radiance.

69. *The Merchant of Venice*, I, i.

70. In Greek mythology, Ariadne, the daughter of Minos, king of Crete, gave Theseus the ball of thread by means of which he found his way out of the labyrinth after he had slain the Minotaur.

71. The quotation is from Molière's *L'amour médecin* (*Love Is the Best Doctor*), I, i, and runs as follows in its complete form: "Vous êtes orfèvre, Monsieur Josse, et votre conseil sent son homme qui a envie de se défaire de sa marchandise" ("You are a goldsmith, Mr. Josse, and your advice betrays a man eager to sell his merchandise").

72. The enlightened skepticism in matters of religion of such thinkers as Hume characterized the outlook of only a handful of intellectuals of the upper classes in the eighteenth century, and was viewed by the less privileged and educated (and thus by most women) as merely another form of atheism. Hume, in the eyes of the people the chief infidel of the age, was consequently the subject of many such anecdotes as the one here mentioned by Hippel. Another anecdote, cited by Dean Ramsay, may serve to clarify further Hippel's point regarding the difference in the religious orientation of women and philosophers:

> The philosopher [Hume] had fallen from the path into the swamp at the back of [Edinburgh] castle, the existence of which I recollect hearing of from old persons forty years ago. He fairly stuck fast, and called to a woman who was passing, and begged her assistance. She passed on apparently without attending to the request; at his earnest entreaty, however, she came where he was, and asked him, "Are na ye Hume the Atheist?" "Well, well, no matter," said Hume; "Christian charity commands you to do good to every one." "Christian charity here, or Christian charity there," replied the woman, "I'll do naething for you till ye turn a Christian yoursell'—you maun repeat the Lord's Prayer and the Creed, or faith I'll let ye grafel [grovel] there as I fand ye." The historian, really afraid for his life, rehearsed the required formulas. [*Reminiscences of Scottish Life and Character* (Edinburgh: T. N. Foulis, n.d.), p. 96]

73. Jean Terrasson (1670–1750), the French classicist and moral philosopher, might well have met the second of the Marquis de Lassay's two wives, née Julie de Bourbon (1668–1710), who appeared occasionally at the court of Louis XIV, where she is described in the Marquis de Dangeau's memoirs as a "femme . . . de grande qualité," in spite of the scandal caused by her separation from her roving husband after only a few years of marriage.

74. After his defeat at the hands of the Russians at the Battle of Poltava in June 1709, Charles XII of Sweden crossed the Dneiper River with his remaining followers and sought asylum in Turkey. In Sweden, meanwhile, where it was not known whether the king was dead or alive, the legislature entertained thoughts of capitulating to the Czar. It was at this point, according to some accounts, that Charles wrote to the senate that he would send them one of his boots to govern them. The incident is now viewed as apocryphal and not included in more recent biographies.

75. The quotation in context reads: "And Jesus answered and said unto her, Martha, Martha, thou art careful and troubled about many things: but one thing is needful: and Mary hath chosen that good part, which shall not be taken away from her" (Luke X:41–42).

76. Hippel here combines the events of Plato *Phaedo* 60 and 118, ostensibly for added effect.

77. Claudius Galenus (ca. A.D. 129–199), Greek philosopher and medical writer, was long considered the supreme authority in medical science.

78. It seems probable that Hippel, his criticism of Voltaire and the latter's religious beliefs notwithstanding, has the Deists (Freethinkers) in mind here. From his previous remarks, we can conclude that he views the religion of women as very much akin to the Deistic concept of true (or natural) religion, which declared the precepts for right conduct and the key to the understanding of God's will for man to lie from the beginning within his own heart, and to be accessible to him through the application of his powers of reason. Failure to apply this reason, however, would predispose him to religious dogmatism and

an existence in a society regulated by laws made for the benefit of the privileged, an existence, Hippel maintains, which would cause men to seek a happier one beyond the grave. Hippel had earlier defended the views of the Deists against Zimmermann's charge of atheism in his book *Zimmermann der I. und Friedrich der II.* (1790).

79. "Despise death and you have conquered every fear" (Pubilius Syrus *Maxims*).

80. The Greeks actually considered Somnes (Sleep) as the twin, rather than the elder brother, of Thanatus (Death).

81. Psalm CXXXIX:9.

82. Cf. Matt. VIII:23–27.

83. A reference to the books on advice to girls and young wives, generally in the form of moral lectures, which were popular in the eighteenth century. Mary Wollstonecraft selects two such books, Dr. James Fordyce's *Sermons to Young Women*, and Dr. John Gregory's *A Father's Legacy to his Daughters* for lengthy analysis in Chapter V of her *Vindication*, entitled "Animadversions on Some of the Writers Who Have Rendered Women Objects of Pity, Bordering on Contempt."

84. On long sea voyages, it was common for sailors to amuse themselves by throwing objects into the sea for whales and porpoises to play with.

85. Through the agency of one Fulvia, then mistress of Curius, one of the conspirators against Cicero, the latter became aware of every action as it occurred and was thus able to thwart the conspiracy and accuse Catiline openly before the Roman senate.

86. Hippel refers presumably to the emperor's wife, Isabella of Portugal. Hippel is understandably critical of Charles V, who so vehemently opposed the Reformation; nevertheless, even Protestant religious historians no longer unanimously concur in their condemnation of this misunderstood ruler.

87. Cf. Gen. I:2.

88. According to the Greek historiographers, Semiramis was the wife of Ninus, the founder of Nineveh, and the daughter of the goddess Derceto. She was considered to be of extraordinary beauty and wisdom. After her husband's death, she assumed the government of Assyria and began a reign so glorious as to prompt some writers to ascribe supernatural qualities to her. Modern scholarship now traces the legend to a historical queen Sammuramat, wife of the Assyrian king Shamshi-Adad, who reigned herself from 810–805 B.C.

89. Charles Geneviève d'Éon de Beaumont (1728–1810) was a secret agent of Louis XV and served at the English and Russian courts. He became particularly well known for his success in assuming a female disguise, and both Hippel and Wollstonecraft, who also cites him as an example of a woman of merit (*Vindication*, chap. IV), seem quite unaware of d'Éon's sex, which was not conclusively established until his death in 1810.

90. "Dangerous leap" (Ital.).

91. According to Plutarch (*Alcibiades* IX), after Alcibiades had had the tail cropped off of his large, handsome, and expensive dog and the Athenians had publicly lamented the loss of the animal's principal ornament, he replied that precisely his intention had been fulfilled: that they would talk of nothing but the dog, and thus say nothing worse about Alcibiades himself.

92. Heinrich Friedrich von Storch (1766–1835) was a German economist and statistician. The observations mentioned are found in his work *Skizzen, Scenen und Bemerkungen, auf einer Reise durch Frankreich gesammelt* [Collected sketches, scenes, and notes from a trip through France] (Heidelberg: Braun, 1787). The school in Paris to which Storch refers was established by Coulon de Thèvenot (1740–1814), an early advocate of tachygraphy, or speed writing.

93. Cf. Hippel's argument concerning the rise of male domination through the sword in Chapters II and III, above.

94. A French statesman and financier (1732–1804), Jacques Necker was minister of finance under Louis XVI and father of Madame de Staël.

The Marquis de Lafayette (1757–1834) was a celebrated French general and statesman who had served as a volunteer officer with the American revolutionary army as a young man. Later, as commander-in-chief of the national guard during the French Revolution, Lafayette sought to restore the monarchy. He once more led the national guard during the revolution of 1830, when he was instrumental in placing Louis Philippe on the throne.

95. In a Roman judicial trial, in controversies requiring specific professional or technical knowledge, an expert (*arbiter*) could be appointed by the magistrate in order that judgment could be rendered by someone better qualified than the average Roman citizen listed in the panel of judges.

96. *Privilegia causae* in Roman law were privileges accruing to the claimant in certain cases regardless of sex or social position, as for example, in the claim of a wife against her insolvent husband for the restitution of a dowry, where the woman was permitted to plead her case before the court herself.

97. From the time of Hippocrates until after that of William Cullen in the late eighteenth century, hysteria was considered for the most part a disease of women, the cause of which was generally assigned to a "displacement" of the uterus (Gk. *hysteros*, "uterus"). Hippel, in implying here that the cause of the malady in women stems from the repression of the desire for freedom in every aspect of their lives, anticipates by a hundred years the modern explanation for the disease offered by the theories of Freud.

The "reports" to which he refers might well be those concerning the march on Versailles on October 5 and 6, 1789, by thousands of the women of Paris, frustrated to the point of despair at the failure of the Revolution to provide bread for themselves and their families, and wishing to take matters into their own hands at long last.

98. Cf. Matt. XIII:45–46.

99. Cf., for example, Matt. IX:18–19, 23–26.

100. Hippel creates a neologism based on the Latin form of the Greek *melanodocheion* ("ink-holder," "inkwell"). His term thus may be interpreted as a "repository for souls."

101. In Greek mythology, Themis was the second consort of Zeus and the personification of the order of things established by law, custom, and equity. She is described as reigning in the assembly of men as well as convening the assembly of the gods by order of Zeus himself.

102. The original text reads *à la Padishah*, i.e., "as the possessor of a harem."

103. Hippel refers here to Jérôme-Charlemagne Fleuriau (ca. 1742–1807), about whom virtually nothing is known except his works. His *Voyage de Figaro en Espagne* [A Sentimental journey through France] of 1785 was ordered condemned to the fire by the French parliament in 1788, presumably because of certain libelous remarks which it contained.

104. Epidaurus, a town on the eastern coast of Peloponessus, was the most celebrated seat of the ancient cult of Aesculapius, the Greek god of medicine.

105. Villacerf is a town in north central France. That such cases as the one here described did occasionally occur is illustrated by the celebrated medical scandal of 1777, in which a girl patient of Mesmer's (see Chapter VI, note 16), Maria Theresia Paradies, refused—whether because of erotic attachment or "Mesmeric attraction"—to leave the house and care of the doctor until the Viennese authorities finally intervened.

106. Hippel here modifies slightly the phrase "edle Einfalt und stille Grösse ("noble simplicity and quiet grandeur") of Johann Joachim Winckelmann (1717–1769), which became the catchword for the ideal of beauty in the German classical period. Winckelmann uses the expression in reference to Greek statuary: "The salient characteristic exhibited by Greek masterpieces is a noble simplicity and quiet grandeur, both in attitude and expression. Just as the depths of the sea remain forever calm no matter how the surface may rage, so the expression of the Greek figures reveals a lofty and sedate soul in the presence of the greatest passion" (*Thoughts on the Imitation of Greek Works in Painting and Sculpture*, 1755).

107. Hippel is probably referring to the cosmopolitanism of the Cynic philosophers, which considered the virtuous man to be above the coercions of the individual state—in-

spiring Diogenes' famous declaration: "I am a citizen of the world"—and the extension of this doctrine to the point of utter indifference to the world which is characteristic of certain Stoics.

108. Roman first names, used in the sense of "Tom, Dick, and Harry."

109. Cf. Matt. IX:4.

110. Cf. Matt. XIX:6.

111. Gen. II:18.

112. Cf. I Kings X:1–13.

113. In the eighteenth century the following anecdote was widely circulated regarding Newton's courtship:

> [Newton], when sitting by an elegant young lady, whom his friends wished him to [court] . . . seized her lily white hand. But instead of pressing it with rapture to his bosom, he thrust it into the bowl of his pipe that he was smoking; thus making a tobacco stopper of one of the loveliest fingers in England; to the inexpressible mortification of the company, and to the most dismal scolding and screaming of the dear creature! [Weems, *Life of Franklin*, p. 27].

While the anecdote was generally repeated as an example of the absentmindedness of the great thinker, Hippel assumes his actions to provide the best example of Newton's utter disregard for the intellectual powers of women. In his Masonic address mentioned above (Introduction, note 50) the Newton anecdote is quoted with the remark that it illustrates precisely the way women are "excluded from all sciences and the fine arts" (*Werke*, X, 241). In the present work, however, he reinterprets the anecdote in favor of the women, and it is Newton who suffers ridicule as the bumbling pedant. The work by Newton to which Hippel here refers is his posthumously published *Observations upon the Prophesies of Daniel and the Apocalypse* (1733).

114. Matt. V:13–14.

115. German: "Schöne Seelen." This philosophical term has a long tradition extending back to Plato; through the influence of such writers as Shaftesbury, Richardson, Rousseau, Wieland, and Goethe it reached the height of fashion in the eighteenth century. Schiller gives perhaps the most detailed definition in his essay "On Grace and Dignity" (1793), in which he calls that soul beautiful or noble which has achieved a full and harmonious equilibrium between moral sensitivity and sense perceptions.

116. Cf. I Sam. 17.

117. In the Italy of the seventeenth and eighteenth centuries, it was the custom for a young unmarried aristocrat to act as escort and companion (*cicisbeo*) to a married noble-woman during the temporary absence of her husband.

118. This argument, which gained some popularity during the Enlightenment, was based on the identification of the soul with human reason and the assumption that this faculty was the possession solely of the male sex. Typical of this genre is Timothy Constant's (pseudonym?) *An Essay to Prove Women have no Souls* ([London]: Sold by A. Dodd, [1714]).

119. Hippel's allusion to Giambattista Guarini's pastoral drama *El Pastor Fido* (1585) and to Ludovico Ariosto's metrical romance *Orlando Furioso* (1515) plays upon a literal translation of the titles: "The Faithful Shepherd" and "Raging Roland."

120. Hippel here refers to a customary form of entertainment at fairs and markets, as well as at village inns of the period, especially for the lower classes, which had no ready access to the theaters. The implication, of course, is that marriage often amounts to a degradation in the woman's status and a forced withdrawal from the active world.

121. I Kings XIX:12.

122. Matt. VII:15–16.

123. Eph. IV:26.

124. Cf. Acts VII:51.

125. The original text quotes the Latin formula *do ut des, facio ut facias* ("I give that you may give in return, I do . . . ," etc.) from the traditional practice in Roman religion of offering sacrifices to the gods in return for favors.

126. When Pythias was condemned to death for a plot against Dionysius I of Syracuse (430–367 B.C.), Damon offered himself to be put to death in lieu of his friend. Dionysius was so struck with this instance of friendship that he pardoned the criminal and asked to be admitted as a third into their brotherhood (Cicero *De Officiis* III. 10. 45).

127. See Chapter III, note 17.

128. Titus I:15.

129. Both Leibniz, court philosopher in the service of the Duke of Braunschweig-Lüneburg, and Christoph Martin Wieland (1733–1813), court poet and tutor to Prince Karl August in Weimar, were celebrated for an intense intellectual activity which transcended the limits of their assigned duties.

130. Cf. I Sam. XVIII:7.

131. Cf., for example, Plato *Apology* 40a. Hippel may also have had in mind Plutarch's essay *De genio Socrates* (*On the Daimonion of Socrates*).

132. Although "Abderite" was already a byword for stupidity in classical times, Hippel here refers more directly to the novel *Die Abderiten* by Wieland, which pokes fun at German philistinism and contains the famous account of a trial arising from a dispute concerning the question whether a mule's shadow is also included in the agreement when a mule is offered for lease. The dispute in this case ends with the death of the mule.

133. Hippel's reference is to the circles of the aristocracy and the middle class.

134. The quotation is presumably a reference to Daniel V:23.

135. Virgil, *Aeneid* I. 218.

136. This and the previous line owe their effect in the original German to a pun on the word *stimmen*: "to vote," and "to tune."

137. Madame Pompadour (Jeanne Antoinette Poisson le Normant d'Étoiles, 1721–1764), the chief mistress of Louis XV, was notorious for her influence at the French court from 1745 to 1764; the Comtesse du Barry (Jeanne Bécu, 1743–1793), was the last mistress of that king (from 1768 on) and exceedingly unpopular with the people for her prodigality. She was executed during the Revolution.

138. A reference to Dulcinea del Toboso, the idealized beloved of Don Quixote.

139. Cf. Matt. VIII:22; Luke IX:60.

140. Cf. Acts VIII:30 and Luke XXIII:34.

CHAPTER VI

1. Hippel refers probably to one of the fundamental assumptions implicit in the economic theory of mercantilism, namely, that the state is justified in exercising its powers in any and every aspect of the national economy in order to secure power and wealth for the nation as a whole. In Hippel's time such strict principles had been applied successfully by Frederick the Great, particularly with regard to the silk industry, in an attempt to bring Prussia's industrial development more quickly to the level of her rivals, Great Britain and France.

2. Cf. Rev. XV and XVI.

3. In the eighteenth century the distinction had not yet been made between the attractive powers of static electricity (described here) and the natural magnetism of certain ores.

4. Numa Pompilius (see Chapter V, note 30, above) was revered by the Romans as the author of their entire religious worship; Solon, the celebrated Athenian lawgiver (638–ca. 558 B.C.), reorganized the Athenian governmental system and rewrote the constitution of that city, eliminating many harsh laws from the earlier Draconian period.

5. See Chapter V, note 132.

6. Hippel's allusion to Genesis III:12–13, followed immediately by a reference to Adam-

ites of his own time, provides an ironic reversal of the doctrine of the true Adamites, a religious sect, originating in antiquity, which rejected marriage and even clothing in its assemblies ("paradises") because its members claimed to have attained the primitive innocence of Adam. The sect reappeared at various times throughout the Middle Ages and again in 1781 after the proclamation of the "Edict of Toleration" by the Emperor Joseph II. Shortly thereafter, the sect was once again charged with heresy and proscribed.

7. The Spartan king and hero Leonidas was famous for his defense of the pass of Thermopylae with only a handful of troops against the entire Persian army (480 B.C.).

8. The statement is perhaps strange in view of the unpopularity which Marie's excesses caused among the French people in the earlier years of her reign. Yet she displayed great fortitude on the outbreak of the Revolution, seeking in vain to induce her husband, Louis XVI, to take decisive measures. She later entered into negotiations herself with Mirabeau after the royal couple had been caught in its attempt to flee. Moreover, Hippel, an ardent monarchist, was also probably aware that during his work on this chapter Marie Antoinette had been imprisoned for treason, a fact which would further contribute to his highly ambivalent attitude toward the events then taking place in France. (See also Chapter V, note 94.)

9. Acts VIII:30.

10. The comparison is to porcelain and pottery after the first baking and before the application of the glaze.

11. Johann Friedrich Böttcher (1682–1719), an alchemist in the service of Augustus the Strong, king of Saxony, invented hard-paste porcelain as a direct consequence of experiments on the vitrification by heat of clays and rocks, and an indirect consequence of his attempts to turn base metals into gold.

12. Cf. Job VII:17 and XV:14.

13. The first quotation in the sentence is drawn from Edward Young's (1681–1765) *Night Thoughts* (1742–46), I, 75. The second is from the poem "Gedanken über Vernunft, Aberglauben, und Unglauben" [Thoughts on reason, superstition, and unbelief], in Albrecht von Haller's (1708–1777) *Versuch Schweizerischer Gedichten* [Some Swiss poems] (1732). Haller, a distinguished Swiss physiologist and botanist, expounded his philosophical ideas in poetic form. Hippel's slightly ironic tone toward a poet whom he greatly admired may stem from Haller's half-hearted acceptance of the principles of the Enlightenment. Hippel's quotation, however, omits the last half of the couplet: "You boast of reason but you don't make use of it," which more clearly reveals Haller's attitude toward this movement.

14. Extensive research has failed to yield any evidence that Friederika Baldinger actually existed; most probably the book to which Hippel refers (*Lebensbeschreibung von Friederika Baldinger, von ihr selbst verfasst. Herausgegeben und mit einer Vorrede begleitet von Sophie la Roche* [Autobiography of Friederika Baldinger, edited and with an introduction by Sophie von Laroche] 1791) is a fictional work in the autobiographical mode, written by Laroche herself (see Chapter V, note 36).

15. The reference is to centripetal and centrifugal force.

16. Although Hippel prefers to cite a more reputable authority for this conjecture, he was doubtless also aware of the sensation created by Friedrich Anton Mesmer (1733–1815) at that time with the cures he allegedly effected through "animal magnetism." Mesmer held that the universe was permeated with an "ethereal fluid" or force which affected the nervous system of men, the control of which (by Mesmer alone) could bring about spectacular cases of healing.

17. John Flamsteed (1646–1719), royal "astronomical observator" to Charles II and the author of the monumental *British Catalogue* of nearly three thousand stars (published posthumously in 1725), to which Herschel and his sister Caroline supplied additions and corrections (see Chapter V, note 66, above). Johann Tobias Mayer (1723–1762), a German astronomer and professor of mathematics at Göttingen, later supplemented this listing with a catalogue of the stars of the zodiac.

18. Cf. Rom. VII:22 and II Cor. IV:6.

19. Cf. Gen. III:19.

20. Cf. Matt. XX:16 and Mark IX:35.

21. Cf. Dante, *Inferno*, III, 9.

22. Cf. Jas. I:22–24.

23. Early in his reign Frederick the Great replaced the system of representation by the provincial parliaments and social classes (*Stände*) with permanent committees which served to keep watch on all matters within the individual provinces and reported directly to the king's deputies. Such a system greatly streamlined the bureaucracy and centralized the power in the hands of the king.

24. Cf. Acts II.

25. Christian Gottlob Heyne (1729–1812), classical philologist and archaeologist, was professor at Göttingen from 1765 to 1812. His editions of the *Iliad*, Pindar, and Tibullus were acclaimed in his own time; his edition of Virgil's complete works is highly regarded by scholars today as well.

26. Hippel here makes a pun on the word *Enten* ("ducks"). In the legal language of the period a Decernent was the official in charge of a legal case, the Instruent prepared the case, and the Referent acted as an advisor.

27. *Noli me tangere* (John XX:17—Vulgate).

28. Hippel alludes to Samuel Johnson's characterization of Lord Chesterfield: "This man I thought had been a Lord among wits; but, I find, he is only a wit among Lords" (*Boswell's Life of Johnson* [1791], II, i.)

29. Matt. XI:15.

Appendix: Rauschenbusch-Clough on Hippel and Wollstonecraft

Emma Rauschenbusch-Clough's study contains an entire chapter on the reception of Wollstonecraft's work in Germany. In her investigation of Hippel's literary indebtedness, she begins by stating that "a diligent search has not brought to light any direct evidence that [Hippel] was influenced by the views of Mary Wollstonecraft" (pp. 202–3). The author then proceeds to ignore this conclusion and embarks on her own detailed investigation with the obvious intent of proving that Hippel was in fact indebted to Wollstonecraft. She states that the *Vindication* was published two years before Hippel's book, enough time for Hippel to read Wollstonecraft's work, reflect upon it, and then to utilize its ideas. Then, referring to Hippel's "plagiarism" of Kant's ideas in the *Lebensläufe*, she claims that it would not have been "foreign to the literary character of Hippel" to draw heavily from the ideas of another author (p. 203). Further, she considers that the divergence between Hippel's views as expressed in the first and second editions of *Über die Ehe* and those of the present work is so great that only if "some striking external influence had been brought to bear upon him" could his change of heart be explained (p. 213).

It is evident that Rauschenbusch-Clough assumes the 1794 Leipzig edition of *Über die bürgerliche Verbesserung der Weiber* to be the first edition, when in fact the work was first published in Berlin in 1792, the year of the publication of Wollstonecraft's *Vindication*. She also concludes that the *Vindication* was finished about the middle of the year 1791 (pp. 204–5). Recent evidence, however, indicates that the work was finished on January 3, 1792 (letter of Mary Wollstonecraft to William Roscoe, January 3, 1792, first published in Eleanor Flexner, *Mary Wollstonecraft: a Biography* [New York: Coward, McCann & Geoghegan, 1972], pp. 276–77). From evidence in the Hippel work—the reference to "today, the 18th of March, 1792" which appears on p. 197 of the first edition—we can conclude that half of the book, and by far the most arduous and theoretical part, was completed by then. Furthermore, we know that Hippel's book was published in the autumn of 1792 (see Schneider, "Hippels Schriftstellergeheimnis," p. 16), and that Hippel had time, in spite of the burdens of his office, to publish two other less important works in that year, which suggests that *On Improving the Status of Women* must have been completed sometime in the summer.

Although the French translation of the *Vindication* was published, according to Rauschenbusch-Clough, before June 1792 (p. 205), it would have been quite difficult, given the upheaval caused by the French Revolution and the dilatory nature of communication and travel in the eighteenth century in general, for Hippel to have obtained a copy of it from Paris earlier than the fall. The German edition did not appear until 1793, and thus is of no consequence here. Furthermore, Rauschenbusch-Clough's assertion that "Hippel would have had time to take cognizance of this new work [by Wollstonecraft] and then to prepare a new edition of his *Über die Ehe* and publish it even in the year 1792" (p. 206) also cannot be proved. As she herself acknowledges, the first notice of Wollstonecraft's book in a review is probably one in the *Analytical Review* for March 1792 (p. 204), and it is apparent from one of Hippel's few extant letters from that period that the third edition of *Über die Ehe* was ready to be offered to the public around Easter (April 8) of that year (letter to Joachim Christian Grot, March 21, 1792, *Werke*, XII, 225). More than likely, then, Hippel's work on the third (and radically altered) edition of *Über die Ehe* dates from the middle of 1791. This conclusion is corroborated by the fact that he ceased work rather abruptly on his autobiography in May of that year, a date which can easily be verified from the text itself, and which Rauschenbusch-Clough inexplicably puts "about the middle of the year 1792" (p. 206).

Thus although Hippel's ideas concerning the rights of women had doubtless been taking shape for some time, he actually began to commit his thoughts on the subject to paper shortly after May 1791, about the time Wollstonecraft first began gathering material for the *Vindication*, for, as she states herself (*Vindication*, p. 106), she had just begun to think of writing the work when she heard of Catherine Macaulay's death, which took place on June 22, 1791.

The likelihood that Hippel could have seen an English edition of the *Vindication* while he was working on the last chapters of his own book is remote, given the isolated nature of the city and the manner in which he worked. Moreover, Hippel, although trained in the classical languages and French, apparently did not read English. It is possible that Hippel heard of Wollstonecraft's work at this time, and it is also conceivable—although highly doubtful—that his offhand and cryptic reference in the fifth chapter to "some hastily sketched piece by a woman" ("ein hingeworfener weiblicher Aufsatz") was written with Wollstonecraft in mind. Nonetheless, the possibility that he had heard of her work at this early date is rendered less plausible by the fact that the term "vindication"—a word most certainly derived from Wollstonecraft, since normal German usage preferred the words *Rettung* or *Verteidigung*—is first used by Hippel in his notes for a planned second edition of the present work, which never appeared (*Werke*, VII, 5).

Rauschenbusch-Clough's claim does not represent the first time that a question about the originality of his thought has been raised, however. Shortly after his death a similar challenge issued from within his own circle of friends, which was inspired by the singular manner in which he worked in order to preserve his anonymity. While he normally worked on each manuscript independently, before publishing it he would send it to Scheffner for correction, further observations, and critical comment. Yet in the case of the *Status of Women*, Scheffner, whose ideas on female emancipation differed greatly from Hippel's, criticized the manuscript so sharply both in public and private that their friendship never fully recovered (see Warda, "Hippel und Scheffner"). Thus Hippel was compelled to seek another confidant, and appears to have found one in the person of his bachelor friend Criminal Counselor Christian Friedrich Jensch. This conclusion is substantiated by a statement made by Jensch to Johann Friedrich Abegg and noted in Abegg's diary during his literary pilgrimage to various German intellectual centers in the year 1798. According to this account, on June 5, 1798, Jensch asserted that he had been a silent collaborator on the present work, principally advising in discussions of legal punishments, and that he had also "played a significant part" in the completion of the fourth edition of *Über die Ehe*, not just in specific passages but throughout the entire book (Abegg's diary entry reporting this conversation is recorded in H. Dieter, "Theodor Gottlieb von Hippel im Urteile seiner Zeitgenossen," *Euphorion*, XVII [1910], 311).

Moreover, on June 20, Jensch made an even more remarkable statement at a luncheon in Königsberg, again recorded by Abegg in his diary:

After the meal Frey [one of the guests present] and Jensch discussed Hippel. The conversation took a very strange turn. Frey and I maintained that Hippel's *On Improving the Status of Women* was one of his worst books, since the superior character traits he assigns to the female sex are simply not grounded in fact. With that, Jensch rose up and said, "If the book is bad, then it is my fault, since I was the one who put most of it together. As far as the content is concerned, I stand responsible for its accuracy, and I still maintain today, and will always maintain, that no man can ever advance as far as a woman can. Women are superior to us in natural talent. They just need to be put in a position from which they can develop [this talent]. It is barbarous and cruel to exclude them from any and all voting rights in society" (quoted in H. Dieter, "Johann Friedrich Abeggs Reise zu deutschen Dichtern und Gelehrten im Jahre 1798," *Euphorion*, XVI [1909], 744).

Since, however, the content and form of *Status of Women* betray Hippel's characteristic touch in every line and thought, we must view Jensch's claims with disbelief. They are all the more reprehensible in that he knew that they could never be challenged effectively by anyone except Hippel himself, who was, of course, in his grave. No further mention of Jensch's claims appears in the critical literature on Hippel.

INDEX

On Improving the Status of Women by Theodor Gottlieb von Hippel (1741–1796) is an important document for historians of women's studies. Virtually unknown to modern scholars, it is made available through the translation of Timothy F. Sellner.

Timothy F. Sellner is associate professor of German at Wake Forest University.

The book was designed by Vladimir Reichl. The typeface for the text is Palatino, designed by Herman Zapf about 1950. The display face is Weiss, designed by Emil Rudolf Weiss about 1926.

The text is printed on International Paper Company's Bookmark paper and the book is bound in Holliston Mills' Kingston Linen cloth over binder's boards. Manufactured in the United States of America.